IN SEARCH
OF A WILD
BRUMBY

Michael Keenan

BANTAM BOOKS
SYDNEY • AUCKLAND • TORONTO • NEW YORK • LONDON

Note: The names of some people in this book have been changed.

IN SEARCH OF A WILD BRUMBY
A BANTAM BOOK

First published in Australia and New Zealand in 2002
by Bantam

National Library of Australia
Cataloguing-in-Publication Entry

Keenan, Michael, 1943- .
In search of a wild brumby.

  ISBN 1 86325 319 X

  1. Wild horses - New South Wales - Snowy Mountains Region. 2. Adventure
  and adventurers - New South Wales - Snowy Mountains. I. Title.

636.100994

Transworld Publishers,
a division of Random House Australia Pty Ltd
20 Alfred Street, Milsons Point, NSW 2061
http://www.randomhouse.com.au

Random House New Zealand Limited
18 Poland Road, Glenfield, Auckland

Transworld Publishers,
a division of The Random House Group Ltd
61-63 Uxbridge Road, London W5 5SA

Random House Inc
1540 Broadway, New York, New York 10036

Internal photos by Mike and Sally Keenan, except where indicated otherwise.
Typeset by Midland Typesetters, Maryborough, Victoria
Printed and bound by Griffin Press, Netley, South Australia

10 9 8 7 6 5 4 3 2 1

Foreword

In the big picture of an environment under siege – from toxic rivers to land clearing on a frightening scale in Queensland – the brumby debate may seem a very minor issue. Yet the anti-brumby lobby has aroused distrust and sometimes hatred in already stressed rural communities, which in turn can create the potential for a weakening in resolve on the need for sound and urgent environmental reform.

I am an active supporter of the establishment and maintenance of wilderness areas where any attempt at land usage would result in irreparable destruction – indeed, in 1993 I donated 50 hectares of old growth forest to the Gardens of Stone National Park. All land is unforgiving, and farmers who deploy poor management practices are soon shown the gate. It's not a bad lesson for the whole Australian community.

Michael Keenan

Contents

Introduction   1

1. Brumbies or Ferals?   7

2. Ghosts of the Frost Hollows   21

3. Brumbies in the Mist   46

4. The Eroded Plateaus of the Suggan Buggan   65

5. The Rescue of Jim Nankervis   90

6. They Was Beautiful   113

7. The Noose   145

8. Blue Duck Retreat   177

9. The Gold Town   195

10. The Permit   215

Epilogue   249

Appendix I   261

Appendix II   264

Acknowledgments   271

There was movement at the station, for the word had passed around
    That the colt from old Regret had got away,
And had joined the wild bush horses – he was worth a thousand pound,
    So all the cracks had gathered to the fray.
All the tried and noted riders from the stations near and far
    Had mustered at the homestead overnight,
For the bushmen love hard riding where the wild bush horses are,
    And the stock-horse snuffs the battle with delight.

– from 'The Man from Snowy River', A. B. 'Banjo' Paterson

Principal brumby populations in Australia's southeastern ranges

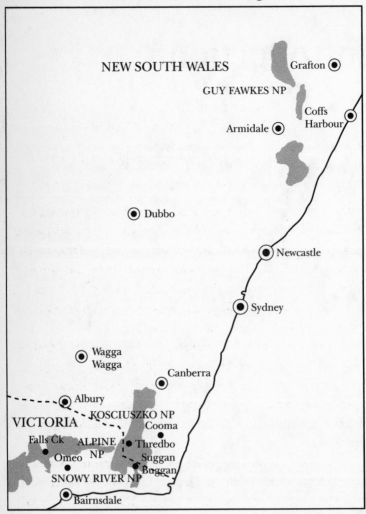

Shaded area = brumby populations

Introduction

And upward, ever upward, the wild horses held their
*   way,*
Where mountain ash and kurrajong grew wide …

In the Northern Territory I have seen them in the stifling savannah woodlands of the Top End. I have seen them when the mist parts and rises in the waterfall country of the northern tablelands in NSW and I have chased them and crashed heavily into the snow on the high plains of Victoria's alpine zone. Only in the arid desert regions of Australia might I be disappointed if I sought them – brumbies.

No one knows for certain when wild horses became known as brumbies in Australia. A popular story is that the term originated with a Major Brumby whose horses were said to have escaped into the wild or been abandoned, but I think it's possible that 'brumby' was an Aboriginal term for wild horse.

Nationwide, brumbies have been part of our folklore since the mid-19th century. They have always been regarded ambivalently. Like so many other introduced animals running in a wild state, wild horses have become a pest in some regions. Debates over whether they should be culled or not relate mainly to issues of animal welfare, not so much

1

a desire for wild mobs to run free. But lurking beneath this debate is the extraordinary bond between horse and man.

At some point in time we moved beyond the predator–prey relationship. We started riding them, probably for speed to hunt other animals. French archaeologists have discovered horse molars in caves with bridle-bit wear, dating back 15 000 years. This discovery suggests that ancient European societies have evolved since the late Pleistocene with the practical help of horses. This is a bond between man and animal that has no parallel. If culture is the product of learning over many centuries, then the fate of horses in modern times must surely awake an old spirit inside us. It is little wonder that there is conflict over what to do with brumbies in the regions where the folklore is best remembered.

Brumby running is a Snowy Mountains tradition which began with the second generation of squatters, in the 1850s. Nowhere else in the world do men gallop after wild horses and catch them with a lasso. American cowboys muster mustangs to corrals and do far more calf roping from horseback than is done in Australia, but they don't lasso mustangs at full gallop in the wide open spaces.

Just what prompted the Australian enthusiasm for such a dangerous activity is anybody's guess, but I have a theory that goes back to early settlement on the Monaro. On the high plains around the central town of Cooma, the early settlers did it tough. It was nothing to do with the soil. Long-extinct volcanoes spewed rich layers of basaltic material over thousands of hectares which weathered into an undulating, fertile landscape. Some of the early settlers were Scottish and not to be daunted by the long bleak winters. What they may not have bargained for was the Monaro rain-shadow and the frequent dry spells. Frontal bearing clouds slam into the alps from the west and the high peaks milk the moisture. The key to survival, the early settlers discovered, was the high grasslands of the subalpine where most of the rain falls. The Monaro squatters became Australia's first white nomads. They took their stock to the mountains for the summer and when they returned in the autumn the home base paddocks were boot high in grass, ready to carry the cattle or sheep through the winter.

In those days the high country was unfenced and there were no government regulations. It appears the owners of the stock simply agreed on grazing boundaries and those agreements eventually were transformed into leases, known as snow leases. There were some small areas of freehold, but after Federation most of the high country was controlled by the NSW Department of Lands. Mounted rangers were given the task of checking that the leases were not overstocked. They counted the stock onto the leases when they arrived from the low country with drovers, checked boundary fences and ensured that the leaseholders undertook rabbit destruction. In 1944 the country above 1500 metres was resumed to form the Kosciuszko State Park. Land resumption continued and in 1969 the last of the snow leases on what has always been known as the northern high plains was absorbed into the Kosciuszko National Park.

The men who watched over the stock were known as the Snowy Mountains drovers. In the alpine zone they received their mail by packhorse from Canberra. Every drover had the same address, 'Mount Kosciuszko', and the mail was left in a community mailbox.

From the stories passed down it appears the mail was the only respite in a monotonous existence. Not many women braved the conditions and the culture at the time didn't encourage them. The tucker was meat and damper, and shelter, one-room huts with a fireplace on a dirt floor. Sudden bursts of sleet and snow were not uncommon even at the height of summer and the dry westerly winds were always cold. Depending on the nature of the terrain, there sometimes wasn't much to do other than watch the stock and tend to the saddle horses. Those left on their own suffered mentally and some went half mad. For the younger men, brumby running broke the dull routine. Aware of the dangers, some leaseholders forbade men on the payroll to engage in the activity. The risk of injury to their saddle horses was enormous, let alone to themselves. But access into the Snowy Mountains was still over rough roads and through spring-fed bogs as late as 1950. The leaseholders probably only made one or two trips from home base during each season, so if the young stockmen wanted to chase brumbies they did.

A veteran of the high country, Gordon Day, told me the yearlings seized by rope were sometimes broken in to become packhorses. They were heavy plugs, he said – stocky horses only suitable for packing. Only the brumbies sired by a thoroughbred or part thoroughbred stallion were suitable for saddle horses. His father, George Day, affectionately known as the old King of the Mountains, managed the NSW Government Chalet from 1930 to 1964. He maintained the quality of the Snowy Mountains brumby herds by introducing thoroughbred stallions. The brumbies from this region have always degenerated into melonheadedness and dwarfism if domestic stallions were not introduced. Darwin's theory on natural selection may provide the reason. The herds in the Snowys have been continually disrupted by man. The best colts and fillies were usually caught, leaving the more degenerate animals to carry on with the breeding. The order of natural selection has only occurred in isolated pockets, where the mountains are either too steep and rocky or the timber too thick for the brumby runners to operate. Alpine veteran Jim Nankervis claims these pockets still exist in the Snowy Mountains. He knows where chestnut-coloured brumbies with white manes and tails have survived for decades. Unmolested by man, it appears a herd will maintain a dominant gene until a fresh gene of hybrid vigour replaces it.

These days, much has changed for the brumbies of the Snowy Mountains – and elsewhere. The snow leases have been resumed to form national parks and wilderness reserves. In the NSW alpine areas, horse riding is forbidden. So too is brumby running – the brumbies inside national parks are protected. Only the National Parks and Wildlife Service has the authority to cull in NSW.

In Victoria the situation is different. Outside the alpine resort areas and wilderness reserves, horse riding and brumby running is permitted from 1 December to 30 April. There are protocols to be observed for both activities.

But the legendary feats of the early brumby runners live on in the popular imagination, as does the idea of the wild horses running free among the snow gums.

Pursuing the story of the brumbies took me deep into the heart of brumby country, with its elusive wild horses, rugged landscape and extraordinary bush men and women.

What started out as a simple impulse to catch a brumby of my own, turned into much more than I could have imagined – a hair-raising adventure that had me crashing down mountainsides, as well as a serious look at the issues that affect brumbies today.

Northern tablelands of NSW
Guy Fawkes River region

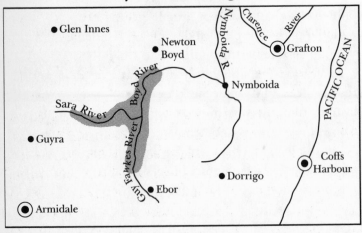

Shaded area = Maximum range of GF brumbies

CHAPTER 1

Brumbies or Ferals?

He was something like a racehorse undersized,
With a touch of Timor pony – three parts thoroughbred
*   at least –*
And such as are by mountain horsemen prized.

The village of Ebor lies on the headwaters of the Clarence River system in New England in northern NSW. Beyond the western edge of the village the Ebor Falls plunge into the Guy Fawkes canyon. The Falls Motel is nearby. At the eastern end of the village is a roadhouse service station. In between there is a hotel, a school and general store. At night there are few lights and on the odd occasion I'd driven through, I wondered whether Ebor would even be remembered if it ever faded from the map. All that changed suddenly on the second last weekend in October 2000. That was the weekend the NSW National Parks and Wildlife Service sanctioned the shooting from helicopters of 600 brumbies in the nearby Guy Fawkes River National Park.

In the New England region the temperate forests on the eastern fall of the Great Dividing Range are home to more than 200 bird species, numerous marsupials, some rare reptiles, dingoes and wild horses. The canyons and lonely land-locked valleys remain to this day sparsely populated by humans, thanks to the precipitous and tangled eastern escarpment. Roads snaking west from the Pacific coast penetrate the highlands in only three places, where long sweeping spurs wind gently all the way to east flowing rivers. So different is the coastal urban culture from the sparse settlements of the rugged interior the only thing the opposing cultures have in common is language and law. The day-to-day living of the highland people has altered little since early settlement, but their numbers have dwindled despite electricity, telephone, television and 4WDs. In the protected valleys of the high country and down where the canyon walls begin to diverge and form valleys of bountiful river flats, the pastoralists run cattle. On the hard granite tops where the altimeter will pass 1500 metres, they run merino sheep. Some of the old hands still refer to the 'northern alps' where the granite tors bow only to the Kosciuszko–Townsend high massif and the Victorian Alps, but the climate is a shade warmer and the winter snowfalls are less reliable.

'It's the windiest road in Australia,' an Ebor highlander said to me one day. 'Coming from Coffs, the driver's exhausted by the time he gets to Ebor.'

Coffs Harbour is on the coast, 150 kilometres away. The tableland city of Armidale lies 100 kilometres to the west. If it wasn't for the combination of fatigue and remoteness no one would ever stop at Ebor. 'Desperate stop,' a truckie mumbled to me in the local roadhouse. 'You land here tired in July or August and you don't switch off. Keep the old girl runnin or the diesel will freeze on yer.' Ebor is high up and bitterly cold in the winter. The westerly winds originate far away in the central deserts of South Australia. Unlike the

Snowy Mountains, where predominant westerlies come off the southern ocean, these are bone dry winds in the winter, facilitating extraordinary drops in overnight temperatures. Maybe the people there are like the Scottish highlanders of old, independent and fiercely proud of where they live. If there has been any capitulation to use motorbikes for stock work I never saw it. They are horsemen and the unborn generation would also be horsemen. It is a perfect environment for the preservation of the Australian wild brumby.

The demanding ring of the telephone echoed through a dream I was having. It was always the same dream. Engaged to ride a horse I never got aboard. Something always happened. I was an amateur jockey for thirty years and the thrill of the race and the thunder of the hooves must have been a form of adrenaline addiction. I have sometimes wondered why it's so deep in my subconscious, because I was a mediocre jockey and for me the gambling often spoilt the simple concept of a horse race. It's the horses of course. I miss being mounted on such beautiful sleek animals, groomed for the occasion and full of hard feed.

I glanced at my watch – 6.30 a.m. Apart from the sowing season in winter and harvesting of the wheat in December, early calls were usually a stray cow on the road or on someone's place, or someone in the family struck down with illness. The young man on the phone announced he was the producer of the breakfast program on a Canberra radio station. Did I know about the shooting of 600 brumbies in Guy Fawkes National Park? What were my thoughts on such an outrage? Could he call me back at 7.10 a.m., after the national news bulletin, for a live telephone hook-up?

I hadn't heard about it. My wife and I live on a wheat and cattle farm called Myall Plains, 20 kilometres west of the small town of Binnaway on the far western division of the north-west slopes. Sal is an avid reader of the daily paper when she can get one and always draws my attention to news releases she knows will interest me, but 20 kilometres is too far to run for the paper every day. By November the south-eastern Australian states are on daylight saving time which puts the ABC television news to air an hour before dark. We run the farm together and the cool of the evening is one of our most productive times. We don't hear the news much once the clocks are wound back an hour. So I was appalled to hear of the slaughter. Horses, for me and other rural folk of my generation, have been an intrinsic part of life. I agreed to do the interview.

There's something of an indefinable time warp between those born before 1950 and those born after. Cultures change not because people wish to change. They change because of technological progress driven by expanding economies. The world I recall from 1947 (I was born in 1943) was vastly different from the one I returned home to on school holidays in 1957. In 1947, Italian prisoners of war were still held on Myall Plains. I never saw one on a horse, but they were good sulky drivers and clever with worn out machinery. Small groups of prisoners, usually no more than five, were farmed out across the sheep and wheat belt of eastern Australia until arrangements could be made for their return to their homelands. The post-war years were dreadfully tough until the upsurge in wool prices, in about 1950. During the war, rabbit populations exploded into plague proportions and, to compound an already desperate pastoral position, 1946 was a drought year. There was no money and little petrol. If rural Australia looked like leaving the horse age behind forever in the 1930s then the years of 1945–50 were like a return to the early 1920s. The one distinct difference would have been farm tractors. My dad bought a kerosene-fueled John Deere imported from America. It had to be started by hand with half a litre of petrol. There was an extraordinary hissing noise while the unfortunate operator struggled with a fly-wheel half a metre wide. When it started it was like a bomb. The station horses took off, the milking cow kicked the bucket and crows in the little pine forest bolted. If you were in the sulky, Violet strode out for 50 metres like a pacer and the driver holding the long reins was jerked to his feet on the rickety platform, leaning back with all his weight.

There were two farm sulkies and they were both harnessed most working days. Big Violet was a grey Clydesdale mare and Kitty was a young black mare. If Dad wasn't driving a sulky he rode a piebald gelding called Pinto. At the age of four I had a Shetland pony called Lou Lou and I still have the saddle weighing about two kilograms. Later I had a bay gelding.

I feel it is important to relate my childhood association with horses because it was vastly different from the weekend pony club experience some rural children are reared on today. Horses were not only involved with the farm on a daily basis, they were still a means of short-range transport. The head man for the Italians, Theo, collected the mail in a sulky and brought in the milking cows. The rabbit trappers fanned out before dawn in several sulkies. As well as working for his uncle's manager on Myall Plains, Dad had a block of his own land five kilometres to the north and left each morning in a sulky with a swag of dogs trotting beside. In 1952 I rode out to meet the school bus and left the bay gelding in the post office yard at New Mollyan. Horses were family. Despite the huge cultural changes in the urban world most Australians now occupy, there are still thousands of Australians alive who were reared in similar circumstances to myself. They will never feel comfortable with the word 'feral' applied to brumbies – the National Parks and Wildlife Service's official term for wild horses today. Strictly speaking, the term is correct. The problem rural people of my generation have is that the modern meaning of the word has gone beyond the dictionary definition. 'Feral' now conjures up images of a dirty and repugnant creature. This is what we collectively resent.

Before the radio producer hung up I did try to explain I had never caught a brumby in my life and didn't know much about them. He had associated me with my second book, *Wild Horses Don't Swim*, released only three months before. He wanted an author and a horseman.

The interview went along smoothly and, despite my lack of knowledge about brumbies, I felt I made a worthwhile contribution to the debate. I explained that wild cattle were easy to catch in trap yards and while horses were smarter, I knew they could be coaxed into bush yards with feed. The operation was time consuming and demanded experience on the part of those involved. There had to be a quieting process. With wild cattle we called it 'tailing'. A stockman would ride amongst the cattle. Initially they always bolted, but the one thing you didn't do was chase them. The rider tailed along behind until he caught up with them again. After a few days the cattle accepted his presence. I imagined tailing to be more difficult with wild horses, as almost any mob in the Snowys and Gippsland had been pursued at one time or another.

The next stage was either random feeding, molasses drips, or in hard country salt blocks were sometimes sufficient. Once the cattle or the horses began to look for the product, the stockmen began putting it in the trap yard. The sight of posts and rails never bothered cattle, but with horses it was a game of patience. I was determined to get across the fact that shooting horses from a helicopter was abhorrent to many country people and if city people were confronted with the grisly scenes, I believed most of them would recoil from it too.

I also pointed out how sad it was that such an ugly scene should be reported across Australia so soon after the Olympic Games. The entire nation, along with tens of thousands of overseas guests and viewers, had applauded our horsemen and women – and the horses themselves at the opening ceremony. We had stamped our proud culture on the world and all those visitors returned home with images of Australia that were no longer authentic.

Finally the interviewer asked: 'Wild horses, can't they swim?' I had to explain that a packhorse expedition of mine into the King Leopold Ranges in the west Kimberley, WA, had been delayed at a river when the freshly broken horses refused to swim. Tired horse handlers were the real problem that day. My Aboriginal friends and I were not in the mood for enforcing horse discipline and we opted to ride down the river until it widened and was not so deep. But the incident gave me my book title.

After a few weeks of intense media interest, the brumby issue simmered down with the lead up to Christmas. The NSW Minister for the Environment, Bob Debus, announced a ban on the shooting of horses in the state's national parks and forests. He said he had listened to and appreciated the distress it had aroused in the community. Apart from the infuriated locals at Ebor it may have all soon been forgotten if it hadn't been followed shortly after by the much-publicised claim by Snowy Mountain's environmentalists that brumbies grazing on the alps around Mount Kosciuszko were damaging the fragile tundra plant species. Fearing another public backlash if any form of drastic action was taken against the horses, the National Parks authority called for public comment on how to deal with them.

The Snowy Mountains region is the most sensitive location in Australia when the topic of horses is introduced. On one hand are the Green activists, who firmly believe horses are the most destructive animals in the Kosciuszko National Park and a threat to the safety of bushwalkers. On the other hand are the horsemen, who claim brumbies are few in number and do little damage. They believe that opposition to brumbies and horse riding in national parks is more to do with cultural division than the environment.

ABC Radio puts an hour aside each weekday for farmers. Following the midday news the producers of the 'Country Hour' cover the farming topics of the day, from diseases in livestock to international commodity prices. It is a serious and informative program for the man on the land, but occasionally a lighter note is introduced. In a telephone interview a veteran Kosciuszko stockman was asked how he thought the brumbies could be caught and what would he suggest be done with them?

The ABC had done their research, for they couldn't have asked a more experienced man. Affectionately known as Dooley, Brian Pendergast has spent his whole life in the mountains. Born in the mid 1930s he belongs to the last generation to ride freely across the Snowy Mountains and he was the last to crack his stockwhip on Kosciuszko and move the cattle down to the winter pastures of the Monaro. In 1973 Dooley featured in the ABC's 'A Big Country' series, in the documentary 'The Man from Snowy River'. The Italian-born director, Gian Manaro, was quoted as saying, 'My God, I've never seen men ride like that in my life'. He had been a captain in the Italian cavalry before migrating to Australia. But Dooley's special skills and knowledge were of brumbies. He rode in what may have been the only brumby race ever held in Australia and fittingly it was won by his uncle, Noel Pendergast. Dooley rode a bluey-coloured gelding roped as a yearling somewhere in the Cascades, southwest of Thredbo ski village. A modest, humble bushman, I had to drag all these stories out of him and sometimes it took one or two stubbies.

On the 'Country Hour', Dooley suggested the brumbies could be trapped in a bush yard using salt blocks as a decoy. He explained that the mountain soils were deficient in salt and when the frosts of late autumn began to dissipate the nutrition in the snow grass, the horses craved it. On the sealed road from Thredbo village to Corryong in Victoria the winter snow used to close the road at Dead Horse Gap for about three months, but in recent years the authorities had brought in snowploughs to keep the road open and used salt to prevent icing on the bitumen. The salt leaches into the soil by the side of the road and the brumbies paw holes to lick the fine granules out of the soil. Deep holes beside the bitumen become a traffic hazard. Deer and moose did the same thing on American high passes and the authorities in that country now use coarse gravel.

When the question was put to Dooley about what should be done with the trapped horses I became riveted by what he had to say. Brumbies caught as foals about weaning age adapted quickly under the human hand. For 150 years horses caught in the bush have been sought after by mountain stockmen. They are hardy and surefooted. Dooley went on to say that some of the brumbies never grew taller than thirteen hands at the wither and made excellent little horses for children. My eldest son, James, and his wife Kari had just made me a grandfather and I had been thinking about ponies. I had James cantering at the age of five. I'm a lot older and far more careful now, but Harry might be riding out on the Kurrajong plains by seven, I thought. Perhaps it would be a brumby, although a lot of preconceived notions about them as a breed would need to be mellowed in my mind before I let a child on one. In any event, I needed new stockhorses and the recreational horse industry had pushed values way above what most cattlemen were prepared to pay. If you paid a few thousand dollars for a motorbike you had it for a decade and it could be repaired. Horses, too, were fetching thousands of dollars – but a new one might be injured and have to be put down the day it arrived on the property.

Was there still a cheap way into horses? The few breeders left, scattered far and wide across the tablelands and slopes of eastern Australia, would say no. Even a small herd of mares – for example ten head – demands a lot of care, and if the handler valued his time by the hour no one would breed horses outside the realm of the lucrative racing industry. On the big western stations it used to be necessary to breed horses. But the arrival of the motorbikes changed everything – not just the use of horses, but also the way modern farmers perceives their role on the land. It's a business now, as distinct from the way of life it was in my father's era.

But, forever optimistic (and sometimes a victim of this), I decided to see if brumby running was the answer, and the Snowy Mountains seemed an obvious place to start.

According to some accounts, brumbies have been

recorded in Australian history since 1804, when a certain Major Brumby abandoned his selection and his horses for a new Crown commission in Tasmania. In those days the tiny British colony didn't extend more than a few miles beyond Camden.

However I feel this proposition is most unlikely. Horses would have had an enormous value in a fledgling colony. Away from waterways, they were the only form of transport and with the First Fleet arriving only sixteen years earlier it's hard to imagine there were many of them around.

I think the origins of the Australian wild horse vary from region to region. They were all either horses which had escaped or been abandoned. In the 19th century the term brumby was thought to be Aboriginal in origin – and I believe this could be the case. There were hundreds of Aboriginal dialects spoken across Australia and there might have been many different names for this new creature the white men had brought. It's possible, too, that the Aborigines had a special name for horses they knew to be wild, especially in Victoria where we know horses were running in the wild in the 1840s. Poet Banjo Paterson certainly believed this term was Aboriginal. One of his poems, 'Brumby's Run', has a little foreword: *Brumby is the Aboriginal word for a wild horse.*

Brumby folklore is more intrinsic to the Snowy Mountains and the Victorian high country than anywhere else, but brumbies are found in many parts of Australia. In Queensland there are tens of thousands of wild horses and in some areas these are such a pest that few people would regard them romantically. West into the Northern Territory helicopter shooting has been accepted as the only viable method of control. In WA's Kimberley region 2000 horses were shot in the mid-1990s on one property alone.

It was the folklore of the southeast that fascinated me from the beginning. Had the spirit of the mountain people survived? One hundred and ten years after Banjo Paterson was inspired to write 'The Man From Snowy River', what was the world of the brumby really like? The outrage from the Guy Fawkes shooting certainly demonstrated that thousands of Australians still saw the brumby as part of our national heritage. It is one issue where there is no dividing line between city and country.

But why do Australians, whether in the city or the country, feel so strongly about the brumbies? Not everyone has had my close relationship with horses, after all. I think Banjo's poem – and the subsequent films – has a lot to do with it. A tale of bush heroes pitting their skills and strength against the rugged Australian landscape and a worthy opponent, 'The Man from Snowy River' epitomises the qualities Australians revere about the bush.

Another influence harder to gauge is *The Silver Brumby* and its sequels by the late Elyne Mitchell. First published in 1958 it has been in print ever since and been read by generations of children, both here and overseas.

It is not appropriate, I believe, to compare wild horses with other feral animals such as pigs. It amounts to degrading the vital role horses have played in human society and history for thousands of years. For example, having studied the final stages of the Palestine campaign in 1917–18, I have absolutely no doubt that relentless charges at Turkish lines by the Light Horse won the war in the Middle East and achieved the surrender at Constantinople. The Turks had superior infantry weapons, greatly outnumbered Allied forces and were fighting on their own territory. What they couldn't handle was lightning charges by mounted horsemen, which overran frontline positions in a matter of minutes.

The Palestine campaign is just one of countless examples of our extraordinary link with the horse. That Australians should be distraught at horrific images of horses being killed with semi-automatic weapons should surprise no one. Brian Gilligan, Director-General of the National Parks and Wildlife Service, was quoted in *The Australian* magazine, 9 December 2000, as saying: 'People might shy from brutal images of helicopter shooting, but experts say it is the most humane and cost-effective method of culling large numbers of animals. Especially when you consider that Australia still uses yellow phosphorous against feral pigs in parts of NSW and Queensland. The chemical burns out the animal's intestines.'

That way of thinking will never be accepted in a culture which has evolved in the British Commonwealth. You cannot expect the community to look upon wild horses the same way they look upon wild pigs. It is an unrealistic expectation and ignores the deep roots of history.

Mind you, I was appalled to read that yellow phosphorous was still being used. It was used widely in the 1960s and it's horrendous. It should be banned.

No book about brumbies or wild horses anywhere would be adequate without at least a brief mention of the Przewalski horse, *Equus caballus przewalskii*. It is the only genetically pure wild horse left in the world. Both *E. caballus przewalskii* and *E. caballus*, the domestic horse, are from the same family, *Equidae*, which split 250 000 years ago.

Polish geographer N. M. Przewalski discovered what came to be known as the Przewalski horse in Mongolia towards the end of the 19th century. It once roamed from the Ural Mountains in Russia throughout central Asia to Mongolia. The horses were even recorded among the famous Palaeolithic cave paintings in France, at the height of the last ice age.

Breeding programs for the Przewalski horse have been set up in Australia, North America and the Ukraine with the intention of releasing them into their original habitat in Mongolia. The Australian breeding program is at the Western Plains Zoo, at Dubbo in western NSW. In 1995 the zoo sent seven mares to Mongolia as part of the international program. They currently have fifteen mares and eleven stallions. With 70 foals born since 1984 and dispersed throughout Australian zoos, Australian breeding co-ordinators are optimistic that one day the Przewalski will roam the wild steppe lands once again.

Of course, the Australian brumby is not a genetically pure separate species – they are simply domestic horses gone wild. But what we do have in Australia is a genuine desire for brumby herds to remain wild. Was the Australian brumby deserving of a heritage status in suitable locations? What was their true place in our culture and what would become of them in the 21st century? Over the next nine months, as I searched for a brumby of my own, I endeavoured to find out.

CHAPTER 2

Ghosts of the Frost Hollows

*And the Snowy River riders on the mountains make
their home,*
Where the river runs those giant hills between;
*I have seen full many horsemen since I first
commenced to roam,*
But nowhere yet such horsemen have I seen.

The story of my search for a wild brumby began in the
Kosciuszko National Park in southeastern NSW. Looking
more like the cold tundra of Lapland than landforms
normally associated with the alps, most of the national park
comprises a high tableland culminating in an uplift on the
western escarpment, beginning at Mount Jagungal in
the north and terminating at South Rams Head, only a few
kilometres west of the Thredbo ski village. This uplift is the
alpine zone, covering less than fifteen per cent of the park's
690 000 hectares. To the south, east and north the land
slopes down gradually into the subalpine. It was in the
north that I began my search towards the end of February
2001.

Dooley Pendergast's interview with the ABC was about

Currango Station and Coolamine
(now national park)

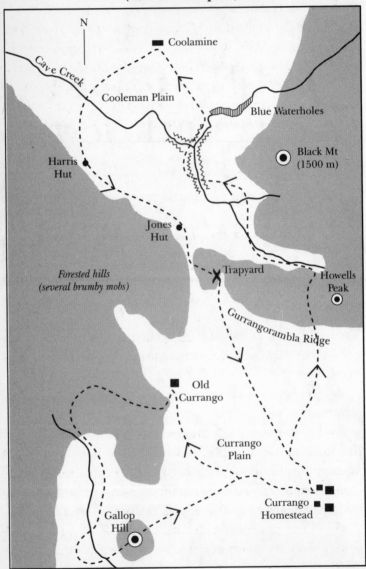

- - - - - - Ted Taylor's brumby trail

mid-January. The weather was extremely hot, with temperatures west of the Great Divide exceeding 40°C. It was hard
to get enthusiastic about anything but the beach. Sal and I
had gone to the coast for about a week and two of our boys,
Nicholas and Tom, had come up from Sydney to join us.
During the week I read Ion Idriess's *The Desert Column*
and Elyne Mitchell's *Light Horse to Damascus*. I had 'horse
storming' on the brain. The wise side of me said chasing
brumbies was madness and the travelling expenses would
quickly accrue to more than the cost of a saddlehorse at auc-
tion. But in the end the sense of adventure was too much.

I contacted Scott Levi at 2WG Wagga. Scott and I had met
twice over radio interviews and we had an instant rapport.
Not over horses – it was our mutual love of the mountains.
I was a veteran rockclimber and Scott was a mountain
stream fisherman. He was fascinated by the long-gone
mountain people of the old snow leases. 'The bushman
caught trout from horseback,' he exclaimed enthusiastically
in his Wagga office.

I told Scott I was thinking of going after a brumby.

'I don't think you can in the Park. I'm sure they're protected.'

'I don't understand,' I said blankly. 'They call them feral
animals.'

As I later discovered, brumbies are indeed protected in
the Kosciuszko National Park, on the NSW side. Above 1400
metres no one mustered cattle or sheep any more. A few
rugged souls chased brumbies and risked a $2000 fine if
caught removing any fauna from the park – feral or native.
The only other horseback riders to enter the park were
genuine nature lovers and photographers.

'Ted Taylor's your man,' Scott told me. 'He's the caretaker
of the old cattle station homestead at Currango. Just a few

days ago he was declared the "Man from Snowy River" for 2001.' It's an annual award, very much coveted by the high country stockman.

Scott introduced me to Ted Taylor in early February and on my second trip to Currango I took my ex-racehorse Malameen down on the old station truck. Currango is a National Park and Wildlife Service guesthouse within the Kosciuszko National Park on what is known as the northern high plains. Horseriding is still permitted over quite a big area in the north and Ted had promised to show me the brumbies from horseback. We'd be riding out from the guest-house, which was the original station homestead. Ted regularly guided horseback riders through this end of the park and his enthusiasm for brumbies was often talked about in his hometown of Tumut, nestled on the banks of the Murrumbidgee River right at the foot of the first big lift into the high country.

Malameen had won six races in NSW and showed promise in Adelaide before breaking down. His tendon healed with twelve months' rest and ever since 1992 I had used him as a saddle horse on the farm. I think he hated the trip to the Snowy Mountains and I didn't take him again.

In single file six horses ambled across the gentle undula-tions of Coleman Plain. Sometimes the iron shoes rung hollow on the limestone, as though a great cavity lay only metres below. Treeless, the plain was a typical frost hollow of the high country. At night, cold air gravitates from the sum-mit spurs of the ranges to the valleys. In the broad upland hollows west of the Brindabella Range the cold air becomes trapped in ancient riverbeds and the severe winter frosts kill off any tree seedlings that may have sprouted in the sum-mer. All that survives is snow grass and bulrushes along the creeks. The snow grass is sweet and full of nutrients. We had arrived upon the plain too late in the morning to see the kangaroos, brushtail wallabies and the little smoke-coloured swamp wallabies feeding out across the hollows. There were tracks and droppings of the brumbies too. Everywhere, horses are known to do well on limestone country. Perhaps the very ancient decay of amphibian life which fossilised over millions of years to form the limestone, still releases nutrients into the roots of the dominant grasses.

Ted Taylor was the trail-finder. Behind him rode four women and I tacked on at the rear. In his mid-60s, Ted was reared here. To the north was Coolamine Homestead and away to the southwest was Old Currango Cottage. He had lived at both places for brief periods when a boy. His father Tom had been a snow lease stock inspector. As we rode along neither place was in sight. They were in other frost hollows. We were headed towards the Brindabellas, the dominant range, with one peak shading 2000 metres. Lateral ranges running off this high blue line in the east formed a complex pattern of low mountain ranges and treeless frost hollows. Ridge after ridge, it all looked the same. The summit peaks of Mount Bimebri and Mount Morgan could be observed from most angles on a clear day, but those peaks frequently buried their heads in mountain mist. Today was no exception. The air hung heavy and to the north the storm floaters had already advanced from the horizon.

We were on our way to the Blue Waterholes. Lying in a limestone gorge, the waterholes had been a popular picnic and fishing spot since the subalpine tablelands were first settled. The four young women riding with us had been talking about a swim ever since the sun had warmed the hollows, with the humidity high before we had even mounted at Currango Homestead. After a barbecue lunch Ted was going to lead us over the Fiery Range to look for brumbies.

He reined in on the lip of a deep gulch. In Australia we call them ravines, but this was not typical water erosion over thousands of years. The limestone roof had collapsed, forming a trench in the plain. He urged his brown mare Bee Bee onto the steep incline and tentatively the women followed. First into the trench was Jill Foster on her big black gelding called Billy. Jill was a ski lodge manager from Thredbo ski village. Julie Bourke followed on a light bay gelding called Arbon Rouge, an aged campaigner from the Melbourne and Sydney racetracks. Julie had a gift shop in Thredbo, in the little arcade across the road from the main chairlift. The most stylish horse of the little group, Echo, was the next to step over the lip. Groomed young horses always looked smarter than the aged stagers and the woman on top was nicely groomed and quite trimmed herself. Her name was Michelle McFarland, a doctor from Jindabyne. Just ahead of me the next rider was Janet Hines, also from Jindabyne. She rode a thoroughbred bay mare called Holly. The mare looked sedate enough, but under a blaze of long red hair Janet didn't.

'I don't think there's any buck in that mare,' Ted murmured on a rare moment the women had pulled away to chat among themselves. 'But there's plenty of spirit in the redhead.'

He was dead right too. Janet had asked me if I would like to flatten Malameen out and give her a race on Holly. In an off-handed way I said her mare wouldn't stand a chance and I was made to bite my tongue for the next two days. Come hail, snow or hell itself, we were going to have that race one day.

Halfway into the deep trench a cluster of boulders appeared, running all the way to the bottom. Ted had to skirt around the obstacle. It was relic of glacial movement during the late Pleistocene epoch. The ice fused the boulders and rocks together, forming narrow tongues of ice and rock which slid towards the floor of deep trenches and ravines. With little stones sliding along with us, we all gathered at the bottom and searched the opposite slope for a better passage.

'I think we'll try and head down this big gutter,' growled Ted. 'At least the fence is washed away on the bottom. Up there where there's a bit of good footage for the horses there's an old fence flat on the ground.' He paused and urged Bee Bee down the narrow watercourse. 'Too much like hard work to roll up the old fences. They're flat on the ground all over Currango and Coolamine and I wouldn't mind a dollar for every poor roo that's been hooked up.'

The fences flat on the ground and the rusty wire trampled into ugly brown bundles upset Ted. We were on land that had been part of Coolamine Station, where his father was reared. His grandfather, William Taylor, took over the management of Coolamine in 1908. The Campbell family acquired it in 1881 and operated it as an outstation of Yarralumla, now the Governor-General's residence on the edge of Canberra. The highland homestead at Coolamine was used as a summer residence by the Campbell family. With so much history attached to these mountains it vexed Ted that the property was allowed to fall into ruin. 'It's only fit for brumbies, roos and such things,' he muttered to me one day. 'If it wasn't for the Kosciuszko Huts Association not even the homestead would stand today. They [the National Parks and Wildlife Service] don't like the past. They seem ashamed of it.'

It was rough going and the women and I were glad Ted was the path-finder. Wombat holes and washouts, like long cavities in an abandoned timber floor, lurked everywhere under the thick mat of coarse tussock. The further down we pushed, the more committed we were – we couldn't go back that way. The steep slope on either side gave way to limestone cliffs and gaping caves. Below one cave, Ted reined in and turned in his saddle. He wore a cream cowboy hat, and with his rugged flushed cheeks there was a trace of the veteran commander about his whole demeanour. It had been earned too. At different times a whole army of men worked under Ted's astute eye in construction jobs, from the Snowy Mountains Hydro-Electric Scheme to earthen constructions deep in the Malayan jungle. But what we all loved was his stories. He brought life to these sometimes drab-looking ranges, where the scenery began and ended with the first glimpse. This was big country and at the turn of the century it was a big empty country. It was the people who had made it memorable and provided some of the folklore Australians still cling to for identity.

'A big old wether, with so much wool on him you had to look at him twice to realise he was a sheep, lived in that cave for about four years, they reckon,' Ted said in his deep voice, and began to smile. 'There was a tourist operator about then. He was based in Tumut. He got great delight out of tellin his guests about the haunted cave. Camped at the Blue Waterholes the more active ones enjoyed a walk, so he'd lead em up here. Apparently this old wether wouldn't make a run for it until a few people got in the cave, then out of the dark he'd come.' Ted chuckled dryly and stared up at the rat-hole sized entrance. 'The tourist bloke reckoned it was just about a mile back to camp. He was never able to time em, but swears a girl returned in under seven minutes.'

We covered the distance in about fifteen minutes. The gutter broadened to form a shallow canyon. It would have been pretty at this stage if it were not for the hemlock. It covered the narrow creek flats at the foot of the cliffs. Hemlock is deadly to everything living – the philosopher Socrates was poisoned by it. I've seen sheep take a mouthful and be dead within three hours, but it would be overstating the danger to include humans unless they deliberately ate it. It has no resemblance to any edible plant. Sometimes horses will pluck at something they haven't seen before, just to taste it. We were all aware of it and urged them along until we saw the tents. Five 4WD vehicles and about 20 people were at the campsite. There was an instant camaraderie of spirit. We exchanged greetings with everyone, but kept our horses moving. Confronted with strange people and smells horses are apt to stop and lift their tail, drawing a swarm of flies to the fresh turds.

Suddenly we were riding beside a river. The dry watercourse ended abruptly at another cave and crystal clear water flowed out of the rocks. If you didn't understand limestone formations you could be forgiven for thinking it was a miracle. On the surface, limestone country may look dry and the chasms and sinkholes create an arid and inhospitable appearance. Geologists call it a karst landscape. But underneath there will be huge caves, some half-full of water, and underground streams will flow like storm-fed rivers. Perhaps the best example in Australia is Lawn Hill on the Queensland–Northern Territory border, where precipitation collected on the eastern Barkly Tableland finally emerges hundreds of kilometres away in a series of waterfalls in the upper tributaries of the Nicholson River.

I couldn't believe it. One minute we were picking our way through boulders on ground so dry and brittle the iron shoes of the horses played a monotonous note like guitars stuck on the bass, then Ted led us belly-deep into a river. I don't think big Mal had ever been in deep water before.

His reaction was to plough through it as quickly as possible, leaving a wake trailing from his rump like a motor boat. Ted chose mid-stream instead of a very steep traverse on rock. The river flowed through a gorge and when we struggled out of it we were on a bend with a nice piece of flat ground and plenty of trees. Vertical cliffs towered above us to heights much greater than before. Ted had selected a very special place for the barbecue.

Horses tied up in the middle of the day in summer don't usually eat. It's sleep time. Still, we didn't take any chances with the hemlock, which was yet to claim this delightful little refuge. We had to pull up a few plants.

There was a scramble for dry twigs to help Ted get the fire alight, and while the flames consumed the dry gum the women gathered around, sitting on logs which had been dragged up to make a camp. It was a regularly used camp-fire site. The long melodious call from currawongs seemed a little too persistent in the noon heat.

'Storms comin,' Ted said, scanning the darkening sky. Not that we could see much more than the sky directly above. 'We're in for a wet backside I reckon.'

'We're half-wet already,' Julie exclaimed. She had her boots off.

'With long legs like yours you should be on Malameen,' Ted teased.

'It's a lovely ride Ted.' She blushed a little as Ted and I stared at her legs.

Concentrating on the riding, it hadn't been easy to think about brumby catching since we left Currango Homestead. I carried a lasso made in Utah, at a place called Moab. It had been an ornament on my desk for eighteen months and I never expected to use it. I needed to get my left hand used to carrying it.

'Thankfully we can still ride in here. So many of the best spots are only accessible by the young and the fit. I can't walk far. What about you, Mike?'

'No – weak knee,' I replied. 'Can walk miles if there's no pack on my back. Loaded with camping gear I'm like a foundered packhorse.'

'Well, we're here now,' Michelle said, seated on the log the way she sometimes rode. If you rode behind and she turned to speak to you, one leg ended up in the saddle. Ted said she had lovely spider legs.

'And we want some better stories from you, Ted. That ram in the cave was a bit lame. You can do better than that.'

'Too clean? Too clean?' Ted exclaimed. 'Well I'll fix that!'

'Oh she didn't mean that,' Jill laughed. If Ted's back got any straighter you could adjust a rifle sight along it.

'Actually I ran into a mate of mine in Tumut the other day. I thought he was past it you know, but he looked different. I said how yer goin? Viagra he said. Get yourself a prescription. Within minutes it's strainin in yer pants. Oh I said, how did – you know, don't like to say her name. Never mind about her he growled. I smuggled the first one to town.'

They all laughed and Ted walked over to his saddlebag to get the steak.

'What are we going to cook it on?' Michelle asked.

Ted produced a rolled up piece of post netting.

'This is our griller,' he announced. 'It rolls up tight and snug for the saddlebag and when you spread it out there's enough room for all the steaks. It's already been in a hot fire. You gotta do that to melt the coating.'

Ted had a special gift for yarn-spinning. Most campfire stories are only good if told cleverly. Days later there are not many worth recalling and if you're having a beer by the firelight you might have difficulty recalling any of the stories. There was one that amused me about a mountain hermit who stuttered badly. Men who lived alone for long periods in the bush sometimes formed a bond with a wild creature. I have been told such stories on several occasions but never one which involved a wild wedge-tail eagle.

Jimmy McNamara was a rabbit trapper and he used to stutter. When he skinned and gutted the rabbits he left the offal pile for the eagles. One eagle began to follow Jimmy around like a pet and got too greedy. Early in the morning he'd fly over the hill where Jimmy was trapping, and eat the rabbits in the traps before Jimmy could get there. So Jimmy set a trap to catch the eagle. But instead of destroying the eagle as almost any other trapper would have done, he clipped its wings. He was just doing this when Ted's father Tom rode up. Jimmy was so engrossed he didn't hear Tom come. For years Tom laughed about the conversation Jimmy was having with the eagle: 'Y–y–you try walking around, you bugger, y–y–you try walking like I–I–I–I got to do, and now s–s–s–see who gets there first!' (Ted added that Jimmy fed the eagle rabbit offal until its feathers regrew, and one day the big bird flew away to a new territory.)

The women had supplied the blade steak and rolls and we all cooked our own bit to suit. Afterwards they left their hats and wandered downstream.

'You guys coming?' one asked.

'Didn't bring a costume,' Ted replied, pretending to be disappointed.

'We didn't either. It's all off or nothing.'

'You won't want me down there,' joked Ted. 'I'm on Viagra. Mike looks like he needs a cool off.'

'Hate cold water,' I got in quick. Freezing water can leave a man mortified.

'Don't be long,' Ted called after them, on a more serious note. 'Them storm clouds are gatherin.'

Ted and I sat down with a mug of tea and talked about brumbies.

'There's only about 65 left on Currango,' Ted said. 'Not many foals about either. I just wonder whether the dingoes are getting a few. If they're in packs they'll have a go.'

'What about the brumby runners?'

'Some young fellas come up from Tumut and give em a chase up. They get the odd one, but it's hell ridin with a rope in one hand, stubby in the other and the horse pickin his own way. Most of em end up in a bog. I think that's why the park protects the horses. They don't want brumby runnin up here – too dangerous for the humans.'

'Seventy horses and perhaps up to 500 roos on 24 300 hectares. What sort of stocking rates did Australian Estates have on Currango?' (Australian Estates Mortgagee Co., a British company owned Currango from 1912 to 1946.)

Ted laughed derisively. 'You're right – there's practically nothin on Currango now.' He took a swig of tea and thought about it for a moment. 'Australian Estates only left the horses here in the winter. Them alone, there was more than 100. But for six months of the year there was 5000 head of cattle on Currango and 10 000 head of sheep. That's why there's such a fire danger now in the summer. One day there'll be the mother of all fires.'

The women weren't long. The water was too cold and they wanted to see some brumbies.

'Mount up then,' Ted said, eager to leave. 'We'll risk it. Pity to ride home now and not see the brumbies.'

We hit the water again and surged through it towards the camping area. Instead of heading back up Cave Creek, Ted took us up into a low range covered in snow gums and a few scattered candlebarks. We didn't walk again. It was trot, canter or half-gallop. Janet took the lead soon after leaving the Blue Waterholes and we galloped to the crest like a Light Horse charge, minus the swords.

At the deserted Coolamine Homestead we dismounted and gave the horses a breather. Jill said she needed a rest as badly as her horse and I did too.

Ted had a special reverence for this place – he was born there. It was the only early settlement left intact in the sub-alpine zone of the upper Murrumbidgee River. I could picture men at the crack of dawn walking from the stock-men's quarters to the tack room, collecting a saddle with a bridle draped across it and walking bow-legged to the corral where probably up to 20 horses milled restlessly, run in minutes before by the horse-tailer. There was an atmos-phere here of people once living in a semi-wilderness, independent from all support services farmers today take for granted. Three years ago 28 schoolchildren from Tumut were given a taste of how vunerable the early settlers were to extreme weather. Defying the advice given by Ted, the teachers directed the children to erect their tents on the creek flats to the front of Coolamine Homestead. The weather changed suddenly and fed by heavy rain the creek burst its banks. The water rose quickly, inundating the tents full of clothes and sleeping bags. Vehicle access was cut off and by the third day food supplies were exhausted. Antici-pating trouble, Ted rode down from Currango with a mate, Paul, to survey the scene. He didn't realise at the time that the teachers had catered strictly for the three-day excursion and there was nothing extra. When he arrived in heavy rain the creeks were still rising. The teachers were becoming alarmed: the parents of the children would be deeply trou-bled when the 4WD vehicles didn't return to Tumut and they were out of food. Ted at once offered to ride back to Currango, telephone to assure the school principal the children were safe and then ride back with some tinned food in a bag.

'The problem was,' Ted said, 'that while the teachers and I were hastily discussing these arrangements it bucketed down. The creek we waded through to get to Coolamine had risen two feet when we returned to it. When we got down to the Blue Waterholes, Cave Creek was a swim job and flowin with an angry swirl. We got through her hangin onto their tails. Paul said he couldn't swim much so by this time it was serious. How the hell were we goin to ride ten miles back from Currango and get over Cave Creek with tins of food? I didn't have a packsaddle or a packhorse.'

Soon after they rode onto some wild pigs. A man used to living on his wits, Ted galloped after a half-grown one and his mate dismounted to look for a stick. Under full chase pigs don't last long. Ted had it bailed up and his mate Paul killed it. A cranky sow came charging back and they killed her too. Bushmen always carry knives. When Dooley's uncle, mountain man Noel Pendergast died, the minister said 'Noel has shut his knife'. It was a favourite saying of the man.

In driving rain the two men quartered the pigs and weighed up the probability of getting back over Cave Creek. Ted's horse Jaheel didn't mind pigs and Ted tied the big roasts, still covered in black hair, to the saddle dees. But Jaheel couldn't carry the weight of two pigs and Ted as well. Meanwhile the smell of the pigs had Ted's mate's horse dancing around as though he were standing on a volcano rim. Ted suggested Paul mount and he pass bits of pig to him.

'Didn't have any trouble with that bloody creek,' Ted

laughed. 'Paul stayed astride in the saddle and if the brown swirl looked like takin em both Paul pushed a bit of pig towards one eye.' Ted shook his head. 'Oh Jesus, that horse swam like a jetboat.'

Back at Coolamine, the pig legs were filleted and grilled. Before the rain started, two days before, the teachers had hurriedly stocked some wood undercover and the children were at least warm in the homestead. There was no electricity or running water.

'Those kids were a bit hesitant at first,' Ted reflected. 'They'd never eaten wild pig. But after the initial taste we couldn't keep it up to em.'

It was summertime and the days were long. Ted and his mate still managed to reach Currango before dark and report to the school principal that the children were safe. That night the rain stopped and mountain streams fell as quickly as they rose.

An ominous darkness was beginning to envelope the whole of the northern sky and we set off for Jones Hut at the canter, Ted leading the way. He said he would have to give the Fiery Range a miss because of lightning. If a violent storm broke there was nowhere to take cover. Instead he led us up the gentle rising slopes of the Gurrangoramble Range, on the western side of the Coleman Plain. Big Mal began to break out in a foam along the neck. He wasn't fit enough for brumby chasing and he was too tall. Snow gums have crooked, low-branching trunks. The trees don't have to be very thick to force a horse and rider into the outer ends of branches. I began to feel a bit guilty for taking him away so far from his home.

Ted took us across a flat top under thick snow grass and a few scattered whipstick snow gums, then down the other side into a claustrophobic ravine, gloomily shaded in heavy gum growth. He reined in at a roughly made brumby trap yard. Some of the bent wooden rails, taken from nearby gums, had rotted at one end and fallen to the ground. No brumbies had been trapped in these yards for several years.

'Thought I'd show you this trap,' Ted said, rolling another cigarette. I always thought smoking reduced lung capacity by half, but Ted sat his horse as though he were reading the paper in his lounge room. The horses panted and we heard the first rumble of thunder.

'The people that did this sort of thing,' Ted continued, 'used to put a couple of blocks of salt in the trap for the brumbies to lick. The trap had to be built in heavy timber like this so the horses didn't spook. Put it up in an open space and they wouldn't go near it. Also the yard needed to straddle a water soak so they could get a drink. Once the brumbies got used to walkin in and out they'd set the trap by railin in the bottom end and attaching an iron gate to the top entrance. The gate had to be an old rusty one or they'd be spooked by it. It also had to be properly hinged and weighted to shut by gravity pull. A length of rope was attached to the trip on the gate, run around the outside of the yard and attached to a suspended hessian bag with a lump of wood in it. A bit of number eight wire suspended from a tree held the bag. To set the bag up on the wire must have been the tricky bit. When the horses came into the yard, lickin the salt, milling around and jostling one another, the bag sooner or later got bumped. When it fell to the ground the rope pulled the trip holding the gate and it simply swung shut.'

'It was a cruel way to catch them,' Jill said, a little disturbed by the bleak, harsh appearance of the yard. With the spring running through the centre it was more like a railed-in ditch. Boggy and uneven, it wasn't difficult to imagine the pathetic plight of the trapped horses.

'How long would they be in there, with nothing to eat?' asked Julie. The women were quite horrified at the spectacle of this yard.

'It was never our way,' Ted replied soberly. 'I brought you all up here for a purpose. I wanted to show you what happens when you officially label an animal "feral". Once you do that it's seen as something dirty and hostile to the country. People no longer care about it,' he paused and glanced upwards at the clouds. 'It was never our way,' he repeated. 'In the days of the leases we either ran em into proper yards on horseback or roped em out in the open.'

A few weeks later a senior spokesman for the huge forestry in the Batlow region confirmed the callousness of bush trap yards. The trappers always intended to go back, but most were itinerant workers on the lower end of income. They lived a day-to-day existence. If a job was suddenly presented they went for it. The trap yard didn't matter much. They were only feral horses anyway.

'It doesn't happen often,' the spokesman, who wished not to be named, said. 'But sometimes we stumble on a yard full of dead horses.'

It was an eerie place with the storm clouds thickening and the light fading.

'We might have to make a dash for Currango,' Janet jested hopefully.

'Don't leave me behind,' Ted warned with a wide grin. 'You'll never find yer way through the swamps on Currango Plain.'

'You make it sound like a death trap,' one of the women laughed.

'There's some ghosts lingerin on that plain,' Ted said grimly. 'You gotta know where yer goin. I rode onto a wellington boot not so long ago. A dingo had dragged it out of one of the swamps. It was so old it was brittle like paper. He was buried alive, whoever he was, taken down under his horse.'

To save time from Currango Homestead to Coleman Plain we had ridden along a track during the morning. Only Ted knew about the perils of the frost hollows off the track.

Threading a different way home through the hills and later the bogs on the plain, Ted led the way. With the menace of the storms mounting almost by the second, we were pleased to be on the move again. We picked our way over fallen timber and ducked the low branches of the snow gums. At the bottom we found ourselves on the northern end of Currango Plain. The storms were closing behind and reluctantly Ted announced the brumby tracking had to be abandoned. Down below the eucalpyt scrub and out onto the low swamp areas we could see the dry watermark of Tantangara Dam and, far beyond, the tall radiata pines around Currango Homestead. Straight across it was only about five kilometres, but we had to follow the undulating ridges to avoid the treacherous low ground. In the spring thaw the long shallow dam filled rapidly if the weir gates were closed. Dry years and extra demands for water caused the dam to fill only on rare occasions. Some said the bogs had always been there. Others said there were no animals to eat the grass any more, only little mobs of kangaroos and wallabies. They claimed the water didn't drain like it should, the vegetation rotted and the seepage entering the creeks was often choked by excessive decomposition which lowered the oxygen levels in creek water. The frogs had all gone. In

April 2001 the water at Currango Homestead was chlorinated, following poor test results on local creek water.

Out on the treeless ridges of this vast frost hollow we rode in a tight group. The horses lengthened their stride – it was the homeward stage. And behind them was a menace. With no trees to obscure our view we could observe the advancing storm. The Brindabellas reminded me of a backbone, with the regular rounded peaks and saddles in between. Only 300 metres lower than Mount Kosciuszko, Bimberi Peak was swathed in a dark cumulous of cloud and the silent streaks of lightning were like tracer bullets in a night battle. We rode on, eager for Ted to break into a canter.

When Ted spotted a mob of wild pigs we did have a lot to worry about. In the blink of an eyelid I perceived the whole scenario. The pigs hadn't smelt us and Ted had already disclosed his relish for pork. My immediate concern was Big Mal. He more than hated them – he was terrified of pigs. Mustering cattle for a friend in the Warrumbungle Mountains I experienced his extraordinary fear of them about 300 metres above the plain. On the racetrack we call eighteen seconds to the old furlong 'half pace'. It's probably about 40 kilometres an hour and that's about the speed we descended. If Big Mal took charge now, a dingo might be pulling my boot out of the swamp.

'We won't go home empty-handed after all,' Ted muttered quietly and took off. The women looked at me.

'No, no I'm not into lassoing pigs.' But I couldn't just sit there. Refusing to race Janet had already disappointed them.

'Come on, we'll trot forward,' I added quickly. 'He'll need help and one of you can take Mal back when I dismount.'

'Get him out of the firing line,' Julie giggled. She was a girl who loved action.

'Look at the size of that boar,' Michelle murmured.

Ted had covered 100 metres on Bee Bee before the pigs suddenly lifted their heads. They have poor sight. When disturbed they will always freeze and test the air. When hunting them with a rifle the trick is to get the first bullet away when they freeze. It lasts about three seconds, then they run like dogs and don't stop again.

There were lots of piglets – we call them suckers in the bush and they're a delicacy. I knew Ted would be hoping one would cower and go for a squat. They'll do that if cut off from the fleeing mob. But on this occasion the sows stood their ground and snorted to draw in their families. They were used to wild horses and showed little fear until Ted was bearing down on them. Tightly bunched they moved like black torpedoes in the long grass, giving Ted no chance. The boar looked impressive, but he led the escape. It would have been a futile charge and all over in one minute if it hadn't been for a half-grown pig which got disoriented in the panic. Ted urged Bee Bee after it. The pig changed course and both it and Bee Bee were coming straight at us. I had already dismounted and flung the reins at Jill.

'Get him back quick,' I rasped. 'Or he'll be runnin with the brumbies, saddle and all.'

I didn't know what I was going to do. My main concern was not to look pathetically useless in front of the women. Oh for a bayonet! I thought. I ran forward, desperately looking for something. I didn't even think to remove my backpack. Then I saw it. An old fence post, washed down in a flood. The pig was closing the gap, coming right at me. Ted had reined in and was having a battle with Bee Bee. She didn't like pigs either. It was a one-sided contest. I raised the length of wood above my head, arms fully extended and brought it crashing down on the pig's skull. The timing was perfect, but the haversack threw me off balance. I followed the post across the pig and tumbled on my back beside the unconscious animal. Bee Bee took dreadful fright at the whole spectacle and for a moment the women thought the Man from Snowy River award winner was certain to be dislodged from his saddle. The poor pig was finally dispatched with a butcher's knife, which Ted carried in his saddlebag. It never knew what hit it.

The women were flushed with excitement. It was almost certain they never again would see a pig campdraft, a rodeo performance and a man killing a wild pig with a bit of stick, all compacted into about half a minute of action. The pig couldn't help being a hated feral and was just unlucky – although the mob which escaped was nailed by the park dingo man a week later, so it only lost a week of being alive. Wild pigs do enormous damage in Australian national parks. With noses especially adapted for digging they plough up hectares of ground searching for roots and bulbs. The exposed ground is often claimed by weeds instead of the original grasses.

In the heat of the moment we had all forgotten about the approaching storm. Black Mountain to the north had disappeared in a squall and forerunning tongues of cloud, the colour of smoke from burning tyres, had drifted onto the lower Gurrangoramble Range. We could hear the wind tearing into the snow gums. There was really no time to quarter the pig, but if Ted and I didn't, it would have to be left – and that was never an option. The wind was upon us before we had the four legs off. I always carry newspaper for padding in the backpack and for firelighting. I wrapped the legs in double layers and shoved it all into my backpack. My only concern was the smell. Would the wind disperse the pig odour enough? There was no way Big Mal would let me aboard if he could smell pig in that haversack. Jill brought him up quickly and without waiting for a response I swung for the saddle. If he did smell the pig it was better to be aboard than left stranded on Currango Plain with an electrical storm about to break. The newspaper must have done the job.

'Let's go!' yelled Ted. 'Jump the little creeks because some of them are boggy.'

We took off and spread out on a long low ridge under thick snow grass. The wind was tossing up the horse's manes, whipping Janet's red Irish locks across her face, and galloping boldly in front of me, Arbon Rouge looked poised to give Julie a taste of his old Flemington form. It was a splendid moment. The ground was firm on the ridge and the lightning was a mile behind. The light had faded into twilight and the rumble of thunder was overhead.

When the first creek appeared we bunched up and eased in behind Bee Bee. Ted knew every crossing. Big Mal jumped so high we would have cleared the highest fence in the Grand National. Michelle's Echo balked, before frog-leaping across. It's a horrible jump for the rider. The horse gathers in its rear legs like a cat about to pounce and launches into the air. The rider goes for the saddle pommel with one hand and holds tight. Michelle had an awkward recovery on the other side, on the pommel itself. For a man it would have been agony.

Ted could not contain himself. 'Landed on yer fanny,' he said with a grin that split his face.

'And bruised,' Michelle moaned. Be careful, Ted, I thought. She's a doctor. If Bee Bee goes head over you might need her.

She had a wild, animated look about her, Michelle. She took the jesting in good humour and her black hair danced in the rising wind, but it was no time to dwell. The dry tops of umbrella grass were airborne, racing past and among the horses like the first snowflakes before the big dumping of a white out. We thundered out of the open grassland and into the needlebush. The snow lease graziers called it 'tear-arse'. It might be native, but like wild pigs and rats no man from the mountains would lament its demise. This was when the jumping began in earnest. Big Mal had warmed up. His neck was arched, head on the chest. If I didn't keep a racing hold on him he would have ploughed through the girth-high scrub and flayed his legs open. We dodged what we could, but where it stood in wide barriers like a garden hedge, he bounded over like an old man grey. It was a wild scene. I rode on the western flank and when I looked across at the other five horses, spread metres apart, the rise and fall of the rumps reminded me of dolphins gliding in and out of the surf. I glanced behind and saw a plain eerily dark in the cumulous of low cloud. Sheets of rain, pale against the darkened horizon, had claimed the ridge where the pigs were. The storm was still a few kilometres behind. We might even get unsaddled before it hit. The Currango pines looked to be under five minutes away. It wasn't the rain that would worry us too much. It was the lightning that might come with the first squalls. Steel shoes lifting and dropping were a dangerous magnet. Once a horse stood still the shoe pressed into the ground and was unlikely to act as a lightning conductor.

Suddenly Ted raised his arm like a brigade leader in the Light Horse.

'Don't jump this creek,' he bellowed against the gale. 'It's real boggy. Yer might go shoulder deep. Watch where I go.'

Bee Bee sank to her knees. It wasn't too bad. It was the spectacle of churned up, quicksandy-looking mud which spooked the horses. Arbon Rouge and Billy were used to subalpine bogs and walked straight through. Echo sprang again and before I arrived at the edge I knew I was in for it. Big Mal sensed danger. I took him back 20 metres and charged the creek, contrary to Ted's instructions. He couldn't stop. All he could do was feign a balk and spring into the air. Focused on driving him through, I took no pommel hold and rose fully a foot from the saddle. When I crashed back into the saddle it was my turn to grit my teeth. Oh to be a woman – sometimes anyway!

The creek was the final obstacle. We galloped onto a dirt road and thundered past the outlying pines just ahead of the rain and lightning. It was every man and woman for themselves now. Horses were rushed into little taped-off paddocks, all of which were sheltered by the pines. Saddles were flung across shoulders and the last one, which was me, made it to cover with about a minute to spare.

Ted poured the Scotch and we both slumped onto a kitchen chair. The rain lashed the homestead and lightning struck nearby, like a shell passing over with a loud crack, then a boom on contact. We'd both been in storms worse than this one, but sitting there with a Scotch in hand and just listening to it was a rare moment of relief. Suddenly we missed something. It was the girls. They had rushed to their own rooms, which used to be the old stationhands' quarters, for cover.

'Will we see them again tonight?' I asked Ted.

'Reckon.' He dropped half the glass and sat it down on the table. 'They'll have a bottle or two of Shiraz over there. I'll keep to the Scotch myself. We better not have too much though,' he added with a warning look. 'Brumby hunt's back on track tomorrow.'

We had another drink.

3 Brumbies in the Mist

*And he bore the badge of gameness in his bright and
fiery eye,
And the proud and lofty carriage of his head.*

The Currango Homestead hadn't changed much since it
was upgraded from a drop-side slab dwelling to the country
weatherboard style adopted throughout Australia. That was
in the 1880s when the station was owned by A. B. Triggs.
In 1912 Australian Estates Mortgagee Co. purchased the
station and built on an extra wing which included the
kitchen and dining room. Nothing else had changed since
then. The main feature of the kitchen was the big wrought-
iron stove, fueled with wood. Ted lit it at daylight and by
7.00 a.m. the two black kettles were simmering. The knowledge of the stove and its warmth helped me get out of bed.
Myall Plains was in the grip of a heatwave when I left and to
awaken to a cold morning was unexpected. At 1300 metres
above sea level, Currango in early March had the same cool
temperate climate as we have in May.

Ted was seated on the long stool up against the back
verandah wall. I could see his back through the window.

46

'Tea in the pot,' I heard him say. His day always started with an early morning smoke, and over the decades smoking had deepened his voice. With his voice and his size he reminded me of a big bear. The night before, dehydrated after our long ride he started me on whisky, followed by rum and then red wine. Like most big men he didn't turn a hair. But like some little men I desperately wanted to keep up, but couldn't. I ended up head over off my chair. The women laughed until they were crying, because I told one story from the floor. So they said anyway. I knew the old stove would draw them up for warmth as well and I expected to be a target of mirth.

'We'll head out to Old Currango today,' Ted said, his voice carrying through the open back door. 'Some brumbies feed out on the plain there. Yer can't chase em for the swamps. That big bay of yours – struth, if he hit a bog and rolled, only hungry dingoes'd ever find ya.'

It was a fantastic concept. Saddle up and ride off in any direction, almost as far as you liked. It reminded me of my year in Queensland in 1994–95, when I had cattle agisted in paddocks of up to 8000 hectares. It was a year of record drought in southeastern Australia. When I returned home it was a while before I enjoyed riding on my own property. Queensland had spoilt me. When I got home and saddled a horse I felt confined to a small space. I could trot to the front boundary gate in a few minutes. It was a state of mind of course. Compared to these young local women I had a tremendous amount of space.

Ted's wife Helen was the first to appear. 'How are you?' she asked. There was a sparkle in her eye and a warmth about her. 'Bacon and eggs,' she said.

'Might have to risk it,' I replied. 'Ted's mounting us all up again.'

'These old construction men are brutes,' she laughed. 'Ted hardly ever touches it now, but he could really drink when he was on the Snowy Scheme.'

'Big camps of men yer see,' Ted rumbled from outside. 'They'd work ten-hour shifts. No women about much, so on the weekend it'd be on for young and old in the canteen.'

'How did you ever get to meet Helen then?'

'Spotted her skiing at Kiandra.' He chuckled deeply, like a bear thinking about honey. 'Never lost sight of her.'

That was all I was going to get and she winked. The bushmen will tell you stories until you throw up your hands, but the deep secrets never emerge. Nor should they.

Ted and Helen were married in 1960 and Ted worked with earthen construction companies for most of his life, doing a stint in Malaya and later Bougainville. In 1996 they tendered successfully for the Currango caretaker contract with the Kosciuszko National Park. For Ted it was a return to the mountains of his childhood and Helen, too, was a farm-reared girl from Tumut. Her family, the McAlisters, arrived in Tumut in 1832 as pioneer settlers.

The next into the kitchen was Mick Davies, the Park dingo man for the northern end and feral pig eradicator. If anybody had a daunting job in the park it was Mick. He had to apply his skills to catching the rogue dingos which crossed the Park boundary to kill sheep on private land, and also wipe out as many pigs as possible. He had three dogs to help him in his battle against the pigs. When a mob was sighted the dogs gathered the pigs into a group, allowing Mick to shoot them all. It was humane and quick. With the elusive dingo it is a very different story and the debate will go on for years, whether to continue with hit and miss trapping or baiting. With the scavenger fox, the baited meat can be buried and no other wildlife appears to be affected, but in the wilds of Kosciuszko simple solutions evade even the experts. Feral pigs root up 1080 baits and with a high tolerance level to the poison they are merely made sick. Some dingos simply defecate on top of the buried bait and move on.

One of the old dingo men in the mountains was Billy Osborne. Lean and hunched over from decades of tracking through the bush, Billy was notorious for his dry wit. He had the knack of making city officials look pretty stupid. Some years before, he'd been given the privilege of driving a senior official from head office around Currango for the day, to observe dingo-catching methods.

'I haven't seen any traps yet,' the official complained.

In a very slow drawl Billy replied, 'You're not supposed to. If they can see them on top of the ground they won't be all that keen to stamp their foot onto the release plate.'

They drove on a little further and official said, 'That stuff in the jar. You call it "dog perfume". I'd like a smell of it. See what it's like.'

'Dog perfume ain't the sort you're thinkin of,' Billy drawled again.

'I'll try it just the same.'

Billy handed over the jar. 'Please yourself then.' The official unscrewed the lid, and inhaled – then spilt the liquid on his hand.

'Stop the car,' he gasped. 'I must have water. Oh God, water please. What a smell. How could there be such a smell?'

'Nothing takes it off,' said Billy. 'Just time. About three days I reckin.' Later that day he said to a mate in a bar at Adaminaby, 'God help the next generation. I didn't tell him it was dog's piss mixed with cayenne pepper, but what else did he think would entice a wild dog to smell around a trap – French perfume?'

Mick went outside and sat with Ted. He didn't smoke though. They were both cold-country men and laughed when I said there was a nip in the air. Just the same, Bee Bee and Ted's beloved Jaheel had been rugged by Ted. Jaheel was the old gelding he was mounted on when a reporter from the *Sydney Morning Herald* photographed the pair, following Ted's 2001 Man from Snowy River award. Both horses had their heads in a feed tin, just beyond the back fence. An electric wire enclosed their little paddock. Beyond was the fog. Cool air had drifted down from the Brindabellas overnight but the frost hollows were still quite warm from the long summer days. The dampness of the plains and the cold air descending created big morning fogs. On the Murray in wintertime the fogs sometimes hung in the valleys for the entire day, gathering heavy cumulous again when a fresh burst of cold air descended from Kosciuszko.

Helen had that wonderful knack of cooking and chatting at the same time. I felt very spoilt. When the bacon and eggs came I was already hungry from the cooking aroma. I felt as though I'd gone ten rounds the night before and lost. I was already on the Panadeine. I hated alcohol. For 40 years I'd wondered why I couldn't say, 'No thanks, I don't drink'. After all, from tender years I'd never had a problem saying, 'No thanks, I don't smoke'.

No sooner had I finished than the two I dreaded entered from the front verandah. It was Michelle and Janet. They'd had breakfast and seemed to be waiting for something. They didn't say anything, but the message on their faces was clear enough: 'We're ready!'.

'Got the track picked out, Ted?' Janet asked.

'I thought the fire trail on the north side of the plain,' Ted said.

'Now wait a bit,' I said, 'I thought we agreed – no race.'

'Oh no,' Janet exploded with glee. 'You changed your mind. You said it was all on. You might have said so from the floor, but you definitely said it was all on.'

Desperate I said, 'It's gotta be level weights. Not fair to race two horses against one another otherwise. I've got no leadbag, so you'll have to gallop in your underwear. There's only two or three kilograms between us.'

'Don't tempt her,' Ted laughed. 'She's very keen to race you.'

Everyone laughed and we speculated briefly on the first running of the Currango Cup with nude riders. 'Boy, the tourists would flock up here for that. Even dry old Billy Osborne would turn up. He reckons anyone who says this place has got scenery must be mad and we need something more interesting than needlebush and dry snow grass.' Ted got up and walked into the kitchen. His face was flushed with the humour of it all and if he'd said it was on I couldn't see any escape. To my overwhelming relief he came to my rescue. 'There was an inch and a half of rain out of that storm. Track's dangerous and the race is off.'

'Next March I'll be back here,' Janet said to me. 'You better be back with a sound horse.'

'The Currango Cup,' Ted confirmed. 'It's on.'

The fog was rolling off the plain like fragments of low cloud as we rode away from Currango. The kangaroos hopped off a little and watched the procession of big mammals. They were used to horses, but always established a 50-metre safety gap. A big buck brushtail wallaby rose to full height under a radiata pine. They were beautifully marked from pale mustard to a light reddish tan. Dwellers of the forests and eucalypt scrubs on the divide's western fall, I never saw more than three or four in a group. At Currango they lived back in the snow gums and grazed in the daytime on the short green pick under the radiatas, ponderosas and Douglas firs. The introduced tree species formed an open woodland around the whole Currango establishment which, as we'd seen yesterday, were visible from many kilometres away, like skyscrapers in an urban sprawl, for the radiatas towered 25 metres above the snow gums. In amongst these North American trees were three restored workman cottages and the stationhands' quarters, a much larger building. Built in the architectural style of the time, it had front and rear verandahs. This is where the women were staying and where we had the party. Late in the night another storm had broken, and in my fearless state I could remember being glad the lightning was flashing everywhere, because I'd lost my torch. It was 100 metres back to the Currango homestead where I slept.

The pork was to be saved for the following night, Ted said. He wanted to hang it in the meathouse and let the meat set. I was pleased about that, because I couldn't remember dinner from the previous evening.

There were two new riders this morning, both from Thredbo. Helga Frolich managed the Ski Patrol Lodge and Sonya Davidson managed the Silver Brumby. I was beginning to think Thredbo might be a nice place to retire one day, but that whimsical notion was suddenly cut short when one of the girls said she'd like to see me on a pair of skis. I think it was Julie Bourke. Be her, all right. She'd be at the bottom with binoculars, laughing herself sick. People paid a fortune to be cold and on a slippery slide. I never understood it, but that was my loss I guess.

The two riders not with us were Michelle and Janet; they had loaded up and returned to Jindabyne. Time was up and they had to go home, disappointed there was to be no race.

Michelle had a birthday party coming up and we were all invited to a moonlight ride in the mountains following the party. 'Following the party' – it would be safer for me to chase brumbies on Currango Plain in heavy fog!

Halfway across the Currango Plain, Ted reined in on a rise and waited until we all assembled around him. 'There they are,' he said. 'About eight of them. I often see them feeding out from those hills.' He waved his arm towards high ridges under scrubby snow gums. The brumbies were mere specks in the distance. In a light breeze the thin layer of fog on the plain had drifted north to the Brindabellas. We rode on, and when we topped the next rise the brumbies were gone. Half an hour later we dismounted at Old Currango cottage and tethered the horses to the front verandah posts with bits of baler-twine. We all carried a piece to save our reins if a horse suddenly pulled away.

There was a lonely, desolate feeling about this place. I saw raw frontier life as a child too, but never isolation like this. We were silent, the six of us, then, as if echoing our feelings, Ted announced the history.

'It was built in 1851 by an Irishman called Tom O'Rourke. He was murdered by a bushranger.

'The place's not haunted though,' Ted chuckled. 'In fact, he wasn't murdered here. This country was too mean for bushrangers to be bothered with, except when they found gold at Kiandra some years later.'

Ted had spent a year here in 1943, during the coldest winter of the century. One blizzard raged for three weeks, and when the snow slipped off the roof of the cottage it formed a snowbank which eventually reached the gutterings. The big wide fireplace inside was the only warmth. Blizzard followed blizzard until kangaroos died in the hundreds, birds starved and most of the brumbies perished. 'They huddle up against one another and go snow-blind,' Ted said. 'Those horses seen on the Main Range summer before last are dead. The big dump in July got em. Pity the armchair environmentalists won't sit up and listen to the bushmen. It would save the taxpayers tens of thousands.'

In 1928 Australian Estates lost 1700 head of cattle in a blizzard on Currango. The lower tablelands and slopes were drought-stricken so the management opted to take the risk and winter the cows in the subalpine. The cold dry air of a winter drought often brings the big snowfalls. In the drought of 1946 Dad built a snowman for me on Myall Plains and in the drought of 1965 we woke one morning to a blizzard, snow bucketing down as though we were at the Thredbo ski resort.

But temperatures in the Snowy Mountains never plunge like those of north America, where blizzards can drop the temperature to −40°C and encase everything in ice. The lucrative Montana cattle industry was wiped out in three consecutive blizzards in 1896. Many of the ranchers perished along with their cattle.

We mounted up again and headed up into the snow gums. Ted was riding his buckskin, Jaheel. The old gelding looked like a twin to the horse used in the film *The Man from Snowy River* based on Banjo's poem and featuring Kirk Douglas and Tom Burlinson. Jaheel was a swamp horse too: like the brumbies, he could smell the bogs. Ted said we had to cross two creeks before we reached firm ground and he let Jaheel find the way. The second crossing was nasty. Jaheel had no fear of it, apparently knowing he wouldn't sink past his belly. Water the colour of black ink rose to the surface as each horse floundered through the bog. Big Mal tried to jump over it and sank to his shoulders. I had my boots up around his neck and locked my free hand on the pommel. The black liquid oozed halfway up the saddle flap but before I could choose which side to bale out to, Big Mal made a mighty effort and launched himself out of it. He was very distressed. Horse and rider build an element of trust over a period of time and I think he was devastated I should guide him into such a thing. Clear of the swamps we ascended the side of a low range and the snow gums walled in the visibility on all sides. Ted asked us not to talk and quietly told us Jaheel would lead us to the brumbies. Ted rode him on a loose rein and Jaheel followed the scent.

It didn't take long. The multi-branched snow gums spread from near ground level and when I stared into the twisted branches very little was identifiable – the grey, silver and light charcoal of decay created the perfect camouflage. Then Jaheel smelt them. His ears went forward and he picked up his gait. When Ted reined in we were less than 100 metres away and they hadn't seen us. A light breeze from the west ruffled the leaves and when we all sat still on our horses, it was curious how loud the sound of wind in the leaves was. The wind carried our scent back down the ravine we were riding up, away from the brumbies.

Ted motioned to me. I dismounted and Jill took the reins.

'We're downwind,' he whispered, when I stood alongside him. 'Sneak up that gully and yer might get a good photo. No hope of runnin them in timber like this.'

I lost precious seconds mounting the telescopic lens on my camera, then, moving like a forward jungle scout, I inched down into some heavy regrowth along the gully. Then I crept uphill and got within 50 metres before the stallion spotted me. He faced up squarely, head held as still as a statue. His mane and forelock were long and shaggy and his thick black tail reached the ground. I had never seen such thick tufts of hair around a horse's fetlocks. He was my first close-up sighting of a genuine Snowy Mountains brumby.

Slowly I scanned the herd through the telescopic lens. I was surprised the stallion hadn't snorted a warning to his mares. He stood there, his eyes glowering down like black coals, but I never felt in danger. I knew if I made no threatening advances I was safe, and the seconds ticked on. The mares were still unaware of me. This was the day camp where they rested. The mares stood with their heads drooped a little, in the sleep position. The two foals were restless. One of them was a bluey-grey, shading to charcoal. It stood behind its mother and I squatted on my haunches to wait for a clear snap. Anyone who has attempted to photograph wildlife will know how frustrating it can be.

Suddenly the stallion snorted and every mare's head lifted simultaneously. The bay foal in clear view whinnied and trotted up to his mother. Then they all broke over the ground like a troupe of ballet dancers, for there was no sound above the wind in the leaves. They glided up the steep slope as though suspended on wire from the tree tops and once again the snow gums dropped the stage curtain. I didn't get my photo.

In single file we continued up on the gentle incline towards the crest. The woodland thinned and we were riding through a soft valley with grass to the horses' knees when suddenly Big Mal stopped and trumpeted out the loudest whinny ever to escape his mouth. He hadn't seen the brumbies before. Apart from Jaheel, I am not sure any of the horses had. But he was the first to see this new mob and he wanted to socialise. Poor Mal had no concept of the reception he would have received from the stallion. A foal whinnied back and next thing the little mob was cantering towards us. Big Mal provided more encouragement and we all watched in bewilderment. How close would they come? There was a dark bay foal and another bluey-charcoal one. The stallion was nearly black and even shaggier than the one we'd seen earlier. He hung back in a thick patch of black sallees, but the mares came within a stone's throw, stopped and gave us a wild haughty lookover. Then before wheeling away, one of the mares answered Big Mal – who was putting so much gusto into his whinnies I could feel his body tremble under the saddle. The chestnut mare mustn't have been able to believe her eyes when she saw such a tall and elegant male. Perhaps she thought Big Mal might challenge the stallion. It would have been a shocking disappointment if he had and won. Poor old Mal was a gelding.

The mares with the foals in their midst galloped back to their stallion. There was some short, loud snorts from him – reprimands, they sounded like. I don't think that stallion wanted a fight, but he didn't like that moment when his mare answered Big Mal's call. In a flash, the little mob of five mares, two foals and a stallion had disappeared into the snow gums.

'Looks like you won't have to chase em after all,' Ted laughed. 'Just ride along and the mares will follow.'

In good spirits we rode on until Ted called a halt in a little glade. We tethered the horses to a few scattered trees and Ted lit a fire on a green patch in the shade of a sallee. The black sallees are the most frost-resistant trees in the Snowy Mountains. It was warm in the late morning and I looked for a gum to put my back against.

'I suppose that was my chance to catch one,' I said, feeling the weight of the previous evening. 'Doesn't seem right somehow. Just foals.'

'They'd have taken yer into thick timber anyway.' Ted broke a few sticks with his boot and placed them around the quartpots. 'If there was a future for the brumbies I'd agree with you. Let them breed up a bit. All my guests at Currango with a heart and a soul want to see one thing – a brumby. A couple of them bushwalkers was striding along the track to the east of Currango Plain one day when old Billy Osborne pulled up in his ute. "Can I give you a lift?" he asked in his slow drawl. "Oh no thanks".' Ted was a born imitator and used a high-pitched tone. '"We'll miss the scenery." Billy looked at these two with great sympathy. "I was trappin dogs here before yer mothers were born. The closest thing to scenery around here is the pub at Adaminaby."'

The women half-lay in the grass. 'I don't think they should be caught here,' Jill said quietly. 'They're such a part of the mountains now. We wouldn't be having this lovely ride if they weren't here.'

Ted dropped some dry leaves onto the fire. The flames shot high and a cinder spat and hissed through the air like a spent bullet.

'That's their future, I'm sad to say. Bullet in the head.' Then added bitterly: 'If they're lucky.'

'But where's the damage?' Sonya asked, in her slightly husky voice. 'What are the horses doing that's supposed to be so devastating?'

'Up on the main range in the alpine region there's no opposition from me or anyone else,' Ted replied. 'A lot of horses up there do more damage with their hooves than their mouths. The tundra plant species are very fragile. But down here –' Ted shook his head. 'No damage at all. There's so much roughage for em you'll never even see a tree ringbarked.'

'Who's going to come here when the horses are gone?' Julie had baleful eyes when something annoyed her. She lay full length, just raised slightly on her elbow so that her hair splayed a little over the snow grass. 'The limestone gorges are lovely, but the rest of it all looks the same. If there are no brumbies to ride out and see, why would you bother?'

'We could go roping the pigs in the swamps,' I suggested, to lighten the mood. I told them the story of *Cities of the Plain*. American author Cormac McCarthy saw the Sierras and the great plains in between with the same heart-eating nostalgia Ted Taylor saw his wide plains and the endless running spurs – once known as Rules Point country – the best land of the snow leases. In both New Mexico and south-eastern NSW it was government acquisition of land that changed it all forever. For those left, the culture was crushed and the land altered beyond recognition. Cormac's cowboys no longer had cattle to rope; instead, they rode up into the sage bush of the Sierras and roped mongrel dogs which had gone wild.

Some of the advocates for more wilderness zones had a disturbing lack of practical knowledge. One woman interviewed on a local radio program spoke with great authority, suggesting that only idiots would oppose her views. She said the parks had to become entirely wilderness to stop sediment flow into rivers and dams. I wondered whether she realised the massive amounts of sediment washed into rivers after a bushfire, which becomes an inevitable consequence once thick scrub replaces grassland in volatile fire regions. Just one episode of severe run-off after a hot fire (which can in some instances remove all vegetation including the roots of trees) could conceivably carry away more topsoil than centuries of exposure to hard-hoofed animals.

A lot of the old hands told me the rainfall had diminished over the past 50 years. But in fact, when I checked the annual records for Cooma since 1899, I discovered that the rainfall had actually substantially increased in the latter part of the 20th century. The old-timers contended that small stream and river flows had receded so much it had to be the result of reduced rainfall, when in fact it was massive moisture extraction by the scrub which had invaded the sub-alpine grasslands since the removal of sheep and cattle. Before white man the Aboriginal people were known to burn the grasslands up to 1400 metres for hunting purposes. Above 1500 metres, fires are sluggish and only run in extreme conditions, such as on Black Friday 1939, when the Mount Hotham Chalet in the Victorian Alps was burnt to the ground.

It was all about a clash of cultural interests and nothing to do with the environment. Of course horses had an impact. Everything we do has an impact, from releasing carbon monoxide from a car's exhaust pipe to flushing the toilet. The impact of the ski resorts on the mountains is enormous.

The quartpots boiled and Ted got his little calico tea bag from his saddlebag. We carried the water in two old gin bottles. I had one in my haversack and one of the women carried the other in a saddlebag. We hadn't planned for a lunch stop. It was to be a late morning tea and then home.

A breeze travelling up the little hollow ran the smoke low to the ground and it drifted through the horses. They were already asleep. We were at the head of a small valley running west. At one time the whole valley had been cleared and the trees were steadily seeding back. There's something about billy boil fires in the bush. I've never left one without some reluctance. We mounted up and followed the valley through to the Currango–Rules Point track.

At Rules Point there was a story that particularly amused me. When the hermits from outlying camps arrived at the pub they got on the grog. There was a bloke by the name of

Jack Oldfield, who always had a skinful and somehow rode home, 20 kilometres from the hotel. In the mountains most men wore spurs in those days, but Oldfield didn't bother with them. Someone helped him mount up one evening and strapped a big spur on each boot. He was too drunk to sit up straight and sagged over his horse's neck. Every time he sagged forward the spurs touched the sides of his horse, which made it dart forward. Oldfield leaned back sharply in the saddle, lolled forward again, and each time the spurs scraped his horse. Most drunks would have filled the air with foul language. Not Oldfield, for he didn't swear. He cried – 'whoops a daisy,' every 20 seconds for 20 kilometres. So the story goes.

Another Rules Point Hotel story was about a station manager called Bung Harris. He belonged to the generation who moved on from horses to motorised transport. Some didn't cope very well. In drink Bung sometimes got very confused. Late one Saturday night Bung stormed into the bar and asked the mob: 'Have you seen a baldy-faced jeep prancin around the bloody place with two white hind legs [rear white mudflaps]?' Bung served with the AIF in the First World War and was credited with some of the biggest overland droving treks from Queensland to Victoria.

A race at some stage was inevitable. I had nursed Big Mal's tendons in vain and I felt guilty later when I thought of Janet. I don't know what sparked it. We were halfway across the plain heading back to Currango when Ted left the track for a short-cut over a high hill. At the foot of it we crossed a creek and Jaheel took off. He was a hard-mouthed old fella. If it wasn't for Big Mal, Ted would have eased him down in an instant, but a message surged through Mal's brain that the starter had released the field. He caught me off-guard and Ted and I met the hill at full gallop. Twenty-seven-year-old Jaheel was a freak of a horse. He didn't let Big Mal get more than two strides ahead and Ted was near double my weight. But fitness told before the summit was claimed by the two old chargers. Helga flew past on Duke and took the prize, which was to be the first to see the view. It was the vastness and emptiness – monotonous snow gum ridges unfolding like an ocean swell and the distant blue of still more ranges – which made us all feel so tiny and insignificant. The girls were only seconds behind and to the sound of heavy-breathing horses and clearing snorts we formed a line on the hilltop and gazed over the wide yellow plains of the frost hollows, and beyond, the noon sun bathed the Brindabellas in ocean blue.

The women went back to their quarters for a late lunch and I had a sandwich with Ted and Helen. I was wondering about my next move when Helen came to my rescue. She had a friend in Tumut who had been on a camping trail ride somewhere south of Khancoban, on the Victorian border. They saw lots of brumbies and the woman who took them out had contacts in Victoria who caught brumby yearlings as a sideline business. I got the local roadhouse telephone number from directory assistance and from the roadhouse obtained the names of the local horse trail operators.

Jackie and John Williams owned and managed Khancoban Trail Rides. On high country safaris, lasting up to ten days if desired, guests were guided on horseback through some of the most spectacular and remote mountain country in Australia. Most of it was on the Victorian side, where the value of horse tourism and folklore is widely acknowledged in the general community. Jackie knew where the brumby mobs were and she knew who went after them. She urged me to attend the Corryong's Stockman's Challenge in April.

'You'll see the roping of the wild brumby!' she exclaimed. 'It's the only event in the world where a wild horse is released into the arena for a mounted rope man to catch.'

The Man from Snowy River Challenge, part of the Man from Snowy River Bush Festival, is an annual three-day event held at Corryong in Victoria. It is recognised as the most demanding test of rugged horsemanship in Australia. Thanks to Jackie, I was finally able to make contact with the Victorian brumby runners. In Victoria, brumby running was still legal outside the wilderness zones at the time of writing.

The Eroded Plateaus of the Suggan Buggan

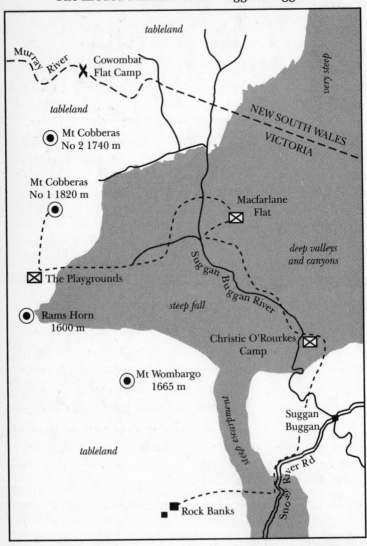

- - - - - Horse trek route

CHAPTER 4

The Eroded Plateaus of the Suggan Buggan

Through the stringy barks and saplings, on the rough
*   and broken ground,*
Down the hillside at a racing pace he went;
And he never drew the bridle till he landed safe and
*   sound*
At the bottom of that terrible descent.

The Man From Snowy River Bush Festival is designed to demonstrate the skills of Australia's rugged stockmen, from roping a wild brumby to cracking a stockwhip. The same men and women who compete in these events will be seen dancing to country and western music later in the evening.

Soon after dawn the various contests began. In the arena a horseman pulled a crowd as he worked a little mob of weaner cattle through gates and towards a tiny yard. Frequently the onlookers despaired for the desperate rider, for the mountain-bred weaners could see nothing but freedom beyond the wire fence.

Not far from the bar (thoughtfully placed in the centre of activities) the whip-cracking contest went on for most of the day. On the end of the leather whip is a finely plaited cracker made of horsehair. Some could fire the horsehair lash faster than Jesse James could have emptied the cylinder in his Colt 45. A stockman's prime tool is his whip. The spurs and the hat are the symbols of the job, but when the lead on a big mob is angling to break or the old cows get to the yard gate and turn, it's the stockman's whip that cracks loud with the last word.

It was the final contests that drew the crowd 30 deep on the arena fence and made a seat impossible to find after noon. The medieval knights of Europe had their jousting, but in our time of peace the warrior horsemen – and horsewomen these days – can rope the wild brumby in the arena, then try their hand at simultaneously riding a buckjumper and cracking a whip. In these consecutive events, stockmen faced one of the world's most arduous horseriding challenges.

In the wild brumby event the rider dodged deadly rear hooves as he dashed around the arena with a lasso in his throwing hand. Not only did the rider have to lasso the fleeing brumby, but he had to draw it in beside his mount and lead it through the arena exit gates. No one succeeded. The best performance was from a Queenslander who swooped upon the brumby with such lightning speed he brought a gasp from the crowd.

The final event was contested only by men as no women qualified. The first to be released from the chute on a wild Snowy Mountains buckjumper was pelted so heavily into the stockade-like fence that the ambulance held up proceedings for half an hour. The plucky Queenslander again took the honours, cracking his whip with more vigour than a lion-tamer while a scrubbie pale bay horse did everything from try to climb to the half moon to catapulting its rump faster than a car could flip at high speed.

Most of the competitors camp on the festival grounds with their horses. There is a carnival atmosphere, brimming with the vitality of a culture destined to fade in the coming decades. Children, some no more than six, canter about on knowing little ponies. In the background mum and dad cook on a portable gas stove and swap yarns with friends. Before four o'clock they drink billy tea and afterwards Victorian Bitter probably tops the list of choice in beer. They sleep in caravans or tents and the horses are part of the extended family. They are placed in little roped-off pens, and with fresh lucerne hay to eat they are as happy as the children. It is not uncommon to see a family standing around a gas stove with a horse's head thrust into the group, as though waiting for a stubby. When the sun dips below the horizon the sound of laughter consumes the grounds, and each little equine group retreats into the privacy of the evening.

A long way from home, I didn't know anybody when I arrived in Corryong. I soon discovered that crowds gathered around 'Banjo's Block' to listen to poetry reading, and it was a great way to meet people. If you had written a poem and wanted to recite it you simply wrote your name on the blackboard and the compere introduced you.

I had a poem, 'The Fighting Ringer and "the Scalding"'. I wrote it in 1963 when I was on Maneroo Station between Longreach and Winton in western Queensland. On the last night before his departure the breaker had a fight with one of the ringers and took a bit of a hiding. There was a big herd of mares on the station for breeding and one stallion. They were rounded up once a year to take off the yearlings. I can recall one morning when six of the freshly broken horses were loaded onto a truck and we were taken out to a paddock to muster sheep. Everyone got thrown that day and had to walk back to the loading spot. It was nearly dark when the last bloke walked in. All six horses were waiting in the corner of the paddock. We must have all been very fit, because I don't remember any serious injuries. The youngest jackeroo was dragged one day by a wild thing called Ginger Meggs. He lost most of the skin on his back, yet got up laughing.

The only person to recite any part of the poem before I took my stand on 'Banjo's Block' was Sally Loane on ABC radio. Sally told her listeners one day she loved poetry with a bit of fire and nostalgia for the bush. Celled up in my tractor while I was working country for the coming wheat crop, I never missed Sally's program. I sent her the poem and was a little overwhelmed when I heard her reading it back to me while I tried to steer a straight line on the dark basalt soil. You can read it in Appendix I.

After my reading at 'Banjo's Block', I got talking to some Victorian horsemen. One suggested I contact Stoney's High Country Adventures, a tourism company based at Mansfield. They weren't brumby chasers, but I was told that the operators might know the names of professional brumby catchers. The suggestion proved to be an instant winner for me. Rachel Parsons, who took the call, managed the trail riding section for the firm. She had a delightful English accent and warmly invited me to join a horse trek into the remote Suggan Buggan area, which spans the NSW–Victorian border, due south of Kosciuszko. It was more than 300 kilometres from their home base at Mansfield. The horses had to be loaded onto a semi-trailer and transported to a property called Rock Banks, owned by mountain veteran Buff Rogers. I had never heard of such an overland movement of horses for tourists, and I think curiosity motivated me almost as much as the promise of a brumby chase. She was taking out eighteen guests from

Queensland. There was a spare horse if I wanted to go. She went on to explain that brumby chasing by the guests was not allowed for obvious reasons, but if I rode independently and not as a paying guest, I could join her on a chase. Occasionally, she and her partner Chris had a bit of a flutter after the brumbies. The riding guests loved to see wild brumbies and if one could be caught it was good business for Konica and Kodak.

Rachel left me with no illusions about how dangerous a brumby chase could be.

'You literally bounce off the snow gums,' she said. She advised me to buy a pair of motorcycle crash kneepads and to bring my old jockey's skull cap. I went one step further and bought a fibreglass vest to protect my ribs and shoulders – I knew what it was like to have nearly half the ribcage broken. The proprietor of the bike shop in Dubbo asked me what race I was buying the gear for. He said he hadn't ever seen anyone my age go in for serious bike-racing. Embarrassed, I told him the race was up in the alps. 'I must have a look at my racing calendar,' he mused thoughtfully.

I left quickly, wondering whether I had gone stark raving mad. Thankfully, most of my friends accept me as eccentric anyway.

Wild gallops were nothing new to me. I just hadn't been in one for many years and I should have been avoiding them. On the flat I had about 1200 race rides. The roughest ride was in the six-furlong (1200-metre) Marthaguy Picnic Race Cup in 1972. This annual race meeting was held on a claypan about 180 kilometres northwest of Dubbo in central NSW. The name comes from a creek, or small river, which flows into the Macquarie. It is one of the principal wool-growing areas in Australia.

The running of the Cup that day was more than just another cup race. The graziers in the area had decided to run the event for the last time. Wool prices had crashed in the late sixties and after four years of low prices many growers didn't feel like financing a race meeting. In years past, the winner had the privilege of keeping the cup until the following year, but this time the winner was to take home the impressive silver trophy for good. In some bush picnic race clubs the cup trophies assumed the significance of a mini 'Ashes', and the cup-holders combed the countryside for strong gallopers. The competition added tremendous vitality to the bush race meetings.

The tracks out in the bush sometimes had a running rail for the final three furlongs (600 metres). I don't think the old Marthaguy track had any running rail. The furlongs were simply marked by two-metre high posts. If your mount ducked inside one it was disqualified. The only new technology was the mobile barriers, towed north from Warren by a 4WD. When the cup field of ten sprang from the barriers onto the claypan track I expected to have an armchair ride from barrier one. The field bunched tightly after the first 100 metres, but in a 1200-metre race that was quite normal. A forward position was always favoured over a rear one. Soon after I realised the outside horses were not merely looking for the lead. The jockeys from the Bogan and Paroo were aiming to force me and one or two of the other runners into the five-furlong post. What they didn't know was the mare I rode was a clean jumper. She was trained privately on a station and jumped logs as part of her fitness preparation.

Both the five- and four-furlong poles were on a 50-degree slant. Cattle had rubbed against them. Faced with the post coming straight at me, I had two options. Go inside of it and be disqualified or jump the lower half of it. In the fierceness of a race you tend to take risks without flinching. I put her at it and she went so high I can recall looking down on the rest of the field. At this point the track had begun to turn. In NSW all tracks are designed for clockwise racing and when the mare's front hooves hit the ground again there was a natural tendency to veer out a little. In racing language it's called 'roll'. She rolled out and collided with the horse outside of her so hard it stumbled and fell and brought down two behind it. Undeterred, the remaining desperadoes applied the same tactics at the four-furlong pole. Again I put the mare at the pole and she sailed over. The horse outside of her somehow got its front legs tangled with her rear ones and fell, bringing down the horse behind as well. The three desperadoes had wiped themselves.

I went on to win by six lengths. A lot of Light Horse charges in Palestine in 1917–18, under heavy fire, would have emerged in better shape than this cup field. Two horses were shot on the track and all five riders were conveyed to the Warren District Hospital by ambulance. The racetrack resembled a battlefield. The shocked stipendiary steward, Cecil Armitage, told me to go home and retire.

'It's too dangerous, son,' he said breathlessly. 'You got a young family.'

The ringleader of the desperadoes was given 'life', which meant his licence was revoked and he would never again be registered by the Australian Jockey Club. Needless to say there was no appeal against the sentence. I never saw him or his two mates in the saddle again.

Today the solid silver cup is back in the hands of those far-western sheep graziers. They resurrected the Marthaguy Picnic Race Club in 1991 and moved the venue to the village of Quambone, 60 kilometres west of Coonamble. Little has changed out there. The same names, many of them Irish, are registered on the racing committee. They all recall when Bright Ingot won both the Lady's Bracelet and the Cup within an hour. Boy, wouldn't Banjo have worn out some pencils! The owner and trainer of Bright Ingot, Mark Beresford, recalled just one trace of humour that day. An old bushman with a one-eyed thoroughbred was asked by the committee if he'd saddle up in the Beaten Stakes, the last race of the day. 'Not if that bloomin jumpin mare's in it,' he growled, referring to Bright Ingot's winning streak.

I thought there would never be another ride like that. Well I was wrong. Twenty-nine years later I found myself in a wild charge to catch a brumby. There's something extremely intoxicating about a hell-for-leather ride. In *The Desert Column*, Ion Idriess wrote: 'What a gallop! Over gently sloping ground – not a leaf of cover – ten times our number furiously blazing at us. For more than a mile those vicious pests whizzed past, ricocheting off the ground, flipping off a man's hat, thudding through a bandoleer. How the old neddies legged it out.'

I met up with Rachel Parsons and her partner Chris Stoney at Rock Banks. The property was about 100 kilometres northeast of Omeo in the Central Highlands of Victoria. There was a yard full of horses with nosebags on when I arrived. Milling around were the eighteen guests, some dressed in jeans and others in an array of expensive riding gear. When the horses had finished the mixture of oats and chaff in the nosebags the saddling began. Rachel introduced me to Ebony, a lovely brown mare 14.5 hands high. She looked perfect.

The guide for the five-day trek was Dean Backman. He

was from Bairnsdale on the coast, more than 200 kilometres away across rugged mountain ranges. Hauling a trailer behind his 4WD ute, Dean had brought one of his brumby-catching horses, called Ernie. He was a very fit-looking grey gelding of thoroughbred origin.

Dean was a farrier by trade. He looked upon work in the mountains as his days off. On a busy day with the hammer and hoof rasp it was nothing for Dean to shoe up to sixteen horses in a day. In a crouched position most of the day and some heavy horses leaning all their weight onto the farrier, it was the sort of work which would take its toll on anybody. Dean loved nothing more than riding the mountains with his lasso, searching for brumbies. In the past three years he had become recognised as Victoria's number one buck runner, having caught 232 brumbies from a horse he called Danny. Dean said he didn't expect to see many brumbies on this ride. A horse column of 24, all with steel shoes, caused a rumble sufficient enough to be picked up by wild horses hundreds of metres away. He had decided to give Danny a spell and ride his No 2, Ernie.

It took a while to get everybody ready. Day one was when horse tour operators really earned their money. There were nervous clients and cocky ones. The cocky ones usually provided the greatest risk of a fall. This group seemed to be something of an exception and Dean was called upon to lead the way about mid-morning. The first obstacle for the riders was the steep descent down Black Mountain to the Suggan Buggan River. Very embarrassed, I had to call a halt halfway down. I had forgotten to bring a cropper and my saddle slipped onto Ebony's neck. A cropper is a leather strap which fits around the butt of the horse's tail and connects onto the rear saddle dees, preventing it from slipping forward. Everyone behind me had to wait while I replaced the saddle, which was uncomfortable and stressful for them on the steep mountainside. Lips pursed and cheeks flushed, Rachel took the cropper off her saddle and put it on mine. She thought her saddle might sit better. It wasn't a good start and I got into more trouble later on. I don't like trail riding. It has always been too restrictive for me.

We camped that night at a reserve called Christie O'Rourke's, on the Suggan Buggan River.

The next morning there was a confident look about the three key figures, Dean Backman, Chris Stoney and Rachel Parsons. Rachel wore a mackintosh vest, black leggings and roller spurs; her gloves were made from the same rubber as you find inside tractor tyres. Over her moleskins she wore fawn chaffs. She rode a bay gelding with a white blaze and black mane. Chris wore a bright green shirt with 'Stoney's Bluff and Beyond' printed above one of the pockets, brown chaffs and roller spurs. Pulled loosely over the shirt, not buttoned up, he wore a black vest. He had a cream hat and Dean wore a brown hat, with black bindertwine for a band. The two of them together reminded me of Butch Cassidy and the Sundance Kid. Rachel teased them both incessantly and often caught the cheeky Sundance's eye. Of the horses, Chris's buckskin, Spider, took the honours.

I admire great riders and people who have the ability to delegate and organise, and 'Butch' ran the operation with the same coolness and efficiency his American counterpart robbed banks and snatched payrolls. Looking after 18 people in a wilderness environment is a heavy responsibility. Rachel took care of the horses, but Chris was the commander.

After breakfast the column formed up and we climbed quickly into the eroded plateau country. A pack of dingoes must have smelt us and the whole pack howled. The tall straight gums accentuated the sound, making someone remark they sounded more like hungry wolves. If you had been alone on foot, you would have altered course. This was wild, lonely country, disturbed only by occasional bands of brumby runners.

There's no warning for a brumby chase. There's a sighting, usually on a creek flat, and the rope is unslung from the shoulder. The skilled buck runner can remove the rope from the shoulder to the throwing hand's forefinger and thumb in about two seconds. This is the only start the brumbies get, as they tend to see the chase horses the same instant the riders see them.

Dean was off. He bounced into full gallop as fast as a racehorse out of a machine. The first 400 metres was along a creek flat with scattered timber and plenty of logs to jump. The brumbies held their lead and scattered into the tangle of gums and scrub, heading for the next tier of the range. I had Chris's mount, Spider, locked into my vision. Dean had got a bit of a break on us, aboard the fast galloping Ernie. Rachel on Mahogany was forging her own track through the scrub. Hot on the trail of the four of us was Peter Watts, who was trail rider assistant. Peter was the driver of the camp-out truck, which carried everything from cold stubbies to bedding. Left behind were the guests.

We burst into a patch of snow gums and within 100 metres I was indebted to Rachel for her advice. The crooked bough of a gum caught my knee. I must have thumped into it at 40 kilometres an hour. Rachel was right; at that speed limbs simply bounced off the sappy timber and confronted by more wide spreading branches there was no time to pay any heed to injury.

All of a sudden we were heading up the steep side of a range. There were just flashes of black and brown whipping through the gums. We had reduced the gap a little, but I

wondered about our mounts' stamina to gallop steeply uphill and not drop out from exhaustion. The brumbies had
no weight to carry. My mare Ebony was incredibly fit. She
stuck with Spider every stride of the way and I wore no
spurs. I hadn't worn spurs for years. It was so steep I half-
expected Dean to pull out. He was only a couple of strides
ahead of Chris, and Rachel was right on my tail. I was too
consumed to see where Peter was. To a conservative horseman it didn't seem possible for the horses to keep it up. We
twisted and turned repeatedly to break the severity of the
climb. Rear hooves flung stones into tree trunks and some
of the big round ones spun out and crashed down the slope,
sending away echoes of rock smashing against rock.

Dean had the brumbies in sight. The rigour of the riding
absorbed every ounce of my concentration and I momentarily lost interest in them. I just wanted to keep up. Rachel
passed me and to my relief Dean switched course to gallop
across the slope. But my heart sank when he suddenly
pointed Ernie downhill. Chris didn't hesitate and both he
and Dean broke away by some lengths. Without Rachel to
follow I might have lost them. I think it was one of the
scariest half-minutes of my life. As every Australian knows,
Banjo's famous poem is about a brumby chase in the Snowy
Mountains, to retrieve a magnificently bred colt that had
escaped into the mountains and joined the wild horses. In
the poem one young man, 'a stripling', gallops headlong
down a mountainside to turn the wild herd. All my life I'd
thought it was poetic licence, until now. The leaps were
huge and I felt sure we raced beyond the equilibrium of
gravity. The centre of weight had to straddle the horse's
shoulders, instead of behind them. Just a slight rear lean
and the mare would have crashed. You had to ride as
though on a flat surface. One slip of a front leg would have

spelt a disastrous headlong smash down the side of the mountain. Dry sticks snapped like starting pistols and stones bounced abreast. In 'The Man from Snowy River' there was thick wild hop scrub and wombat holes and the mountainside was far steeper, but if ever there was such a ride I was having a taste of it now. I vowed I'd never take such a risk again – an American mustang runner once said, 'A rider's grave is always open', and never had it seemed truer.

At the bottom there was no respite and I began to breathe heavily, almost gasping for air. A crevice loomed and Rachel sailed over it. It was over four metres wide and when Ebony sprang for the opposite bank I didn't think she would reach it. The top half of her made the rim and desperate scrambling with her front legs saved a nasty tumble into a nearby waterway, lined with jagged rock. Exhaustion struck me quickly after that. Rachel's ponytail bobbed out of view in a thick tangle of snow gums.

I caught up a few minutes later. I had to cooee to locate them. They were at the bottom of a ravine, in thick timber. Dean had his lasso over the head of a dark brown mare and had the other end of the rope wrapped around a tree trunk. The mare was straining back against the rope, but breathing quite normally. The lasso had a big leather eye, which prevented any choking. She was pregnant and when I got closer I could see she was melon headed. A deformed head was a reasonable indication she had mated to the same stallion her mother had fallen pregnant to. At face value, the inferior quality of this animal would provide some support for those who demand the eradication of all brumbies. What they seem reluctant to acknowledge is the order of natural selection. Inferior colts never have the strength to fight for and win a group of mares. The inferior fillies will fall

... when the droughts come, or the blizzards ..., they will be the first to perish. The process ... selection works in all species.

...er rode back to collect the guests and about ten ...inutes later most of them were busy with cameras. The mare was the ugliest horse I had ever seen, but the enthusiasm for photos demonstrated the awe wild brumbies inspire in Australians.

Dean released the wild mare. It was impractical to take her along with a tourist group.

Later in the day there were a couple of unsuccessful brumby chases. The brumbies were spooked and on the alert. A buck runner and his wife were operating one day ahead of us, scattering the little mobs. It was awful country. The lead horse shied and we all steered around a copperhead, coiled up with the sun catching its translucent eyes. They lie on the bare track where the soil is warm. In the soaks, black snakes skidded through the horses' legs.

Above 1200 metres the plateaus were covered in snow grass and scrub wattle. Most of the time Dean followed a 4WD track, but occasionally a shortcut was necessary to avoid kilometres of riding, and the horses were forced to do more high-stepping over logs and fallen trees than a circus pony. The guests ducked branches and clutched their hats, but they didn't seem to mind; this was what they had paid for. It wasn't Chris Stoney's choice of terrain. The spokesman for the eighteen guests had specially booked a trek through this area. On the map he showed Chris where they wanted to ride. Nowhere else in the world could a large group book a five-day trail ride and show the operators on the map where they were to be taken.

We camped that night at McFarlands Flat, a few kilometres south of the NSW border and the forbidden territory of Kosciuszko National Park. The buck runner and his wife had caught two well-grown foals. The frightened animals were tied to trees and the couple planned to ride out of the mountains next morning. They had come to capture a couple of ponies for their children and were delighted with the result. Brumbies were shot in this country and as miserable as the two foals looked, snatched from their mothers, their lives would be far more comfortable and secure on a Bairnsdale farm than on the eroded plateaus of the Suggan Buggan.

By the light of the campfire I inspected the damage to my body. The knee was okay. The motorbike pads really worked. My right ankle was black and the whole foot had turned purple. The lack of swelling indicated there was no hairline fractures. But it was enough. I had done my first and last brumby chase. As far as I was concerned it was for young men.

I remarked casually to Dean I was abandoning my plans to catch a young brumby. He said he had one on his farm which would suit me perfectly. It was a light bay gelding, caught near Christie O'Rourke's reserve. Born and reared on the Suggan Buggan suggested it had genes made of steel. Dean had already gelded him and taught him to lead. I could have him for $500 and Dean would look after him until I found time to make the 900 kilometre trip to Bairnsdale. I didn't own a two-horse trailer. I carted my cattle to market by truck and when horses had to be moved they went by truck too. It was such a long trip in a truck I decided Sal and I would have to make a holiday out of it. In the mountains of Victoria that wasn't difficult to plan.

Before I left the group next day Dean made me a member of the Victoria Alpine Brumby Runners Association. It was a bit like taking out a jockey's licence with no intention of ever appearing in the jockey's room, but when the certificate arrived I put it away so carefully, I haven't seen it since.

Buff Rogers collected me at a reserve called the Playgrounds. One of the early explorers had seen Aboriginal children playing by the creek. The Biduelli tribe had been gone for 150 years.

'Did you learn anything?' Buff was a tall man with a deep voice. Now in his 60s, he had spent all his life in the Victorian high country.

'Buck running's not for me,' I replied. 'Not even in the movies will you see anything a lot more dangerous.'

Buff didn't answer for a while. In his 4WD station ute we were slowly threading our way through the big mountain gums to the Rams Horn. To the north were the dual peaks of the Cobberas. These three were the only alpine peaks in Australia with sharp, rocky profiles.

'We never ran the brumbies like they do today,' he said at last. 'Striking daylight, or last light, we'd get em onto the big open flats. If you get close enough and go hard, the young ones get so confused they run all over the place. All you need is a good horse. He homes in and you pop the lasso over the head. Not hard if you got a horse that knows what to do.' He paused and turned towards me with a wide grin. 'The smart horseman's a good campdrafter. That's the skill that counts. Forget the tearaway bush racing and this mad galloping in the scrub. It ruins a good horse. Soon or later they get broken down. Sooner or later the riders get smashed up. They've all got busted knees and some have arms that don't bend, or their wrists are full of steel plates. It's madness.'

I agreed with him and told him about Dean's offer.

'I thought I might call the brumby O'Rourke. Dean said he caught him near Christie O'Rourke's reserve.'

'There's a lot of history attached to the O'Rourkes,' Buff said. 'It's rumoured that the name Suggan Buggan is Gaelic. No one knows what it means. I'll show you an old manuscript when we get home.'

Some months later I contacted a friend of mine in County Cork, Ireland. 'Suggan' meant fragile, she told me. One interpretation was a fragile rope, made from straw. Buggan was thought to mean 'small' in Gaelic. In a slab cottage in the 1830s, no neighbour for maybe 50 kilometres and the fierce Biduelli people resenting white invasion of their country, it was little wonder the O'Rourkes called their new home Suggan Buggan.

'How many cattle do you run on the mountain lease?' I asked. I have always felt it rude to ask someone how many cattle they ran. It's not far short of asking how much money they have, but in this case I excused myself. I knew Buff's mountain lease was only a minor part of his whole grazing operation. Rock Banks was a substantial freehold property, but the Crown mountain leases in Victoria had various limits on them. Buff had a seven-year lease. Some were as tenuous as twelve months.

'Only about 200 and they're only up there for about four and half months,' and he added with a grin. 'Not many on a 100 000 hectares.'

'You got a pig and dingo problem like Kossie?'

'No pigs on my lease and I take full credit for it,' he said dryly. 'Right behind the seat is the equaliser. I caretake about 162 000 hectares in total and nothing gets the chance to breed up and harm this country. I do it single-handed. What's the park up over the border in size?'

'About 607 000 hectares I'm told.'

'And enough staff to mount a marching salute for the Governor-General.' He pushed his hat back a little. In the higher altitude it was cooler and I wound up my window. I don't think Buff felt the cold much. He had his elbow out. 'I don't go up there now. My mates are gone and the whole place depresses me. The worst thing they've done is lose control of the dogs. They're crossing the border in hundreds. At calving time I have to bring the cows into the small paddocks where I can keep an eye on things. I always found, and my dad and grandfather before me, you get the fewest calving problems when the cows are out in the hills, left alone.'

Half an hour later we arrived back at Rock Banks, where I had left my car. It was a picturesque property of rolling downs 1000 metres above sea level. It could have been the soft undulating hills north of the city of Orange or the stud chequered upper Hunter Valley around Scone, both in NSW, but when it came to driving to the nearest town for food and station supplies, Rock Banks was as isolated as some of the cattle stations in North Queensland. It took more than two hours to drive to Omeo, the nearest town, on a rutted dirt road.

Buff asked me in for a cup of tea and produced the O'Rourke manuscript for me to browse through. I was still reading it three hours later and Buff graciously asked me to stay the night.

The O'Rourke estates were held in the county of Kildare in Ireland. In the reign of Queen Elizabeth I (1558–1603) the Gaelic clans in Ireland were overwhelmed by superior forces. Oliver Cromwell had artillery and when he invaded Ireland he was met with only primitive weapons such as the pike and the sword. Any clan prince who refused to acknowledge Queen Elizabeth I as sovereign was taken to Tyburn Hill for execution. The O'Rourke prince, Sir Brian na

Murtha O'Rourke was executed in 1591 at the hand of Oliver Cromwell.

The princes refused to submit to English rule and, rather than face certain execution, some fled to France, Russia and Austria. Their noble status was often recognised and they were accepted into the military elite in those countries. Nearly two centuries later General Count Joseph Korn-cliefvitch O'Rourke was one of the first Russian generals to expel French Napoleonic forces. His portrait hangs in the Hermitage Gallery in St Petersburg, Russia. In France, a Count John O'Rourke was promoted to a 'Peer of France' by King Louis XV for military service to France.

Most of the O'Rourkes remained in Ireland after Cromwell's invasion. Their land was confiscated and they were forced to remove the O from their proud name, but they never gave up the fight. In 1798 the county of Kildare became the mother of Irish Republicanism. The movement was in contact with the new French revolutionary government and in the same year three French troop-carrying ships broke the British naval blockade. Despite French assistance the rebellion failed and the outcome was another catastrophe for Ireland. Six thousand people were deported from the County of Kildare as convicts and one of them was Michael O'Rourke, aged eleven. He arrived in Botany Bay in 1802. Over the next two decades several members of the O'Rourke family migrated to Australia as free settlers.

After some years of roving in the colonies, the brothers James and Christie O'Rourke finally settled at Wulgul-merang. In 1838 Christie took up the run he called Suggan Buggan and James extended his landholdings to include Black Mountain in 1840. In 1842 something seemed to go wrong with the O'Rourkes. The infamous Ben Boyd arrived in this remote area and historical records reveal him as suddenly being the owner of both runs, but not for long. Ben Boyd had his cattle speared. More than 150 head were killed in a single raid. It was never documented, but the Irish families in Gippsland appeared to get along better with the Aboriginal tribes than the British ever did. Whether they formed closer bonds because there was a common oppressor, or whether it had something to do with the Catholic faith, nothing at the time was written on the subject.

Like all regions in Australia, the Monaro has its share of oral history and folklore. It doesn't appear the Monaro had any famous bushrangers, but if all the stories about Ben Boyd are true the Monaro was exposed to one of the most swashbuckling characters in early colonial history. As well as suddenly acquiring a lot of land, it's rumoured he also acted as a land agent for one of the most elite British families in the colony. If my sources are correct, some selectors were forced off at gun point. However, there is no written documentation. In 1848 his personal land empire crashed and his swashbuckling lifestyle continued in the Pacific. A whaler as well as a land entrepreneur, he is supposed to have put to sea in one of his vessels anchored at Boyd Town near Eden and deliberately wrecked it on an island. He is said to have abandoned the craft and crossed the island on foot to an awaiting ship. His creditors thought he had drowned. He was never seen again, anyway. Somewhere in the middle of this Wilbur Smith-style intrigue is the truth.

What happened at Suggan Buggan in 1842 no one knows. While Ben Boyd controlled it he had an overseer stockman called Cranky Paddy and a hutkeeper known as Suggan Buggan Ned. It appears that as early as 1846 the O'Rourkes were back in possession. Christie's son David introduced 70 mares into the valley and two stallions. They went wild almost from the start and provided the genetic base of the Snowy Mountains brumbies. The Suggan Buggan River valley is no more than a long day's ride from the southern ramparts of the alps.

In 1902, the last of the O'Rourkes left the Wulgulmerang area and the Rogers family took over Black Mountain Station, which by then included Suggan Buggan. In 1933 the station was split and the smaller portion became Rock Banks. Decades later Suggan Buggan and much of the original Black Mountain Station was absorbed into the Snowy River National Park. The park authority maintains the old slab schoolhouse erected by Edward O'Rourke in the 1840s. Descendents of David O'Rourke's horses have never left.

'Did you ever run brumbies?' I asked Buff next morning over breakfast. We sat in a kitchen warmed by a fuel stove, about an hour after sunrise.

'There had to be a quid in it for me to be bothered,' he replied, a huge mug of tea hidden between both hands. (The evening before he had served a meal which would have fed me for two days. He told me not to worry when he noticed I was struggling.) 'Ken Connley and I caught 120 for the Commonwealth Serum Laboratory in '77. We caught em in the snow on Cowombat Plain. Left the trailers below the snowline and head and tailed em eight or ten at a time, loaded em and let them go in a paddock here.' Buff paused, topping up my mug of tea. 'It was the worst year of the cattle crash. Big bullocks were only making 80 bucks a head at Newmarket, so when the contract was offered Ken and I accepted and got stuck into the job. Ken has a farm down at Benambra. He's a crack hand at the rope. You want to see good lookin wild horses he might take you up into the alps.' He grinned, 'Our Alps, I mean – Victoria. We got the snow brumbies. They never leave the top. When the big snow comes they dig for grass.'

No one working in the laboratory 24 years later knew why so many horses were suddenly needed. Maybe there was a disease scare and details were never released. Today, draught horses are held on a research station farm to produce antibodies for such virulent diseases as strangles in horses and tetanus for both humans and horses. In addition, snake antivenin is made from horse blood serum. Small doses of the venom are administered initially and, as the doses slowly increase, the horse develops antibodies to the venom. When the dose is large enough to be lethal to a human, the horse has developed sufficient resistance to supply blood for serum extraction. It is a simple procedure. When fresh blood is deposited into a container, the red blood cells and the other forms of protein clot and coagulate at the bottom. The clear liquid entirely separates from the clot and is known as the serum. A number of horses are involved as each venomous snake species has a different venom. The eastern brown has severe clotting components, whereas the venom of the death adder attacks the central nervous system. (I had fun imagining each draught horse being named for its particular specialty – Tiger Snake, King Brown, and so on.) Animal liberationists should have no concern. These horses would never feel anything more than a pin prick and are providing a security in the bush we didn't have decades before. The build-up of mice in the central west of NSW during the late 1990s led to a rapid multiplication of deadly snakes. In half a century before this I could not recall spotting one to two snakes each day in the spring. Sensible farmers never kill them, for they and the hawks are our defence against devastating mice plagues.

In India the worship of the cobra is not mythical nonsense. Natural scientists declare that without the cobra the sub-continent would be overrun with rats, infecting entire populations with mass killer diseases like bubonic plague.

I left Buff Rogers with a firm intention to go home and abandon the brumby quest. My riding jaunts in the mountains had been educational to a point and a lot of fun at times. Sally, my wife, hadn't been included much in these jaunts, so I took her down in April to show her the high plains and try some trout fishing with Ted Taylor. The fishing was a disaster. If you've ever been a spear fisherman you won't fancy being crouched and uncomfortable in a cold wind, trying to cast a fly into a gloomy subalpine creek. When Ted later produced the whisky bottle there was only a nip left. Golly, could you blame him! But the next day he took us for a ride on the southern end of Currango Plain. No more than 20 minutes from the guesthouse we spotted a herd of brumbies walking towards us. They had been feeding on the Currango Plain and were slowly filtering back into the cover of the snow gums, where we happened to be riding. As it was towards noon and thinking it was an unlikely location, I had left the zoom lens behind. It seems to always be the case with amateur photographers. While I was cursing myself Sal was able to watch the brumbies stroll past, just 70 metres away. The wind was with us. The moment was virtual proof that brumbies survive on smell and hearing, although our camouflage was good. Our greatest concern was Big Mal. If he saw them he'd trumpet his head off in greeting, so he was made to face away from them. Sal's Billy saw them. He was a cunning old chestnut. Contrary to my argument, famous horse handler Monty Roberts claims the American mustang has extraordinary sight.

Sal loved the mountains and the brumbies sparked more passion in her than I could muster. The day after that ride we began the long trip home to Myall Plains. We decided to deviate slightly and see something of the steep western fall. Instead of passing through the towns of Tumut and Cootamundra we would go through Tumbarumba and Wagga.

Not far from Tumbarumba we came upon a herd of brumbies grazing in open woodland. It was on the Batlow road and the horses had made themselves at home around the Forestry Commission base. All the mares had foals at foot and the shaggy stallion stood away a little, warily watching the car. I dropped into 4WD and crossed the ditch on the side of the road to get Sal in position with the zoom lens. The brumbies' coats were so sleek and healthy it looked as though someone had shampooed and brushed them. The foals lay in the sun, raising their heads in a nonchalant manner to take a peep at the intruders. The mares simply twitched their ears and tried to pretend we weren't there.

'Don't give up on them yet, Mike,' Sal whispered, as she fitted the second roll of film. The issues surrounding brumbies were complex and murky. I had told her I was going to collect the brumby gelding Dean Backman had offered me and then write off the whole exercise as an interesting experience. But it was never going to be as easy as that. There was a nagging conscience prick every time I thought about the Guy Fawkes shooting. There were newspaper articles about how brutal the killing was. It wasn't about wild dogs, pigs or feral cattle – it was horses that had been shot up in such a cruel exercise. Resist it I did, but it took me back to childhood when horses were a part of the family. On the western stations right up until about 1975 you could count on three things happening every day no matter what: the rising of the sun, the milking of the house cows and the running in of the stockhorses.

No, Sally was right. I'd got into something I couldn't just walk away from.

5 The Rescue of Jim Nankervis

The wild hop scrub grew thickly, and the hidden
ground was full
Of wombat holes, and any slip was death.

I heard a lot of campfire stories during my time in the southeast ranges. Some of them were haunting and chilling, like the one about the two Irish tradesmen who were brought in to build a stone cottage on Wollondibby Station, about 20 kilometres east of Thredbo. Upon completion of the job the Irishmen were paid 25 pounds in cash. They left very happy. That night they were both murdered at a lonely campsite not far away. Their ghosts are said to haunt the lovely cottage, which has been restored and is visible from the Alpine Highway. Then there are the rescue stories: men critically injured in pockets so remote that their fate was usually a foregone conclusion. But sometimes there was a miracle and I believe the saving of Jim Nankervis's life at Dead Horse Gap was one such miracle. The story was first told to me by Gordon Day whose father, George, was involved.

The hut at Dead Horse Gap was built in 1938. Sadly, it

was torched in the early 1970s. In the 35 years the stock-men used the hut a qualified doctor was only ever known to be present for one night. That was the night Jim Nankervis was carried in unconscious.

The Nankervis brothers took over Tom Groggin Station from the Pierce family in 1930. The freehold portion of the property was quite small for those days, being only 1200 hectares along the Murray River. It was the high country lease that made the station so valuable. From the freehold boundary the Nankervis country stretched to Lake Albina (2000 metres) north of Muellers Peak and southwards to the Pilot, which in a direct line is 38 kilometres south of Lake Albina. There were no fences and they kept their cattle west of the main divide. In the same general area the McGuffickes, Taylors and Mackys were running cattle in the summer months. The Taylors walked up more than 2000 bullocks to fatten on the snow grass. Each herd was shep-herded by stockmen and they often congregated at the Dead Horse Hut, which was on the Nankervis lease. There was an unwritten rule: first up in the late spring had to kill a beast for meat and hang it in a tree. In the cool of the high altitude the meat lasted for a month. On one occasion the first stockmen to arrive only had cows and calves and needed meat so desperately they shot and skinned a brumby. They stewed it up and were happy enough with it. When they departed no note was left on the quartered meat and the in-coming men cut off steaks thinking it was a steer. There was a big row over it. There were no women and no grog was allowed. Meat became almost sacred to the mountain horseman.

Jim's father, Harry, was the principal of the Nankervis brothers partnership. When it was time to move the cattle into the alps for the summer, Harry would hand over the job to the partnership's stock manager, Leo Byatt. While still a teenager fresh from school, Jim joined the droving team in the late 1930s. After the initial droving from Tom Groggin Station, Jim was put in charge of a draft of cows and calves which were walked onto Abbotts Ridge near Mount Townsend. He laughed when I put it to him that he was the herdsman on the roof of Australia.

'I enjoyed riding those alpine crags for a couple of days, until the cows settled down. But you wouldn't want to be up there for any length of time, sleeping in a swag. It was always cold at that altitude. The odd day, maybe, was like late spring at Groggin.'

Despite his casual way of talking about the old days in the alps, Jim truly loved going up there among Australia's highest peaks. He doggedly contends that Mount Townsend is the highest of them all. I perceived an almost personal vexation that Kosciuszko takes the honours as Australia's highest mountain. It's as though an old friend has been deprived of the prize.

'The explorer Strzelecki only climbed Townsend,' Jim said to me in his home at Corryong. He was the fittest looking man in his 80s I had ever seen. ' "Rocky and predominant amongst all others" was the quote in his diary. There's boulders as big as houses up there. Kosciuszko's a dome with a clear surface. And I know about the survey done up there too. They hung lights on nine peaks and did their levels at night. No chance of a mistake that way. They found Townsend was higher, all right. I was poking around with the cattle. That's how I knew about it all.'

'Why wasn't it altered?' I asked.

Jim smiled sardonically. 'History – Kosciuszko's always been Australia's highest mountain. It was shut down – taboo.'

In 1946 Jim's love of the alpine peaks almost came to a tragic end. He was camped at Dead Horse Hut with a couple of stockmen. It was March, early autumn. Apart from range riding and looking out for strays, there wasn't much to do until the alpine mustering began, when all the cattle would be moved down to the low country. On 12 March, about a week before the mustering started, they had just finished a late breakfast when George Day from the Chalet rode in. The Chalet was a government tourist resort about ten kilometres to the northeast via a bridle track up over the Rams Head Range. George had with him two guests, one of them being a doctor. The other was Reg Williams from South Australia, better known today as R. M. Williams.

George was an almost fanatical horse lover. In the summer his staff saddled 50 horses every day for guests. He loved the brumbies and often released thoroughbred stallions into the wild herds to try and halt inbreeding. While George Day was king of the mountains the brumbies were sleek and high in the wither. On his days off he loved nothing better than a brumby chase.

At Dead Horse he and his guests dismounted for a billy boil from the Nankervis fire. They had barely got comfortable when in rode Noel Pendergast and Ernie Bale – both young stockmen then.

George announced that he wanted a roan colt and he knew there were mobs of that colour running on the Cascades. How about a brumby run? George's suggestion was met with enthusiasm by Jim, Noel, Ernie and Reg. The doctor opted to remain at the hut and the two other stockmen headed off on a boundary inspection.

The Cascades is the name given to a broad sweeping slope coming off the ridge line of the Great Dividing Range to Cascade Creek. On the western fall, it drops away in a gentle meander of spurs for over three kilometres. The snow gums and candlebarks create an open woodland setting in stark contrast to the steep forested slopes rising from the Jacobs River on the eastern side of the Great Dividing Range. The Nankervis bullocks loved foraging in this area, as did the brumbies, and for a good old brumby chase the Cascades was some of the safest terrain in the Snowys.

On a little knoll north of Jerusalem Hill Ernie Bale spotted a mob halfway between the top and Cascade Creek. He volunteered to ride quietly down, get below them and from the crack of his stockwhip drive them upwards to the waiting horsemen. All agreed it was a good plan and four horsemen waited on top while Ernie rode down. The whip crack echoed along the range and in the space of a couple of minutes the brumbies were thundering over the summit of the Divide. The mob split when they spotted the horsemen and Noel Pendergast and Reg Williams spurred their mounts to be abreast of George Day when he took off after the bigger end of the split. They didn't have much space in which to collar a yearling before the wild mob scattered into the fearful tumble of the Jacobs River canyon.

Noting in the passing of a second that the others had focused on the bigger bunch, Jim set off after the other group. The chase took him over the shoulder of Jerusalem Hill, past Purgatory Hill and then, near Paradise Gap, something happened.

There were two brumbies caught in that flutter. No one remembers who caught them. They were each halter-tied to a tree and the four men sat around on some boulders to wait. It was late morning, coming on close to lunchtime.

The first thing they saw was what all mountain horsemen dread – a saddled horse, trotting around bewildered and lost. Very disturbed, it took off when the men tried to catch it and made its way home to Tom Groggin. Where was Jim? Everyone had been so focused on the brumby chase they didn't know for sure which way he had gone. Brumbies grazed across the Divide every morning and evening, marking impressions in the snow grass in all directions and making tracking difficult. Tracking a shod horse in thick snow grass demanded the keen eye of an Aboriginal tracker, able to distinguish the faint sharp edges from ordinary hoofprints. A galloping shod horse actually cuts blades of grass, but the tracking is painfully slow and a last desperate option when searching for someone injured, especially when Jim could have been several kilometres away. It was nothing for a young stockman to chase a particular yearling he wanted for up to four kilometres. If he fell soon after the scatter he might be anywhere within 200 hectares. If he fell after three kilometres the search area widened to a massive 2500 hectares. Grimly, they began to search for Jim.

They rode around Jerusalem Hill and Purgatory for hours. Ernie Bale knew Jim Nankervis well and told the others he would not have galloped down onto the Jacobs River horror slopes. Something freakish had happened. They would find him unconscious or with a broken leg somewhere on the top. They cooeed until their lungs hurt and then just before sunset, George spotted a thin spiral of smoke. It was Jim. He had regained consciousness and upon hearing the cooees he lit up a tussock of grass. Stockmen always carried matches in those days.

The four men were stunned by the severity of Jim Nankervis's injuries. 'He looked as if he'd been scalped, his hair was soaked in blood, one eye had popped and he could barely see,' George Day told Gordon.

How Jim was carried back up the mountains to the Dead Horse Gap Hut remains a minor mystery. It was dark and they had some difficulty locating the gap. Jim believes the smell of smoke from the campfire finally guided them in. He also thinks he was put on one of the saddle horses semi-conscious, led by one rider and held in the saddle by another. Another version is that someone galloped back for the doctor and a packhorse. Whatever happened, the resourcefulness of those men saved Jim's life. He would not have survived the night without the emergency first aid and constant attention of the doctor. The facilities available at Dead Horse Hut also played a role, with bunks, clean water, lighting from lamps and numerous clean vessels for the doctor to use.

Gordon Day, who was reared at the Chalet and was taught by George to become a fine horseman, told me the hut was solidly built from mountain ash and had a slab floor and verandah. It was one of the most home-like of all the mountain huts. Since the burning of the hut nearly 30 years ago a handful of lost skiers have perished for the simple want of shelter. How many may have lived if the hut had not been destroyed will never be known, but despite the skill and knowledge of the doctor that night, Jim wouldn't have survived without the shelter of the hut. The wanton destruction of huts in the Snowy Mountains has been one of the most senseless acts of vandalism in Australian history, and it will never be known who was responsible.

By the time the rescue party reached the hut, Jim's condition was critical. The doctor managed to replace his eye back into its socket, but the skull formation of the socket was fractured. The night was so dark no one could attempt to ride the mountain trail to the Rams Head spur until daylight. It was a 600-metre lift in altitude and steep all the way. At daylight

George Day headed for the Chalet, called an ambulance and waited. It was possible to get a vehicle off the Summit Road (from Jindabyne to Mount Kosciuszko) and up towards Merritts Spur if a horseman rode in front, selecting a track. Meanwhile, Jim had to be lifted out of one of the deepest valleys in Australia. He does recall brief moments of the rescue and says that he was lifted onto the rescue horse behind Reg Williams and was conscious enough to grasp Reg's waist and hang on. The rider of course would have had to somehow hold Jim steady all the way over the next eight kilometres on very steep rocky terrain.

The mountain trail to Rams Head was thought to be too steep for safety and Jim was taken along the old stockroute to a point level with where Thredbo village now stands. Then they zigzagged up a wide buttress which was to become the main Thredbo ski run. It was steep for a horse carrying an inert man, but relatively free of stone, allowing the horse to secure a good footing in the snow grass. Merritts Spur was the top.

Jim Nankervis was hospitalised for three months in Sydney and in the early period his survival prospects were rated as slim. When I met him at Corryong in 2001 he was in great health and still operating a farm. He's a little sensitive about what happened that day in 1946. He told me a falling branch hit his head.

Jim was very lucky. In 1921 Charlie Woodhouse died from head injuries when his horse fell during a brumby chase in the same area. His saddled horse turned up at Ingebyra on the Jindabyne–Omeo road. A search was mounted and Charlie was found unconscious at a place called Long Plain. He died on the way to a Sydney hospital. It was a bitter irony that Charlie had survived three grueling years with the Light Horse in Palestine only to die in this way.

More than fifty years later I was in the same area. The men and women embroiled in the brumby issues plaguing the Snowy Mountains were all agreed on one thing – the Jacobs River and Pilot areas were overstocked with wild horses. I wanted to have a look for myself. But there was another reason I wanted to see the area: where did Banjo ride to gather his inspiration for the poem? After all, it was the poem that still captured the imagination of a nation and helped make horses a symbol of our bush heritage. One thing for sure – it wasn't 'down by Kosciuszko' that Banjo rode. If you wanted to find the vague, almost mystical realm of the Snowy Mountains brumbies, you had to visit the uninhabited tablelands south of Thredbo.

Riding with me was Helga Frolich and Julie Bourke, both of whom rode with Ted Taylor and me at Currango in February, a couple of months earlier. Julie's partner, Bazz Dennis, the Thredbo chairlift manager, was also with us. I rode a free-moving mare and led a packhorse, both borrowed from a polo player.

Early in the day we crossed over the Moonbah Ridge and reached the Barry fire trail near Lady Northcote's Chair. At Mill Gap we stopped at Brov McGufficke's old camp. Brov was related to Richard and Freddy McGufficke. With winter approaching, Brov had retreated to the low country for a few months. He was the last of the mountain hermits and the Kosciuszko authorities permitted him to keep two horses, even though his snow lease had expired. Asked once if he went to the Second World War, he replied there was no war to go to, though his father had talked about the Great War and many of the local horses had been loaded onto trains for that war effort. When I dismounted in this peaceful valley, walled in by forest-clad mountain ranges, it wasn't difficult to imagine someone living through the Second

World War without knowing it ever happened.

At the Mowamba River crossing we left the fire trail and pushed on towards the Chimneys. Helga was the guide. She had often ridden the trails with Brov and when he lived at Mill Gap in the warmer months she kept an eye on him, riding out from her little farm near Wollondibby about once every two weeks.

The trail blazing was difficult and I didn't look forward to being left on my own. After lunch Helga and Julie would head home and leave me to find my way with a compass. It was the bogs that made it so hazardous. If it wasn't for the brumby pads some of the small streams coming off the timbered slopes might have been impossible to cross. It seems deep bogs have a different smell from bogs which have a bottom and the brumbies nose around until satisfied where it's safe to cross. The surface was always hard to read and when the lead horse, which was Helga's Duke, baulked at a brumby crossing we always knew we would flounder through, belly deep. Sometimes the bogs were 50 metres wide, stretching right across the narrow creek flats and forcing us to ride onto the steep slopes. Here we were met with a species of thick green wattle two metres high. Brov McGufficke had cut a horse trail through the wattle some years earlier, but it was almost overgrown. On occasions we had to spread out to find it. Slipping around in the scrub with a packhorse made for some very uncomfortable riding and I began to realise how easy it would be on the return ride to lose the trail and end up in the wrong valley.

About midday we rode out onto a wide plain and on the far side there was a little mob of brumbies. I took the field glasses out of the saddlebag and scanned the mob for the elusive silver ones. Two nights before I had seen the classic silver brumby at the Dead Horse Gap pass in the headlights of my car. It was a stallion, with black mane and tail. He was heavily built, almost like a draught horse. The horses I was seeing now through the field glasses were an uninteresting lot. They were all bays and indistinguishable from the station horses once common on western stations. There was a miserable yearling with them. He seemed to be a reject, for when the mob moved on he stayed and watched us and when we got near him I thought he was going to tack on and be a bit of a nuisance. He certainly thought about it.

We reined in under the umbrella of a thick copse of black sallees. It was a lovely spot for the horses, sheltered from a cool draught of air creeping down from the high range to the north, and plenty of old snow grass. It was early May and the Thredbo locals were looking to the western sky for the first snowfall. I felt cold and remarked the snow might soon come. They all brightened up every time you uttered the word snow. The thin whiskers of cloud gathering on the exposed tops looked promising enough, but they thought it was too early in the season.

'I think you know all the stories in this neck of the woods,' Julie said warmly. 'Apart from a park ranger handing you a summons to appear in court, what more can you gather riding west from here?'

I liked Julie. She spoke her mind and had a feminine, unobtrusive way of probing secrets. These women had the knack of making a man question himself, without feeling humiliated. Dreamers liked me had to be brought to earth from time to time.

'It's the poem "The Man from Snowy River",' I said, a little abashed. I had intended to keep this to myself. 'If Jack Riley ever saw a young stockman turn the brumbies single-handed, I reckon it was a gallop off the top of the divide near the Cascades and down the horror granite of the Jacobs Fall.'

The true location of Banjo Paterson's epic poem is still hotly debated right across the southeast ranges. The theory I do reject is the one that claims Paterson witnessed or took part in a brumby chase far from the upper tributaries of the Snowy River. A writer myself, I don't believe he would have done that. In regard to location I think all his poems were genuine.

'The Man from Snowy River' was first published in the *Bulletin* magazine in 1890. It is a magnificent work with extraordinary clarity of description. Only once in the entire poem does Banjo use a metaphor, 'and he bore the badge of gameness', which suggests to me that the poem was inspired by the combination of a person and a scene and written spontaneously, while he still felt the passion of the moment.

Jim Nankervis and I had talked about Banjo's poem at great length. He wouldn't have it that Jack Riley, a local stockman, was the basis for the rider in the poem.

'Oh, he couldn't ride much,' Jim said. There were no grey shadows about the issue with Jim and you had to respect his opinion. Jim's family owned Tom Groggin Station where Riley lived for the latter part of his life.

The official launch of Corryong's annual Snowy River Bush Festival is always held at the graveside of Jack Riley. Despite scepticism from many quarters, the people of Corryong have no doubt that Riley inspired Banjo to write the famous poem and the evidence is compelling.

In the summer of 1890 Walter Mitchell from Bringen-bong Station took Banjo on a camping trip to Tom Groggin (then owned by the Pierce family), on the upper reaches of the Murray River. The station's caretaker was Irishman Jack Riley, who was well known among mountain stockman as an eccentric bush character. No one knew the mountains better than Riley. Ten years earlier he had tracked down and rescued Christie O'Rourke, who was missing in an area now known as the Pilot Wilderness. O'Rourke had been injured in a horse fall.

Riley lived alone at Tom Groggin and was delighted to play host to Mitchell and Banjo. With the summit crags of the alps only a few kilometres away, he led them along the horse trails to Mount Kosciuszko. The brumbies were rarely seen in the alps. It was nearly 50 years since David O'Rourke had lost control of his horses and the successive generations, with the infusion of genes from many wild stallions by this time, knew where the big winter snows fell. The brumby country then, as now, was the much lower tablelands of the Cascades and Pilot Wilderness. Jack Riley took his guests there and it was there that Banjo would have seen the stupendous fall into the Jacobs River gorges. The river is a minor tributary of the once mighty Snowy River and from the Cascades tablelands it drops 1000 metres in 24 kilometres, gouging out some of the wildest and most rugged country in Australia. Despite its steepness, it was brumby country too. The O'Rourkes' old station, Suggan Buggan, was only 30 kilometres downstream from where the Jacobs spilled into the Snowy. Jack Riley had spent many years on the Snowy before taking the job at Tom Groggin and in the evenings when Mitchell and Banjo were camped at his hut, he related some extraordinary stories about those wild days. I believe it was a combination of Jack's stories and the wild Jacobs River country that inspired Banjo to write the greatest of all his poems.

For me, the poem itself provides the evidence: 'Where the hills are twice as steep and twice as rough', and 'Where the river runs those giant hills between', or, more convincing of all: 'Where the mountain ash and kurrajong grew wide'. On southern, shaded slopes, mountain ash will grow as a sprinkling among other eucalypts as low as 300 metres above sea level, but the kurrajong seedling cannot survive severe frost. Above 800 metres the seedling can only survive on an elevated spur where the cold air each night sinks to the valley floors. Also, the kurrajong is never seen where annual rainfall is higher than 800 millimetres, which in itself rules out the whole of the subalpine and alpine zones.

Banjo must have been impressed with Jack Riley as a colourful source of mountain folklore, for he returned eight years later with Tom Groggin's owner John Pierce. That visit inspired Banjo to write 'Johnny Riley's Cow', which was published in 1898.

The Jacobs River gorges and the Pilot Wilderness were not always blessed with heroes and legends. There was a dark side to the mountains as well. There were murders over miserable amounts of money and duffing was rife. When Charles Carter took up a tiny selection of 200 acres not far from Mount Pilot, in 1910, he had no idea he had plonked himself into the middle of territory plundered by cattle thieves. He was a harmless though eccentric hermit, but those rogues of the bush were not prepared to risk his eyes. They took a horse with a clearly visible brand on its shoulder and shot it outside Carter's hut. Then they butchered it, to make it look as though Carter had killed it for meat. The hide was left hanging over a rail. Carter was away at the time and when he returned the police were waiting for him. It was one of the most miserable frame-ups in Australian history and Carter was never able to prove his innocence. He was jailed for two years.

People from near and far always contended Carter was innocent. He was one of those pathetic bush hermits who was thoroughly decent and totally alone. Twenty-eight years later he returned to the Pilot Wilderness country and moved into an abandoned building put up by a tin mining company. He built a stockyard and once again educated his caught brumbies to become packhorses. The folklore suggests he moved back as an old man to take deadly revenge on those who framed him, who themselves had become old men, but could never pull the trigger. Carter died at the tin mines in 1952, alone to the end.

There is a harshness about the Snowy Mountains region. In pioneer days the natural hostility of the land moulded tough individualists. Today their descendents still hold much of the freehold land away from the national park area, but in the shadow of the mountains, communities are deeply divided. The old families remain, most of them dispossessed of their snow leases and living on restricted areas of freehold land too small to be viable. Many have been forced to turn to the towns for work and some simply carry on, living a Spartan, hand-to-mouth existence. The new arrivals have a different interpretation of life on the land and different priorities. They have income from other sources and display signs of affluence not shared by the pioneer families. Some care for the land with convincing commitment and others brutalise it. Starving, malnourished cattle are a depressingly common sight around the Snowy Mountains in the wintertime. On one occasion my companions and I were ordered to park a truck in the centre of the road rather than at the side. The road ran through a paddock where there were 100 starving cattle. The farmer said the truck was blocking the sun from the grass.

The blue of the sky had been snatched away while we had our sandwiches and billy tea. The little rocky peaks of the Chimneys were swallowed in cloud.

'Looks like the forecast you heard was right after all,' Helga said, disappointed for me. I had wanted to wait a day or two, but the man who owned the horses had other matters to attend to and I had to ride out, take a quick look at the Cascades and the Jacobs gorges and get back the next day.

'It's only a mile and a half to the Jacobs,' I said. 'I'll decide there, but it doesn't look good.'

We mounted up and headed down a creek called Tea Tree. It started to rain, and half an hour later when we reached the banks of the Jacob it was pelting down. I had my swag rolled up tightly in a horse rug on top of my pack-horse. The rain fell so heavily I couldn't see the sleeping bag remaining dry. My heart sank at the thought of going on alone in such conditions and was grateful to Helga when she prodded a decision.

'This river will run a banker in no time.' She had to yell to be heard above the hissing sound of big droplets striking the ground and the noise of the fast-flowing stream.

'I'll abort,' I said. 'I'm not going over.'

I had good reason not to cross, too. Veteran mountain stockman Dooley Pendergast from Jindabyne (who I'd first heard on ABC radio) had only days before told me an unforgettable story about the whitewater of the Jacobs River. In the early 1960s Dooley used to help some of the snow lease holders drove their spring market cattle to Bairnsdale on the Victorian coast. It was an overland drive of more than 250 kilometres.

'They were wonderful days,' Dooley began. He was a jovial man with a rubicund complexion and greying hair. 'I feel lucky I saw the end of the era. Mates would risk their lives for each other if called upon. I remember two packhorses getting swept away while crossin the Jacobs in '64. A lot of the lease holders used to drove their sale cattle to Bairnsdale. The store market down there in Victoria was always stronger than Cooma in those days. In the spring of '64 I gave Teddy McGufficke a hand to walk down 200 head. My uncle, Dudley Pendergast, rode with us as well as a big Scotsman by the name of Victor Connis.

'The snow up high was meltin and if you got a warm spring day followed by heavy rain those mountain streams come down overnight. Usually we had some warnin because if it rained on the top we got it too. This day we didn't. We didn't know there'd been a storm up there. We just did what was almost routine at the camp on the Jacobs and that was yardin the cattle on the other side for the night. There was a back up supply vehicle as far as the Jacobs and that's why we always camped on the eastern side. The mornin followin we threw on the packs and went the rest of the way leadin packhorses.'

'Sounds like the water was cold,' I said, thinking of the millions of tonnes of snow that lies above 2000 metres well into the spring.

Dooley nodded.

'I'm gonna tell yer how cold. That mornin we woke to see a river with a strong flow. Nothin more. We went about our business and packed up. Victor elected to go first and take the packhorses across. He led the lightest of them and the other two followed. Just as he got to the opposite bank we see a wave surging down on em. Victor hadn't seen it, but his horse and the packhorse were nearly out when it struck. The other two horses were swept away like corks. They went about 50 yards before being swept into a backwater of rubbish and logs. One horse sank quickly. The packs were just too heavy for him. The other one must have got a bit of footing on a boulder or sheet of rock. Only his head was out, that poor horse. By gee it was a miserable sight and it all looked so hopeless. How do yer rescue a horse from drownin when they weigh 800 pounds?'

Dooley raised his eyebrows and his eyes glinted.

'Well, to our horror, Victor said he would. I mean, in our eyes Victor was headed for a certain drownin. Teddy protested. He threw up his arms and yelled "No, Victor, no!". But there was no stoppin him. He stripped to his underpants and dived straight in. We thought he was done for. Well, talk about swim. He ploughed through that boilin, dancin water and when he reached our side he wanted a rope. Teddy tried again to get some sense into him, but arguing was fruitless so we got the rope Victor wanted and belayed him back into the river. He skidded down a tree trunk and let the current wash him towards the packhorse. God knows how cold that water was off the snow. We were cold enough with our clothes on. When he got to the packhorse he opened the nearside pack underwater and wrenched out a bottle of rum. He had it in there on the quiet. Teddy didn't allow grog on the job. Then we couldn't believe our eyes. He scrambled up onto an island boulder and gulped down half the bottle. Someone told me once it was a bad thing to go and drink spirits when yer as cold as he would have been. They reckon the two skiers found dead on Bogong died after they drank rum. They found the bottle beside them, still nearly full. But Victor had half the bottle.

'"Oh mother of the beads," Teddy gasped. "His soul's on the way to the Snowy."

'Next thing Victor was back in the river and he put the rum bottle carefully back into the pack.

'"We gotta get that pack before he has the rest of it," said

Ted. Anyhow, the rum must have done him some good. He got the two packs off in a flash, unclinched the saddle and tied all three items to the rope. We pulled the stuff in fast, I can tell you. Free of everything the horse began to struggle and floundered out into the current. We thought the poor thing must still drown. It sped downriver for 100 yards before it got its feet onto the bottom. With great relief we watched that packhorse struggle out of the river. Meanwhile Victor's disappeared under the water to get the packs off the other horse, which we knew had to be drowned. Victor could only get one pack out and it happened to be the one with the money in it.'

'Victor didn't know about the money?'

'Dudley and I didn't know either. That pack was Teddy's private one. He had 2000 pounds in there.'

Two thousand pounds was a fortune in those days.

It was just as well I decided to pull out. To reach the top of the Divide after crossing the river there was a steep 600-metre climb. The horses would have started sliding before I got halfway. On the return ride, visibility dropped to 200 metres and the small creeks had become raging torrents. To avoid bogs already under sheets of water, Helga opted for a short cut, entailing a steep descent. I had never thought of horses skiing downhill, on all four hooves. I wouldn't have believed it if I hadn't been forced to sit on one. It was tempting to dismount, but the horse would have skidded over the top of the rider. A couple of times the packhorse, Baldyface, careered so fast down the slope I was forced to drop the lead rope.

Two hours into the return ride the weather began to clear again. The mountains are always volatile and unpredictable.

But if I doubted my decision, every creek crossing

re-affirmed the wisdom of the instincts. The water reached our knees, and if the horses had been forced to swim the ferocity of the current would have swept them away.

In a pragmatic sense, not much was gained that day. Only on reflection later did I feel I had shared something, perhaps a moment only, with these great old stockmen who had known the mountains in the golden days.

Thanks to Helga we were all back at Thredbo about 9.00 p.m. having hot showers, followed by a Shiraz. She managed the Ski Patrol Lodge and for me it was a home away from Myall Plains. Some months later Helga guided me to the Cascades on foot from Dead Horse. It was just a walk. Compared to my beloved Warrumbungles there was almost nothing to look at. It was horse-riding country.

'You should have gone up to Teddy's hut,' Jim Nankervis said to me, when I was telling him the story of the failed ride. 'There used to be stockyards there too. You could have seen the storm out and stayed there the night.'

'Helga knows the hut. She said it's in ruins. The roof's gone.'

'Oh I haven't been back to the Big Boggy for years and years,' Jim said. We were having coffee in his sitting room. Jim had come in from the farm to meet me. In his eighties and still farming! His son lived out on the farm and Jim had moved to town.

'A strange thing happened out there one day,' he began. 'Stock have got a sixth sense we don't have. It was in '43. We took 100 cows and calves up from Tom Groggin in two stages. Stopped on the Leather Barrel the night before and had them on the Boggy by midday. The other blokes were going to leave and go back to Groggin. I was to stay the night and make sure they were settled before I left. But the cattle were very disturbed. Didn't want to eat much and you can imagine how fresh the feed was. The cows kept calling their calves and the boss, Leo, decided to stay too. It was a beautiful clear evening. We expected to see a big frost in the morning. Sometime after midnight it was bucketing down with snow. There was a small hole in the roof and so much snow fell through there was a pile on the floor like a big pavlova. Outside there was three foot of snow. Golly, what about the cows and calves, we thought. Our feet were draggin in the snow and we had a job to tell where we were going. The cows had gone! We later found them with their calves back at Groggin. They knew.'

We yarned on for most of the afternoon. Jim told me that the 1939 fire was the most devastating event in the history of the mountains since first settlement. It burnt the stockyards, some of the huts and all of the old cockatoo wooden fences. Dead Horse Hut survived the fire. He was bitter about the torching of it in the early '70s.

'They blame the old pioneer stockmen for erosion and loss of some plant species,' Jim went on. 'But it was the rabbits that caused all the destruction. The men were away fighting in the war and they took over. It wasn't us at all. But you can't tell that today to anyone under 50. They weren't alive and they can't image what it was like.'

I knew exactly what Jim was talking about. In 1947, aged four, I watched a rabbit drive accumulate so many in an acre of netted yard the ones on the bottom suffocated. I got into the yard and so many of the rabbits used my tiny body to claw upwards for air, that I had to be rushed to the Coonabarabran hospital with more weals than a cat-o'-nine-tails could deliver. Discharged from the army after the Second World War, my father arrived home to 9000 acres of bare dirt. A citified friend ducked behind a tree and wiped his bottom on the only plant still standing – stinging nettles.

Today the same property, Myall Plains, has a greater diversity of wildlife than the national park in the nearby mountains, thanks to the prevalence of water, and young trees are sprouting of their own accord. Anyone who thinks that only national parks provide a healthy ecology is seriously out of touch, and if they successfully agitate on that theme they risk depriving the national economy of millions of dollars. Without a healthy, vigorous economy, Australia will never be able to adequately fund national parks.

The homeland valleys and canyons of the Guy Fawkes brumbies

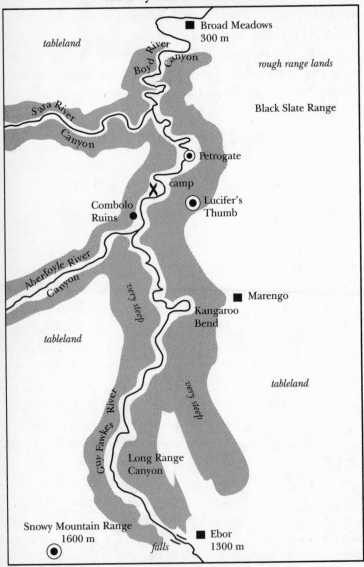

Note: Ernie and Billy Maskey's 'Why Worry' was somewhere along the Sara River

CHAPTER 6

They Was Beautiful

On a dim and distant hillside the wild horses racing
yet ...

Old sentiments die hard. I picked up a disturbing story from a 70-year-old man. For two decades he had promised his sons a ride across the alps, from Dead Horse Gap to Kiandra. Time was running out and he wanted to remain true to his word. They unloaded their horses at Dead Horse about five o'clock one morning in the summer of 2001 and followed the old bridle track up Bogong Spur. Leading packhorses, they rode straight into a park ranger near the top of Kosciuszko at about 8.00 a.m. They kept riding. The ranger radioed Jindabyne alpine headquarters and reported the intrusion.

The race was on. The old man and his middle-aged sons became the fugitives and the park rangers the law enforcers. If the park authority sought the eradication of disease spreading feral pigs with the same fervour they pursued this tough veteran of the mountains, the last pig would have been taken 20 years ago and a netted boundary would be in place. One of the rangers tried to commandeer a helicopter already under hire. The hirer point blank refused to hand it over. Meanwhile, the old mountain man remembered the steep trails of the Geehi side and escaped.

A few days after this story was related to me, I heard about a helicopter incident that convinced me a tragedy in the park is inevitable unless specific codes of apprehension by park rangers are cemented into legislation.

It happened in the Jacobs Ladder area, not far from where the Jacobs River meets the Snowy. It's a little north of the twisted gorge country Jack Riley rode in his prime and it's a favourite haunt of the brumbies. I don't think Banjo Paterson saw this area, except in his vivid imagination from what Jack Riley told him. It is awful country. The towering, broken walls of rock, rise like giant ugly scars. Not even the narrow river valleys can provide a little fertile patch. The brumbies must wander into these ravines to escape the catchers. The bed of the Snowy River is boulder-strewn under tortured, miserable species of wattle. Lake Eucumbene had taken 90 per cent of the flow and where a once mighty river flowed the hardy scrub now takes up more space than the water. It is a depressing place. Dooley Pendergast told me that young men from Jindabyne drop into the Jacobs Ladder ravines to look for brumbies, mainly because in there, trouble with the Park authorities is most unlikely. The area was considered to be Kosciuszko's outback. Dooley Prendergast's son Dean nearly died here. Like Jim Nankervis, he had his eye knocked out of its socket. He almost drowned in his own blood while a mate, Garry Caldwell, rode for miles to seek help. But the National Park authority had forbidden horse riding long ago in all but the very far north of the park, and those desperate to ride in open, unfenced spaces, choose this God-forsaken place of hell gorges, briars, blackberries and copperheads that waited around every corner.

Garry and Leisa Caldwell and their friend Glen Simons were on a special mission this day. Garry wanted to find the old mountain hut where his great-grandmother was born in the 1850s. A lover of photography and local history, Leisa hoped to photograph it, and along the way she hoped to catch some brumby snaps.

Despite the daunting country and the difficulties the pack-horses were having with the briar and the blackberries, they were more than happy with the way the day was unfolding. Garry's ancestors had been riding the mountains for generations. Robbie, his father, remembered the stock days when the mountains were not covered in thick scrub and the blackberries didn't rip at their leggings, but not all had been lost: kookaburras chuckled loudly from the river trees and redneck wallabies darted for cover. The wallabies never went far. When they felt safe they would peer through wattle branches and watch the procession of horses pass. Leisa thought about the photographs she might get and wondered how far down the Snowy they would ride by lunchtime. She was always searching for shots of the brumbies along the river. No one had ever managed to photograph the brumbies in the water, drinking. She thought that with their multicolours, shaggy manes and long tails it would be a beautiful, rare photograph. One worth waiting for, and in a cloudless sky, butterflies catching sun on their wings and birds singing, she was faraway in something of a dream world when a throbbing sound disturbed her thoughts.

The horses were the first to react. Their hearing is far superior to that of humans. The riders patted them and spoke to them: 'It's all right. It's all right.' But the throbbing sound rose until it was a reverberation on the cliff bands overhead. At 140 kilometres an hour the helicopter had the speed to take them by surprise. All of a sudden it was hovering over them, the updraft sucking at their clothes, their hats spinning away like Frisbees and the horses exploding in terror. To them such a machine sparked indescribable fear; a monster bird predator about to tear every ounce of flesh from their backbones. They plunged, skittered and reared. The packhorses broke free and the packs crashed into trees. The riders tried desperately to catch them, but their own mounts spun in fright and hit tree trunks, and the riders were savagely scratched from brittle low branches. Then the helicopter moved on.

Confused and shocked the men caught the packhorses and quickly tied the mare Jessie to the slightly calmer Ned, a big bay gelding. Leisa flooded Caitlin's ears with soothing talk. She loved this filly of hers and even through the thickness of the saddle Leisa could feel the uncontrollable quivers running in spasms through the little horse. Leisa's own hands were shaking and she fought to control the initial stages of shock.

Garry took charge and headed uphill. They had to get away from the river. The helicopter had moved away somewhere, but if it came back and they were still near the river they could lose a horse. If one panicked, threw the rider and galloped into the gouged, rocky floor of the river, it was almost certain to break a leg.

The ranger giving orders to the pilot must have expected the horsemen to wait near the river while the helicopter looked for somewhere to land. He apparently had no idea of the fear and mayhem he had inflicted on both the riders and the horses. Then Leisa heard the helicopter coming back. The noise of the giant rotor chopping at the air filled the gorges and great ravines for kilometres up and downstream. They could abandon their horses and be safe themselves, but they loved their horses and would no more leave them than throw a child into a raging stream.

This time the helicopter came in lower. The dust stung their eyes and their mounts crashed through the underbrush in blind terror. The packhorses, with the mare tied to the tail of the gelding, smashed into trees. Again the pilot pulled away and now truly terrified, Leisa stared skyward for direction. What did they want of them?

The helicopter landed in an open patch on the riverbank and, subdued by terror, the little group gathered their horses once again and proceeded towards it. The packhorses were tied to tree trunks and left behind. Packs had been ripped off by the branches and some of the harness was broken. Yes, under state legislation horse riding, by-and-large, is illegal in national parks, and rangers must pursue intruders, but they had been chased and apprehended like violent criminals.

The state law was read out to them aggressively, and the rhetoric and orders intensified the chilling quality of the encounter.

The helicopter returned the way it came, back to the landing pad and the air-conditioned offices. The ranger claimed to be searching for feral pigs and just happened to spot them but possibly someone had reported the riders either heading off towards or entering the park. The arid and ugly ravines of the Jacobs Ladder are an unlikely environment for pigs. Under pressure they will survive anywhere that has water, but the vast swamps and soaks higher up would have much more appeal. Apart from brumbies, the feral animals that had happily adopted the Jacobs Ladder habitat were goats. When the cruelly-shaken Leisa, Garry and Glen rode out, they saw goats grazing nonchalantly on the higher terraces. The rangers in my home territory, the Warrumbungles, had eradicated all the feral goats from incredibly rugged and steep terrain. In Kosciuszko, deadly hemlock crept further into park creeks each year, St Johns wort threatened to carpet the subalpine in 20 years and wild dogs were forcing struggling farmers to abandon their farms. Meanwhile, the priority was apprehension of horse riders whose only crime was to enjoy the wilderness on their beloved horses.

The contempt for horseriding groups in the Kosciuszko National Park troubled me throughout my research for this book. White man and the creatures he brought with him have altered the Australian landscape forever. If a few people want to ride their horses through the Jacobs River canyons or across the subalpine of the upper Murray tributaries, they ought to be allowed to. In the big picture they will alter nothing, now or in the future. It is miserable beyond belief that people should be denied such simple pleasures. I can understand the protection of the alpine zone, but the rest of the park should be available to horseriders.

Parks Victoria has struck a wonderful balance and I hope the anti-horse lobby in Victoria doesn't spoil it. Horses are still used in Victorian national parks for surveying and monitoring, transport of equipment (packhorses), search and rescue, ranger patrols, control of cattle and vermin control. There has even been a recommendation to Park management, in view of the closure of more tracks, that they consider expanding the role of the horses on environmental grounds. Horses have the ability to travel across country, they are silent and unobtrusive, unhampered by weather, can carry loads up to 100 kilograms and their physical impact is minimal compared with that of 4WD vehicles. In search and rescue operations, humans on the ground interfere with the scent and make it almost impossible for tracker dogs to perform efficiently. In addition, searchers can move so much faster on horseback.

We must not forget that the vehement opposition to horses in national parks is derived from the cultural antipathy of a vocal minority, and that the claim horses do enormous damage has not been scientifically proven. An impact study on the Mount Bogong massive in the Victorian Alps compared the impact of bushwalkers and horses and was unable to conclude that one was worse than the other.

After hearing the Caldwells' story I lost all enthusiasm for riding in the Snowy Mountains. At Currango you had the wide open spaces for riding, but for a man more inclined to rope up for a rocky spire than gallop over boggy frost hollows, those cold high plains didn't have a lot of appeal. I'd missed my chance with the brumbies. Ted Taylor had set up two close encounters: on the first I was too slow with the camera and on the second I didn't have the camera with me. Maybe I would have better luck in the Guy Fawkes River National Park in New England, northern NSW. According to the media reports, about 80 per cent of them had been shot in the October 2000 massacre, but there were still enough mares left for a herd recovery. That is, if the local New Englanders could prove the horses had heritage significance. It was rumoured that the Guy Fawkes brumbies had direct genetic links with the breeds used in the Australian Light Horse.

Finding the remnants of the Guy Fawkes brumbies posed quite a challenge and that appealed to me. The roadhouse at Ebor proved to be a fruitful source of information about local identities. The whistleblower on the carnage at Guy Fawkes River National Park was Greg Everingham, a station manager who lived a few kilometres east of the village.

When I located his telephone number and gave him a call he offered to organise a four-day packhorse expedition to the Guy Fawkes River. The only vehicle access was from the Grafton side, entailing a long haulage with the horses followed by a hard ride to reach the canyons. The Guy Fawkes River National Park is principally made up of a twisted tangle of river canyons and flat top tablelands. He said he hadn't been down since all the media coverage over the shooting and was keen to have a ride through the canyons to see what horses, if any, had survived. When I told him I had read somewhere that some 70 horses were thought to be still down there he was very sceptical. We arranged to meet on 14 June.

The New England region was home to the first cavalry troop outside Sydney. In Sydney the first enlistments were made in 1885 and the Upper Clarence Light Horse was enlisted a year later. In 1889 the various troop units across country NSW were welded into a regiment, the New South Wales Cavalry Regiment. The regiment first saw action in the Boer War, 1899–1902. In 1900 the 6th Australian Light Horse Regiment was formed with headquarters in Armidale and in 1906 it became the New England Light Horse. In 1914, at the outbreak of the First World War, volunteers were called for to join the Australian Imperial Force (AIF), which caused a considerable drain on all Light Horse regiments. For war purposes the Armidale-based regiment became the 12th Light Horse and in 1917–18 served in all the major battles for Gaza, Beersheba, El Mughar and Damascus in the Palestine campaign.

The Australian war horse had been selected under breeding programs since 1830, when horses from the colony were exported to the British army in India. In the 1830s most of the horses were bred in NSW and were known as 'walers'. They were bred to be 14–16 hands at the wither. The initial breed was English thoroughbred stallions joined to mares with genetic links to the draught horse. Over the decades, the genetic pool was deliberately widened to produce a hardy horse, suitable for the unpredictable stresses in a battle environment. Such breeds as the Welsh pony, Timor pony and the wild brumby were introduced to refine what became known as the 'classic waler', with fine clean legs and bone, wide barrel-like chest, short back and a broad head. Unlike the thoroughbreds, the waler could hump weights for long distances, endure searing heat, survive on any available grass and, if called upon, unleash bursts of speed only marginally slower than their big cousins.

Few breeding records apart from those of pure thoroughbreds were kept in colonial times. To make a credible assessment of the Guy Fawkes brumbies' origins demands a knowledge of New England history – and common sense. Walers were bred in the region and there was some infusion of the famous Saladin stock. Saladin appears to have been a genetic freak. His sire, also called Saladin, was mated to a mare by the famous imported stallion called Eclipse. The result was a filly and old Saladin was then mated to her, producing in the younger Saladin the closest genetic double-cross possible. Such a mating usually produces a weakling or obvious genetic defects such as melon head. Instead it produced a magnificent creamy palomino-type stallion, with an extraordinarily dominant gene colour that has survived for more than 100 years. Saladin's sons were coveted by stock-horse breeders and the Saladin breed extended throughout the Northern Tablelands. In 1947, about 80 years after Saladin was born, one A.G. Stewart was quoted in a Central Coast newspaper:

Perhaps the close breeding of these famous horses kept their colour and stood the test of time on the rough north coast range country. There is no seedy toe, no sand cracks or corns, no sidebone, no sprung tendons or splints; and when you look at their back legs, no spavin or curb. A good-skinned, strong galloway with nice hair in mane and tail, mostly creamy in colour, good enough in the shoulder to carry a saddle without a cropper and sprung enough in the ribs to dispense with the necessity of a breastplate. No day too long – up to 14 stone in the mountains.

Saladin's stock was particularly sought after in the eastern watershed of the tablelands. It was always cattle country in the land of the waterfalls and strong, sure-footed horses were essential. In New England there was always a tendency to stick to traditional breeds. Used in the cattle industry, the breed was subjected to the boom and bust cycle which dogged the Australian cattle industry in the early days, more so than it does now. In bad years, cattle were not even mustered on some stations and the new drop of yearlings on the mares would be neglected in some back paddock. On the big stations in the steep country, neglected herds became the northern tablelands brumbies, carrying the flag of Saladin in the creamy coats and lovely grey tails and manes.

Saladin was such a vicious buckjumper he was sold by his original owner, J. K. Mackay, to another stud breeder, who was responsible for the wide dispersion of the stallion's genes. There is a story from one of the Light Horse charges in Palestine that makes me chuckle and think it was the ghost of old Saladin, who almost made it into the 20th century. The horse was called Bill the Bastard, because every time the brigade leader signaled the charge he dropped his head and bucked for the first 50 metres. It probably saved Major Shanahan's life, for Bill the Bastard was always one of the last horses to gallop into enemy artillery range. The storyteller selected Beersheba for his yarn, but there were hundreds, possibly thousands, of individual Light Horse charges against the Turks in Palestine. On this occasion Major Shanahan was well and truly in the rear. Bill the Bastard had bucked for more than his usual 50 metres and the Major galloped upon four unhorsed comrades. Without rescue in the desert sand these men would last only minutes under heavy enemy fire. Major Shanahan put two on behind him and one stood in each stirrup. In a labouring gallop Bill the Bastard took all five troopers to safety and galloped himself into military history. My bet is that Bill the Bastard was a brumby.

The packhorse trek into the Guy Fawkes canyons promised to be a nail-biting adventure for me. I bought the Ebor 1:100 000 map and plotted the course from where Greg said we would unload the horses. The contours showed we would drop 800 metres in four kilometres. That's approximately half the drop into Arizona's Grand Canyon, which is reputed to be the world's deepest canyon. Height doesn't bother me if I am rockclimbing, but on a mule going down into the Grand Canyon the descent was a scary experience.

Greg invited me to stay the night with his family, and early next morning we loaded up three Guy Fawkes brumbies and one palomino-type mare that he had bought for his young daughter. At nearly 1400 metres above sea level the frost lay heavy across the Ebor highlands. The sun pushed through the mist, promising a little warmth when the slanting rays grew stronger.

Most of Greg's horses had been caught in the canyons along the Guy Fawkes River. They were all creamies and buckskins. It was as though the ghost of Saladin would haunt the canyons forever. Greg was going to ride Survivor, the last colt taken from Guy Fawkes, and a stylish grey mare he called Gravel would carry the packs. My packhorse, too, was a Guy Fawkes brumby, called Daisy. Greg had recently declined a Saudi offer for Daisy. The amount offered from the Arabs was not disclosed, but a journalist reported the figure was in the thousands. Daisy had soft eyes and big twitching ears. You got to love her within a day's ride. The strong little mare I was to ride was called Straps, bred in the Merriwa hills.

Riding with us was Errol Hibbert, a very good friend of Greg's. Hailing from the coastal plains just inland from Coffs Harbour, Errol was a saddler, contract musterer and cattle farmer. Like a lot of Australian bushman he was taciturn by nature, but his eyes were everywhere, and when he spotted me struggling with the packhorse girths after we had unloaded the horses and were saddling up, he promptly came to my assistance. Sowing wheat two nights before I had kinked my back lifting bags. The stars had disappeared with the onset of a rain band and I was hurrying to get the last block sown before the rain. I didn't make it, but that's grain farming. When I returned from Guy Fawkes I had a few hectares left to sow.

We mounted up and, each leading our own packhorse, single-filed onto a bush track which led into a forest of New England blackbutts. Once on the razorback we seemed dwarfed by the immensity of the central canyon. The hazy blue of the ranges claimed every horizon and, staring down past my offside stirrup iron, I vividly recalled the great drop of Arizona's Grand Canyon. There were no well-worn trails here. Greg was the trail blazer and I wondered soberly how steep it might get.

The razorback ridge terminated abruptly and Greg's white hat dipped out of sight. Errol followed and I tacked on behind him. There was very little loose gravel and the horses secured good purchase in the soft soil. It was very steep and Greg zigzagged, but compared with the loose rocky slopes of the Suggan Buggan country the ride down wasn't too bad. The New England blackbutts gave way to stringybarks with a light mingling of mountain grey gums. Midway down the she-oaks appeared, suggesting the spur we followed all the way to the bottom held little soil moisture in reserve. On either side of the spur the canyon walls grew more and more intimidating as we eased our way down. I was last down and when I reined in behind the two men Greg urged his colt across the Guy Fawkes River.

We crossed the river countless times before reaching Greg's campsite. It seemed a lazy-flowing river, though Greg assured me it often wasn't. One of the risks attached to camping in Guy Fawkes was the mood of the river. A storm on the tablelands produced a banker within hours, marooning those caught on the wrong side. If we crossed where there were bits of boulders and a strong flow the stream was only ten metres wide. Where there were beaches and sandbars we waded into a wide expanse of water and when the horses stepped into holes ripped out by currents we emerged with our boots wet and dripping. A trace of water leaked into my boots, but with the continual movement of the horses and the breathtaking scenery a bit of cold water went unnoticed. What I had difficulty ignoring was my back. The ride down had jarred it badly. I had expected the pain to intensify when I started to ride and had put some Panadeine tablets in my shirt pocket in readiness. I carried a waterbottle on a military belt. Halfway down I got five tablets into my hand and used the water bottle to wash them down. It was probably why I never felt the cold water when it ran through my trousers in the river. In fact I loved the ride along the canyon floor and never once thought about why we were there. A pair of eagles circled above us at one point. We debated what they were. Greg said they were wedge-tails. I thought they were one of the sea eagle species, owing to markings I hadn't seen before. Mobs of grey kangaroos hopped away from the shade of the apple gums near the river and drifted into the stringybarks on the lower slopes, which rose gently from the river flats to connect with the sudden uplift to the canyon rim. The canyons were not lined by unbroken granite cliffs – it was more a complex tangle of exposed rock and hardy vegetation.

Sometimes we crossed expanses of pure sand, like a pristine beach, and I think Daisy must have rolled in them as a wild foal, for she never missed the opportunity. I knew a bit about packhorse rolling and had packed accordingly, placing my eggs in an army mess plate. Some crossings were devoid of any sand. We rode through river oaks and out onto slate rock screes, the iron shoes of the horses loud enough to drown out the babbling of water rushing over rock.

In the winter the cobble-like screes are slow to dry when water has dripped off some animal. The first telltale trickle of water was from a dingo. It was so fresh that droplets of water still lay on saucer-shaped rocks, and where the dog had shook itself the fine spray lingered on the cobbles. The second was from a wild horse. At least one was still alive.

Greg reined in at the campsite flat about 4.00 p.m. It was a wide flat on a bend in the river. There were several huge river red gums and their seedlings had begun to regenerate the original forest, which had been cleared in the days of the cattlemen. Many of the new trees were less than ten metres high with perfectly straight trunks. Those growing apart from other young trees were ideal for horse tethering. Greg's system for settling down horses for the night was the best I'd ever observed. A rope five metres long was attached to a halter and the end tied to a tree using a big loose loop locked secure by a non-slip bowline knot. The knot simply followed the horse as it fed around the tree. The horse got plenty to eat and never tangled in the rope. If the horse was a known rogue he hobbled it as well. He said he didn't like hobbling in wild stallion territory. If the domestic horses were attacked during the night the hobbled ones could be seriously injured.

With only six days to go before the shortest day of the year we were all busy trying to get a comfortable camp set up before dark. First up Errol lit a fire and we gathered wood. It was tempting to roll out the swag near the fire and call it a day, but it would end in misery. First the heavy dew would descend and wet everything, followed by a white frost turning the dew into a film of ice. There were no short cuts and it was nearly dark when the three of us finally sat down to boil the billy. I poured some rum into my pannikin, knowing I couldn't keep taking Panadeine five at a time.

Both Greg and Errol were very quiet. They had been riding through these canyons for years and were used to seeing lots of horses. Greg hadn't been back down since his involvement with the media after the shooting of the horses by the National Parks and Wildlife Service and I think he had secretly expected that a few little mobs would have wandered in from the more remote canyons. The lack of tracks suggested they hadn't.

'When did you first hear about the shooting?' I asked Greg. I had my back up against a big log, not far from the fire. The overhead trees were still, not a leaf fluttered and the canyon chill was ominous.

'Well, the shooting commenced on the 22nd,' he said thoughtfully. 'I got a call from Ernie Maskey about three days later. I hadn't heard a thing. I live too far from the canyon rim to hear rifle fire. Ernie said he'd heard a lot of distant reports like gunfire. He rang to see if I knew anything.' Greg paused and stared bleakly into the fire. With the light fading the flame shadows were beginning to dance on the trunks of nearby trees.

'My heart sank when he told me. I had a pretty good idea. Anyway I called Errol and he was here at daylight with his truck. We loaded up and got down here a little bit quicker than we did today. It was terrible. We couldn't believe our eyes. It was the height of the foaling. Mares with foals half born. It made me spew up. Everywhere, bloated and stinking bodies of horses. Sun-baked shit caked around the bullet holes where the slugs slammed into their guts. They were meant to be heart–lung shots, but when horses are bolting and the pilot's trying to weave around spurs that rise almost from the river the best marksman in the world couldn't pinpoint bullets. The bullets hit them all over the place. One stallion had more bullet punctures in his legs than anywhere else. He'd dug a bit of a hole underneath himself. Then the flies told so much of the story. Blood must have spurted from these running horses like water escaping from a polypipe crack, and the flies were still on the blood trails, dried black by the sun. There were millions. The smell in the canyon was overwhelming and we gasped at the prospect of all this rotting flesh leaching into the river.' He stopped and looked at me grimly, to be sure I understood the significance of what he was about to say.

'The Guy Fawkes is a tributary of the mighty Clarence,

you know. In terms of supply to populations it's the second most important river system in northern NSW.'

'What was Ernie Maskey's reaction when you told him?'

Greg was silent for a moment. He had been drained of any emotion months ago. 'They was beautiful,' he replied slowly. 'That's all he ever said.'

Ernie Maskey had Aboriginal blood from distant connections with the local tribes in the 19th century. His grandfather had a canyon lease called Razorback which was left to his father and, born in 1932, Ernie was reared there. His whole world was the Guy Fawkes River canyons and the creatures that lived in them. Their land ran onto the Sara River, a tributary of the larger Guy Fawkes. In latter years Ernie acquired a lease he called 'Why Worry' which he operated jointly with his brother Billy. Nearly all their stockhorses came from the canyon brumbies. No fence was ever erected between Why Worry and the national park. The brumbies along the Sara wandered onto Ernie's property at will and he looked upon the horses as his own. He was very proud of them. He enjoyed nothing better than sitting around a campfire and telling the younger generation of local horsemen, like Greg Everingham, about the origins of the wild horses. All the blood links went back to Saladin, he told the younger men. There were no better stockhorses in the world.

We were all weary from an early start. Vegetables were boiled and meat cooked on a griller. By eight o'clock Greg and Errol were in their swags and I stared into the flames, contemplating the long night. About midnight a wild stallion struck. There was a tremendous rumpus from the horses and Greg raced out amongst them with a torch and stockwhip. The powerful beam located the stallion immediately. He was trying to drive the mare Gravel away. Greg didn't crack the whip, for fear of panicking the tethered horses. He whacked the stallion across the rump once and it bolted into the night.

'It's a good sign,' Greg said. 'Maybe there are some survivors.'

I snatched a little sleep and tried to prepare for the final hours before dawn. We knew the temperature would plummet. Glen Innes, which often recorded the state's lowest temperature, was only 50 kilometres away in a straight line. Days later I heard it dropped to –8°C that morning. The billy was full of water and froze rock solid. At daylight I tapped it on a boulder to fracture the ice and got a fresh fill from the river. Our camp was a good ten metres above the water and down on the river the fog had not lifted. It was a bone-cracking cold down there, possibly as low as –12°C. According to the map we were still 600 metres above sea level, I hurried back to the fire before the water froze again.

By the time the billy boiled the sun had arched over the canyon rim and cast a brilliance onto the river fog. High up, puffs of mist hung on the cliff bands, like white flowers on an arid background. On the flat the horses stood as ghosts in the frosted glades. They were cold and the green feed in the open woodland lay under a dew frozen to ice.

We had a quick breakfast and saddled up. Before mounting we took the packhorses down to the river for a drink. They didn't need to come with us so we tethered them to forest trees with plenty of grass.

'From here down was one of the favourite haunts,' Greg announced as we mounted. 'If there are any left we should see them this morning.'

Before the first river crossing we had ridden onto the skeletons. The bones lay in thick patches of grass fed by the decayed flesh and intestines. None of the skulls had a bullet hole. To our increasing horror we examined bullet shattered pelvises and leg bones smashed by rapid fire.

That morning, drinking a mug of tea by the campfire, Greg had a robust colour in his cheeks. An hour after departing the camp he was ashen-faced, like a man coping with the funeral of a close friend. Errol was tight-lipped and more silent than ever.

'They must have known it was foaling season,' Greg said bitterly, his chin on his chest and Survivor picking his own way. 'But then again, what do they know?'

It was the pathetic little pile of bones and tiny skull mingled with the large pelvic bones of a mare which prompted Greg's rhetoric. He had photographs from the day he and Errol discovered the bodies and using trees as markers it was not difficult to pinpoint what skeleton belonged to each horse photographed.

We crossed a wide expanse of river – a gravel plain of blue-charcoal slate under shallow water. Emerging, we rode into the deep shadow of the river she-oaks. Behind us rose Lucifer's Thumb, with the summit rocks ablaze in the sun. I was momentarily sidetracked by the scenery and when I looked ahead again Greg had vanished. With no packhorse to lead he was free to move quickly.

'If he finds a little mob he's going to hunt them back towards us,' Errol explained. 'Give you a close look at them.'

Greg knew their favourite pockets and the footfalls of just the one horse were more likely to arouse curiosity than fear. We knew any survivors would be easily spooked. The sound of a helicopter would be more terrifying than bolts of lightning to these horses – like elephants, horses have an extraordinary capacity to remember.

Downstream towards the Sara River the canyon expanded into a deep, wide valley. The near-perpendicular range on either side was no less impressive. Seen from a cattleman's eyes this was excellent breeding country too. The Guy Fawkes and its tributaries might have generated in excess of three million dollars in beef sales in 2001. It would have been export income, without which a nation falters and spirals towards bankruptcy. Argentina, the largest beef producing nation in the world, would probably give up territory to be foot and mouth free the way Australia is.

In my view, the locking out of the cattle industry from the Guy Fawkes canyons and river valleys is academic policy which the nation can't afford – the national social service programs and defence deployments are already over-stretched. We rode on. There were tracks of kangaroos, dingoes and a few horses. There were no tracks of bush-walkers and it was the peak walking season for this region. In summertime the canyons are insufferably hot and dan-gerous: a lightning strike from a dry storm, wind and the flames would outrun the fittest bushwalker.

Our stirrup irons slid through the thick dry grass. It promised to explode into sheets of flame from the first lightning strike in late spring or summer. The brumbies had been a buffer against the fires by consuming the inflam-mable red grass. In some parts of the NSW tablelands it's known as the fire grass. Districts like Mudgee and Gulgong greatly fear bushfires when the grass hays off. Firefighters had been trapped and burnt alive on several occasions during the 20th century. I foresaw a future for this magnif-icent region no different from what I had observed in the King Leopold Ranges in northern Western Australia. The west Kimberley mountain region was being inexorably destroyed by hot, annual fires.

Greg was waiting for us at an old trapping site called the Rock Wall. During the process of erosion over millions of years massive rock deposits had been formed, like low bridges across the canyon. In time the river cut through them, creating narrow gorges. It was a perfect bottleneck for trapping horses. Using nets, the National Parks and Wildlife Service staff and local horsemen used to catch up to 20 horses in a single run. The net was erected where the brumby pad exited a gorge. Horsemen chased the mobs towards the gorge on the side left open, and when the last horse had galloped in, a man left in hiding pulled a net behind them, shutting off any escape. The ocean trawler nets, purchased from Townsville fishermen, were attached to an overhead cable with snaplinks. The rock wall secured one side of the trap and on the river side the net was already up. In 1993 28 brumbies were caught at the Rock Wall site, but in subsequent years the method had mixed results. The report by Dr A.W. English for the National Parks and Wildlife Service on the 1999 attempt commented that haltered horses were tethered behind 4WD vehicles and dragged up the escarpment. For the sake of animal welfare, the system had to be abandoned.

'There was one small mob feeding on the flats,' Greg said, when Errol and I rode up to him. 'I didn't see them. I only know from their tracks.' He paused, dispirited as ever. 'The skeletons are everywhere.'

We rode on towards a feature called the Petrogate, a minor peak set apart from the range. On the way, Greg turned away from the river into a side valley.

'Favoured little valley, this one,' he said quietly. 'They used to foal in these pockets. Notice the fire never came through here. There's no scorch or char on any of the trees and it's old grass.' He sat his horse in silence and I heard some insects in the trees overhead. There was a cold anger in the man. 'There was plenty of feed. They didn't have to kill them.'

'That little group we saw on the long weekend before the shootings looked in great nick,' Errol confirmed. 'Pity we didn't get those youngins that day. All dead now.'

'We saw these three mares with foals, Mike,' Greg added. 'Lovely creamies they were. It was my fault. I said to Errol, let's give them another month on their mothers before we take them.' He shook his head in despair and spurred Survivor to walk on.

At the Petrogate we stopped for lunch and boiled the quartpots for tea. We went on chatting and in the warm sun our alertness dissipated. Suddenly the grass was alight and the noise of the flame was like a blast of wind in a corridor. We had forgotten about the little quartpot fire. Windjackets were unzipped and ripped off. It took a couple of minutes to beat out the flame and this was June, in a temperature of less than half the mid-morning temperature in December.

On the way back to camp we meticulously inspected every pile of bones Greg could find. From a count of 52 skulls, only one had a bullet through the forehead. One of the surprises in the English report was the claim that the 'heart–lung' is the preferred kill shot, not the head. Those of us with wide and long experience in the shooting of large animals know the heart–lung is an imprecise target and only causes instant death when the bullet hits the heart. It is a target of last resort. A few years ago I had to dispose of a cow that charged horses or bikes. A head shot was impossible and I went for the heart. The bullet was placed correctly, but she unleashed a ferocious charge and hit the side of the vehicle. Five seconds later she was dead. That was a lung shot very close to the heart. It's a very untidy kill shot. If a helicopter shoot must be done it is preferable if the pilot runs the mob until they begin to labour and stand

Dean Pendergast with a rare silver brumby caught on the Snowy Plains.

Typical snow brumbies with their shaggy winter coats.

Ted Taylor, caretaker of Currango Homestead.

Outside the deserted Coolamine Homestead L-R: Mike (on horseback), Ted, Michelle, Julie.

Brumby chase: competitors at the Man from Snowy River Bush Festival show off their skills.

Jim Nankervis (L), with Mike at Corryong, lived to tell the tale of his amazing rescue.

Roping the wild brumby at the Festival.

The Suggan Buggan bathed in mist.

Ken Connley (L) shares a campfire joke with Dean Backman.

Chris Stoney with a brumby foal roped in the Victorian Alps.

Rachel Parsons with the black mare.

Fording the Guy Fawkes River in our search for surviving brumbies.

Greg Everingham on Survivor, the last colt taken from Guy Fawkes before the October 2000 shooting.

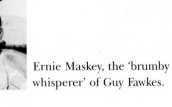

Ernie Maskey, the 'brumby whisperer' of Guy Fawkes.

The Blue Duck Inn: a welcome sight for travellers.
Inset: the inn circa 1920. (COURTESY, BLUE DUCK INN)

A wintry gold-mining camp, 1890s. (COURTESY, BLUE DUCK INN)

O'Rourke and little
Feathertop at Myall
Plains.

Sal with Feathertop.

still for head shots. A marksman not capable of shooting a horse through the forehead at 200 metres (in good conditions) can't shoot.

I know what I'm talking about. At Holsworthy firing range in the 1950s, under the supervision of the Australian Army, the cadet squad I was rostered into fired at targets over 500 metres for up to four days straight. Many of us are partially deaf 40 years later, from rifle range report. But most of us became so good that when the score for the day looked like rising above 85 per cent the anti-rifle camp cadets fired over the top of the targets. If you scored more than 85 per cent on any one day you were sent to Singleton army base for three weeks' rifle camp. I trained with about 60 boys in their late teens and knew 20 of them could take consecutive bullseyes on what was termed 'rapid targeting'.

The disturbing discovery from the bone inspection was the bullet fracture of many pelvises. A 'finish off' shot would never be placed through the pelvis. This type of targeting suggested a crippling shot to bring the animal down and return minutes later to deliver the kill shot. In other words the horses were fleeing, trees got in the way and the twisty nature of the spurs and steep rising gullies must have made it impossible for a marksman to deliver a first sighting kill shot. Had I been ordered to do the shooting and had the stomach for such an exercise, this is what I would have done. In Guy Fawkes or any other canyons of the waterfall country, it would be nearly impossible to do it any other way. In other words, helicopter shooting in such areas should not even be considered.

To add weight to my conclusion, the location of one skeleton particularly distressed the three of us. An adult horse had galloped into one of the main gullies coming from the top. Near the river it was steep and rocky. Halfway up it was a rockclimb and for the second half it became a vertical fissue in the cliff face. This horse had entered the second stage. A capable rockclimber myself, I was using my hands by the time I reached the skeleton. We could only ponder over the terror this poor horse must have experienced to get so high. If we had found several skeletons in such unlikely locations we may have been able to conclude carcasses had been moved away from the river by helicopter. In the report it was stated that was done. The skeletons we found on the river flats and crosschecked against Greg's earlier photographs, indicated that no skeletons were removed from where we rode. But it is a serious and honest report, so I can only conclude carcasses were lifted away from the Sara River flats. We didn't ride the Sara.

We had given up hope of seeing any live brumbies when we heard the sound of a horse approaching, a galloping horse. A big bay stallion was bearing down on us. We turned to face him. Survivor struck the air with one front leg to warn the wild stallion. The little colt was just a baby, but the mare under saddle was his. The bay stopped on raised ground, but only revealed his head. He was looking down at us. It was a clever bit of strategy. He could see everything and all we and the horses could see was the top of his head.

'He's assessing whether we're a threat,' Greg whispered.

With highly focused intensity, he appeared to stare at each horse and man unit individually. Daisy, my packhorse, was coming into season. Had she been with us there would have been trouble.

The stallion stood his ground for about a minute and then returned to the cover of the grey gums at the same speed he had approached us.

'There'll be mares up there,' Greg said. 'Not a word now. We'll ride in there where he's gone.'

The mares weren't far. Three creamies and two buckskin foals. They were very flighty from the way each mare faced up, head held high. There was 100 metres between them and Greg's colt. The stallion stood boldly out to the front. I got the feeling this fellow would attack if roused. One of the foals swung onto his mother's milk and the little silver tail could be seen to waggle as he began to suck. The other foal ducked in behind his mother. It was a typical social group called a harem. Groups of stallions only were called bachelor groups. I had seen one such group in the Suggan Buggan. One stallion had been very assertive. He knew there were mares among the riding group and wanted them. Weight of numbers seemed to drive him off.

The stallion was a big horse for a brumby. He stood nearly sixteen hands. His head was wide and game looking and he was barrel-chested. Any stockhorse breeder would have been happy with this bloke. I wanted a photograph, but I was just too far away. To ride forward on the dainty mare I was riding would have been about as safe as riding towards a lion about to defend his pride. We waited and I think all three of us were a little uneasy. This was a stand off. Someone had to back off, and after three or four minutes the stallion did. He snorted loudly and tossed his head. The snort from a wild stallion is not one you'll ever hear from a domestic horse. It's sharp and intimidating. Something deep within your own instinct triggers the adrenaline.

After the warning snort he trotted briskly towards the mares, tossing his head again, which was definitely a signal for them to move on. They disappeared quickly into the timber and we thought he would go too. Their direction was towards a canyon wall and we were riding away upstream, back to the camp. We had only gone 100 metres and we heard him coming, full gallop. Greg suggested we didn't stop and the stallion tailed us for 300 metres. If he'd wanted the mare he would have attacked. He was seeing us out of his territory. I couldn't think of another creature in the animal kingdom that would behave in this manner, but no doubt there are, particularly among the primates.

For some people, and I am on the edge of the bracket myself, the shooting of horses is not as distant from the shooting of people that we would like it to be. It's not a rational revulsion as man has been killing and eating them since the Paleolithic period in Europe. The native Americans are known to have made the American wild horse extinct, a breed which probably evolved from the early Asian *Equus*. In America there was even a native zebra (*Equus simplicidens*), but altered environmental conditions rather than the first Americans may have led to its extinction.

Back at the camp we watered the packhorses and set about preparations for the evening. I made a rum damper. Probably a waste of rum, but feeling a bit stressed after what I'd seen, I relished the prospect of drinking rum and eating it at the same time. Camp ovens are a bit heavy in the packs, so I always use a billy. You grease it liberally with olive oil then tip in the rum, an egg, salt and self-raising flour. Water is added to knead the flour into a moist dough. The end result is a giant scone. It has a rum flavour and is delicious with blackberry jam.

I had just slid the damper from the billy when two men burst over the riverbank, leading their packhorses.

'Had to stop a couple of times and spell the horses,' Allan Cavanagh said, surveying the camp from the saddle. 'My two haven't had much work for a while.'

Allan was a cattle breeder from the Dorrigo Plateau. Now in his 60s, Allan had been catching Guy Fawkes brumbies for station stockwork since he was a boy. He was also chairman of the Grafton Rural Lands Board. Behind him rode Fred Marsden, a cattleman from the waterfall country further east towards Dorrigo. Both men had ridden into the national park to meet me and express their views on the brumby culling and the massive aggregation of declared wilderness.

'Find a spot for the horses and have a mug of tea before you set up camp,' Greg suggested to them. It was an hour before sunset.

There was disquiet on the upper Clarence tributaries. More and more leases were being acquired by the National Parks and Wildlife Service. Some had been pastoral and others forest leases. The Guy Fawkes River, Washpool, Chaelundi, Nymboi–Binderay, Cathedral Rock and New England National Parks comprised more than 250 000 hectares of de-stocked forest. Allan's concern was the build up of scrub under the forest canopy and the disappearance of fire trails.

'There'll be a fire one day so bad the valley people won't get out,' he said grimly, taking a seat on one of the camp-site logs. 'All the roads in and out of the valleys are slow. You can't fight the mountain fires. It's stay put and hope for the best or get out. I am worried so many of the fire trails have been let go. In the pastoral days the men used them to burn breaks.' He paused, staring gloomily into the fire. 'We're doing our damnedest to get along with them, but it just gets worse and worse. You know the fire bill last year was two million and it burnt itself out.' He shook his head. 'The waste – it goes on and on.'

Allan was jovial man by nature. After a quick mug of tea he made up a bit of a canvas shelter for himself and was soon back by the fire telling stories. Fred nodded gravely whenever the brumbies were mentioned. He was a horse lover. The tether-to-tree method wasn't good enough for Fred. He put up an electric fence so his two could walk around and feed. It fascinated me how everyone had a different solution for bedding down their horses.

'Do you know where I'll find Ernie Maskey?' I asked Allan. 'If I could talk to him I may find out the Maskeys' secret. They alone seem to be masters of brumby running.'

'When Ernie's crook he's in Glen Innes, but there's no phone. There's a phone connected at Why Worry.' Allan smiled. 'But you'll be lucky if it ever answers because they sleep and eat out in the bush. They're oldtime bushmen and that's the core of their brumby running skills.' Allan had brought his swag over for a seat and opened a bottle of red wine. 'Ernie's grandmother was a fullblood Aboригine who reared a big family with one of the Cobleys at Razorback near Newton Boyd. Don't know what became of old Cobley, but she reared those kids on her own to be smart bushmen. They could track and ride anything. One of Ernie's uncles used to sell broken-in brumbies on a regular basis at the Dorrigo horse sales. They were popular among cattlemen in the district for their hardiness and surefootedness. The colour too – lovely buckskins, yer know.'

He paused to pour himself a pannikin of wine. It was starting to get dark.

'Anyone like a drop?'

It smelt good and I tried a little of it. My back was much better and I felt I could ease off the rum.

'You'll have to ask Ernie for details when you catch him somewhere,' Allan went on. 'But the Cobley men descended from that Aboriginal woman were apparently brilliant at getting those brumbies. They knew the terrain and at any given point they knew where the brumbies would try to break. Sometimes they had a boy in hiding to block the path of a fleeing mob. They rounded them up and yarded them like we would cattle.'

Allan was a natural storyteller. His family had been on the plateau for four generations and what he didn't know about the local area wasn't worth knowing.

The next day, when we rode much further down the river, still looking for brumbies, we entered a broad valley walled in with cliffs. Allan reined in at a ruin. It was the site of the old Combolo Station homestead. The only thing left standing was an orange tree with fruit on it. We each picked an orange. It was a beautiful valley, empty and wasted. If there had been smouldering coals among the ruins any of us could have been forgiven for looking nervously around, but this was a lonely place and no one came here anymore. Even the rangers only passed over in helicopters.

'The Brown family lived here,' Allan said quietly. 'No one did more than those people to produce such magnificent wild horses. It wasn't intentional of course. Horses escape from time to time in this country. Here they began with stock from Saladin, thoroughbreds and even Clydesdales. It all began down here in 1850.' Allan went on to relate this history.

Two brothers arrived at Marengo in 1850, on the canyon rim. An explorer, Major Parke, traversed the plateau to the east of Guy Fawkes in 1835 and became the first settler. The winters were long and hard at 1200 metres, and in 1861 Henry Brown selected Broadmeadows Station on the canyon floor. Above Broadmeadows the Guy Fawkes and Sara Rivers join to form the Boyd. In the days before bores and heavy earth moving equipment, selections along rivers were highly sought after. In 1880 Henry's son David set up Combolo Station. Tight, precipitous gorges up above

Broadmeadows, where the water from the river sometimes lapped vertical walls on either side, made horse travel very difficult if the river flow was up a little bit. The only good track out of Combolo was a 650-metre lift in six kilometres on a single spur snaking out from the cliff walls. The station must have been one of the most isolated in eastern Australia. It was little wonder lonely white men in this region sought Aboriginal women, despite the huge disparity in cultural background. White women were understandably reluctant to enter the frontier, for they knew they would often be left alone for days on end, sometimes weeks. In the 1850s at the headwaters of the Guy Fawkes River, a small run called Bald Hills was the scene of a raid by a tribe hostile to white occupation. Three women, a baby and a shepherd were speared. But sometimes passion overrides all fear and creates stories. Relinquishing governess duties at Government House in Parramatta, Mary Ann Monahan married David Brown and arrived at Combolo Station in 1880. She lived there for most of her life.

The spirit of this woman must have captured the imagination of women living at Combolo for the next three generations. The Combolo Hutkeeper's wife, Mrs Carney, was left on her own for weeks when the men walked the cattle down through the gorges and on to distant markets. She had three young children. The mail arrived at Marengo once a week and to collect it was a day's ride. The children were tossed up like monkeys onto a big Clydesdale packhorse and they all set off for a day out, up 850 metres to the post office. Perhaps only in Switzerland did people have to climb so far to collect their mail.

In the 1930s and 40s another Brown woman was known to lead a packhorse 100 kilometres into South Grafton, do her shopping, catch up on the gossip and return the same day. I may have been suspicious of this story if I hadn't ridden a 'seven mile an hourer' on Maneroo Station. The horse was normally ridden by an overseer. Some of those western horsemen knew how to teach horses to walk along at an extraordinary rate. I was instructed to fix a floodgate on a fence exactly seven miles (eleven kilometres) from the station yards. The gelding walked it in an hour. Mrs Brown would have left Broadmeadows Station about 4.00 a.m., arriving in South Grafton about 1.00 p.m. She would have been back home about 2.00 a.m. the following morning.

The MacDougall family took up country in the Guy Fawkes area as early as the 1860s and appear to be the only original family remaining. Family records have been carefully kept for 140 years and throughout this long period there are references to wild creamy horses. In 1915 there was mention of a large herd of grey horses living on one of the tributaries of the Guy Fawkes River.

Allan Cavanagh was great company and I was sorry when we parted on the fourth day. He convinced me that the area fondly known as 'the Gulf' has wonderful heritage value and that something has to be done to save the remaining brumbies. Fred was a practical bushman and had always believed that something had to be done to reduce the brumby numbers. He could never understand why the authorities didn't pay local horsemen to do the job and keep right out of it themselves. He and I often talked about wildlife in general and plant species. Fred was very knowledgeable about the waterfall country.

When the party split up Greg, Errol and I put our mounts to the task of climbing out of the canyon and returning to the station. Survivor was one of the most striking young colts I'd ever seen. Greg suggested I catch a filly in the Snowy Mountains and when she was mature enough she could be mated with him. I had made arrangements to go out with Dean Pendergast in the early spring. Maybe he could catch a filly for me. Greg and I might start a whole new breed of brumbies.

CHAPTER 7

The Noose

*I warrant he'll be with us when he's wanted at the
   end,*
For both his horse and he are mountain bred.

Ken Connley from Benambra in Victoria has roped and
caught more brumbies than anyone else in Australia's
southeast ranges. With more than 1400 going under the
lasso, his tally is undoubtedly a world record for a lone man
catching wild horses, whether it be mustangs in America or
criollo horses in Patagonia. Off a horse he called Ace, he
had caught 364 brumbies. Ken and Ace featured in the film
The Man from Snowy River, doubling for Jack Thompson
during a daring gallop through the snow gums.

'I'm booked out with deer shooters,' he said, when I
called him at his Benambra home in late June. 'I can give
you a handful of names. They know the alps because at one
time or another they all rode with me. I taught them.'

I wanted to photograph the snow brumbies and see if they
were having any harmful effects on the ecology of the area.
With nearly half a century of field observation behind me,
I felt well qualified to make an environmental assessment.

The Victorian Alps

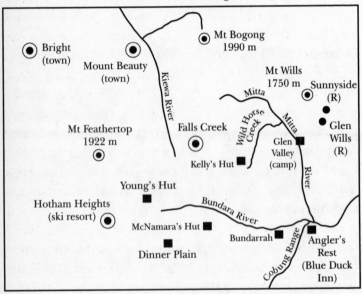

(R) = ruins

The Victorian government had adopted a more moderate and sympathetic approach to the cattlemen of the high country than was ever demonstrated in NSW, but the mountain people were worried the remaining snow leases were about to be resumed. The new government had its share of supporters who were against admission of horses into national parks and there were some very outspoken Greens in the various environmental advisory committees. If the mountain people were to retain their way of life it was vital the government hierarchy was not influenced by misinformation campaigns. Like other extremist groups in the world, a very small and bitter minority stooped to bacillus methods to influence government policy and the forming of legislation. One such case occurred in the Murray River, along the Victorian and NSW border. An environmentally-conscious journalist was invited to report on horse manure pollution. About an hour before the unwitting journalist arrived a truckload of manure was unloaded upstream. Fortunately common sense alerted the journalist and the article was abandoned, but the attempt at vicious distortion was real and worrying.

Ken went on to say he would contact me if he had a cancellation. But it seemed unlikely. Deer hunting was a booming sport and this was the hunting season. The fallow deer were breeding up throughout the far southeast ranges of Australia and many bushmen predicted that populations would overtake those of brumbies. The deer were more elusive; they thrived in the thick undergrowth that was becoming more and more a feature of the mountain and valley country under 1000 metres, and it was nearly impossible to lure them into bush yards. The trophy hunters focused on the samba deer imported from India in the 19th century. A wide set of antlers from a stag, mounted above the fireplace or in a study, was the ultimate reward for the hunters. It saved the state the cost of culling them.

I finally gave up on Ken. He was always out. On his answering machine he left the following message to callers: 'Hi there, Ken Connley's Alpine Adventures. Well it looks like I am not about. I could be out fishin with Jungle George after a 14 lb rainbow, or I could be in the high country chasin brumbies with Dean [Dean Pendergast], or I could be stalkin a big samba I seen the other day, or I could be workin me arse off on the farm tryin to keep this great country of ours goin.' Resigned to not being able to go with him and with time running out, for I had a west Kimberley trip planned in August, I worked through a list of names given to me in the Benambra Hotel when I had stopped there for a few drinks in March. A bloke called Larry Smith said he'd take me. For a fee of $150 a day he agreed to provide a quiet horse for me to ride and take me into the alps from the Mount Wills side, which is due east from the skiing resort of Falls Creek. I explained I didn't wish to chase brumbies; I just wanted to ride along quietly, take photographs and observe how the brumbies survived in the snow. We agreed to meet on Thursday 5 July on the Mitta Mitta River at a camping ground called Glen Valley, just south of where the vanished towns of Sunnyside and Glen Wills once lay with a combined population of 2000 people in the 1890s.

In 1888 a government surveyor reported the discovery of tin ore on the southern slopes of Mount Wills. Two years later another report claimed the ore-bearing area was two and half miles wide and 35 miles long. The manager of the company newly formed to mine the tin declared the deposit was larger than Broken Hill. Strong investment backing for the mining venture was demonstrated in the share prices.

One pound shares soared to £120 at the height of the boom. The Victorian Secretary for Mining was commissioned to undertake a thorough assay of the geological material and the surveys and assessments were found to be flawed. The collapse of the share prices must have taken a greater toll than the long freezing winters.

It was the discovery of gold which briefly saved the towns. The O'Connell brothers made headlines when they weighed more than 1000 ounces, taken from the Yellow Girl mine.

In the 19th century the Australian climate was much cooler than it is today. For weeks on end the much higher Sunnyside was almost buried in snow two metres deep. On occasions the town ran desperately short of supplies and it was a relief when packhorses from Omeo with light loads floundered through the snow to bring in fresh vegetables. There was always plenty of flour, but the risk of scurvy in the alpine mines was a serious problem. It was little wonder the towns were surrendered to the ghosts of miners after Yellow Girl was closed in 1915, when the call to arms for the Great War dislodged the manpower. The lower town of Glen Wills had a modest revival in the 1930s from gold and timber, but in 2001 next to nothing remained.

Stories like the one about a man freezing to death inside his hut at Sunnyside and being partly eaten by his starving dog didn't fill me with a lot of enthusiasm for the ride. I was heading into country 500 metres higher than Sunnyside. The locals kept saying the big snow was coming 'any day now', and I had a fear of the cold which went beyond rational thinking. I was pleased when Larry arrived on time and I no longer had time to dwell on my phobia.

Glen Valley is about 65 kilometres south of the village of Mitta Mitta. The mountain road, mostly dirt, winds over a steep pass at Mount Wills. I stayed overnight in a hotel at Mitta Mitta and left next morning for the rendezvous. When Larry turned up he told me another two riders would accompany us. He had organised a full-on brumby run.

Larry was a handsome man of middle height in his late twenties. He had a shrewd look, unusual for that age. There was a hungry drive about him. He said the horse he originally had for me was found to be lame yesterday and unable to contact me, he had loaded up another one. From the wavering of his eyes I knew this wasn't the sort of horse I wanted. With some difficulty, I suppressed my anger. He had altered the arrangements without any consultation and I was paying him. I wanted to observe the wild horses, not chase them. I also had no protective gear. Never dreaming the arrangements would be ignored I left everything at home. I was nervously anxious about not having my skull cap. A veteran casualty of the racetrack, I had been gravely warned against getting injured again.

I had to think quickly, because a ute towing a trailer had just swung the final bend before the river. The trip from Myall Plains was more than 800 kilometres, and if I aborted the whole exercise was a waste of time and money. Larry had also travelled quite a long way in an old truck. He came from somewhere in the hills out of Buchan, not far from Buff Roger's home territory. There wasn't really an option: I had to go along with Larry's plans and just try to avoid injury.

I expected two men to emerge from the 4WD ute, but I was astonished to see that one was a woman. Women with personality are a tremendous asset in the camp – men tend to refrain from excessive drinking and will consider the welfare of their horses a little more. But a lot of restrictions can also come with a woman. You can't swear – there's often plenty to swear about on hard bush rides. You can't dismount and pee on the spot. Instead, you have to tie up and walk away. It's no good telling the others to keep riding, because the tethered horse will fret and pull away. A dubious horse and now a woman. My apprehension doubled.

The bloke's name was Bert. About 1.8 metres tall, there was a hint of great strength and an unyielding disposition. He didn't simply look at you; he fixed you in a hard, uncompromising stare. The woman was called Sophie. In my experience, only the most feminine women are blessed with the name, but this Sophie was a cool, tough horse lady.

My decision to go on with the program had been made while the horses were still aboard the truck. Now, watching my mount come off, it felt like watching my own coffin come out of the hearse. A racy-looking thoroughbred's fine on a railed-off racetrack, but chasing brumbies through the snow gums on a stud-bred horse was extremely dangerous. He'd been raced somewhere and seemed a fractious type. There was a lot of bush racing in the ranges, both sides of the border. Some of the tracks described to me sounded horrendous. When I began to saddle this horse I had visions of bolting out of control towards Falls Creek and irate ski patrol officers hot on my heels.

Larry rode a thoroughbred too. He was a lovely light bay with a white blaze. Bert's horse was a strong stockhorse type. The horse had to be to carry his weight at full gallop. The young woman rode a stylish grey gelding with a distinct Arab head. In the 1970s my best saddle horse was a three-quarter Arab. I lived in the Warrumbungle Mountains in those days and he was the most surefooted horse I ever rode.

I helped with the horse unloading and we immediately began rigging up the packhorses. When Bert had finished packing the big bay gelding Larry had brought for him you could barely see the animal. I think he may have had a motto: 'No matter where you go, take your woman and all the comforts of home.' The frying pan on the ground was unnoticed until the overall strap had been reefed down, so he jammed it in under the huge bedroll. Larry and I shared the other packhorse and our combined gear was about half the size of Bert's.

Fittingly for the occasion, the trail hugged the banks of Wild Horse Creek for a few kilometres until we swung away and climbed steeply into the mountains. Just as the cold intensified with every 100 metres gained, so did the nature of the forest change. Above approximately 1200 metres we left the broad-trunked candlebarks, stringybarks and grey gums and entered the world of the impressive white-trunked manna gums, along with a mingling of the tall, smooth-barked snow gums. The snow gum, or white sallee, is all one species, *Eucalyptus pauciflora*, but the species varies greatly in appearance depending on altitude and tempera-ture. In the subalpine it is a beautiful tall gum with scribbly patterns on the bark. The shades of colour in the bark alter with the season, varying from clean white to olive green. At the limit of the treeline the same trees become gnarled and twisted. In the final stage of our climb we passed on from the tall trees to a tableland plateau covered in stunted snow gums on the ridges and the more interesting black sallee trees on the edges of the frost hollows.

Riding through a sunless land under steel grey skies, a biting wind tilting our hats, I decided only drunken poets and city greenies could look upon this mountain plateau environment with any passion. I was getting hell, too, from the packhorse. Larry said he had a pinched nerve in his shoulder and Bert brusquely tossed me the rope. Leading an unwilling horse on a skittish half-mouthed mongrel is exhausting. Over a few hours it would have tested a man decades younger than me. I didn't bother asking Larry what he called my mount. For me, 'Hammerhead' was spot on. They were bastards in tropical waters around harbours and this was a bastard of a horse. He wouldn't stand when you went to mount and if you reined him up he threw back his head like a mallet. Larry had a black eye and I overheard him tell Bert that Hammerhead had given it to him. I mounted by running alongside, one hand holding the pack-horse lead. The next three days looked bleak and I spent most of the day wondering what the hell was wrong with me. All the telltale signs were there at the beginning, but still I went on with it. Hours later I was too committed and grimly accepted what I'd fallen into. Bert chillingly conveyed the quality of the camaraderie when the first snowdrifts had begun to appear in the protected hollows. (I use the Spanish word 'camaraderie' because I felt that I would have been safer with the bandidoes in Mexico's Sierra Madre. It is said even the bandidoes respected the crucifix.)

'What's in the second pouch on your belt?' he asked, trying to break the boredom of the ride. 'Never seen a man carry two knives.'

I would have preferred not to say. 'It's a Mexican cross,' I replied reluctantly. 'I always carry it.'

'Some sort of Jesus thing?' Bert guffawed.

There was nothing malicious about Bert. He was just a stockman, but the crudeness of the remark shook me. I had mixed with some rough men in my time, but this style of insensitivity was very rare.

'Yer, that's right,' I said quietly.

'We'll test it up here,' laughed cheeky Larry.

Bert only smiled. He may have been slightly superstitious and had no desire to mock something he didn't understand.

It was almost dark when we arrived at a slab hut. Larry had been talking about the hut. He got the television forecast before leaving home and there was snow coming. Bert wasn't very interested. Reared at Adaminaby in the Snowys, a snow squall to him was no more than a sun shower to the rest of us. Sophie didn't talk much and left no clue as to where she came from. If I had been hoping for that feminine, chatty relief around the campfire I was going to be disappointed.

For me the appearance of the hut out of the gloom was like a big motel with neon signs after a long lonely stretch on the road. Hammerhead was still running sideways and the over fat packhorse was thoroughly fed-up. I couldn't wait to dismount and tether them out. I hadn't discussed the overnight arrangements with Larry, but assumed tethering was the only option we had.

Nearing the hut we realised a darker greyness surrounding the hut was not mountain mist. It was smoke. Someone was in the hut and then Larry spotted two horses standing like frozen shadows.

'Anyone about?' yelled Larry. We waited as sleet began to fall, the dark flowing in as fast as a Kimberley tide.

'Anyone there?' he yelled again.

I saw Bert look at Sophie. 'Let's move on,' he said with a finality in his tone. 'We'll set up camp somewhere.'

We urged our mounts back into the snow gums and the dark. The sleet settled on the fringe between Hammerhead's ears and I brushed it away from my crotch the way a stockman in the old days would brush away cigarette ash.

'I know a place,' Larry said confidently. 'Be better than the hut too.'

When we stopped again it would have been pitch dark if it had not been for the rise of a half moon. The sleet had stopped falling and the mist was thin, letting some of the moonlight through to the ground. I could see a log barricade of some sort.

'It's an old brumby-catching yard,' Larry muttered as he dismounted. 'I'll check it out with a torch. There'll be some repair work needed for sure.'

Stiffly I eased myself out of the saddle and immediately began to lighten the load from the packhorse. I didn't feel very sorry for the plain bay gelding. I had a sore right arm from pulling him along. Bert and the girl got to work on starting a fire. Everything was damp from sleet showers and they had to gather dry leaves from around big logs, where the wind had blown them into protected crevices in the wood.

Larry went to work on the bush yard. He had the inherent knack of moving quickly and only minutes passed before he announced the smaller of the two yards secure. The big yard had to have electric wire run on one side. Larry had the wire and the small batteries in one of the packs. When I queried about tethering out on a halter he mentioned the wild stallions. We were well inside brumby territory.

The routine is always the same with alpine bush camps. Fire alight first, horses rugged and fed, tents or shelter erected and then the cooking. The horses were fed with nosebags. When the packs had been clinched down on the packhorses at Wild Horse Creek it looked impossible for anything else to be loaded on, especially when the horse rugs had gone on over the top of the swags. Then Larry lifted out of his ute butts of horse feed. Haybale twine was secured so it couldn't slip and a knot with double thickness used as a loop to go over the packsaddle hooks. Each packsaddle had four hooks and a fifteen kilogram butt of horse feed was slung from each one. It was ingenious for its simplicity.

I volunteered to be cook. There was nothing selfless about

it. I hadn't done any yard repairs and I didn't want to be the one putting a meal on the following evening. After ten hours of brumby chasing I'd be lucky if I was interested in food. I cut up a kilo of steak and dropped it into boiling water flavoured with beef stock. In another billy I boiled potatoes and in a smaller billy I had fresh beans ready to go on the fire later.

The ground felt like cement to walk on. It was frozen and Larry said we were only a kilometre from the snowline. In a normal winter the camp would have been under a metre of snow and they never usually camped this high. Most of the successful brumby running was done in the winter.

Feeling the cold in my bones, all I could think of was scalding black tea. I had rum in the pack, but exhausted I knew two nips would drop me on my bottom. No one else was interested in tea. The woman did what the men did. They were good mates and it lightened the sombre atmosphere of the camp to hear them jest with one another. Bert offered me a stubby and I should have accepted. Instead, I collected a couple of empty billies and set off for a creek about 150 metres away. On the way in the horses had a drink when they crossed it.

It was a clear track through the snow gums, but out on the frost hollow where the creek was the track was overgrown with snow grass. There was no track at all and it was pitch dark. Heavy cloud had rolled in again and if the forecast held true the snow would come any minute. Where the horses had crossed the water looked dirty. I had a powerful torch and walked downstream looking for a pool of clean water. Where the creek narrowed the water ran a little faster and I found a hole so clear I could see the pebbles on the bottom. I filled the billies and headed back to where I thought the track cut through the snow gums. The track didn't show up where I expected to see it and shining the torch in a full circumference nothing looked familiar. I was standing under a wide spreading black sallee which I would have noticed on the way out. The creek had shifted direction when I followed it, probably only 20 degrees, but enough to throw my sense of direction. If I walked far in the wrong direction I was in serious trouble. Finely built, I wasn't confident I could survive a night in sub-zero temperatures. I had matches and may not have been anxious if Bert hadn't been so long trying to start the campfire. He was an expert bushman.

I cooeed as loudly as I could. Under cloud cover I felt certain my voice would carry 150 metres, despite wind ruffling the snow gums. There was no reply. I cooeed again and again to no avail. It's moments like this when it's hard to keep cool. Ted Taylor had often talked about the ghosts of the frost hollows, and here I was in danger of becoming one myself.

The temperature was below zero. Along the creek I had noticed the ice forming where the water was still. I tried to remember something – something that would show up in the torchlight. There was a post, I recalled. It was an old strainer post, the last relic of a pioneer fence. I only had to walk back into the frost hollow to find the creek and if I walked out for a hundred metres, shining the torch, then returned to the creek to orientate a different direction each time I had to eventually spot the post. It took about ten minutes, but it worked. Forlorn and lifeless as it is, I'll never forget the shape or the height of that post.

Back at the campfire the two men were grinning and there were a couple of empty stubbies at their feet.

'We wanted to see if the cross worked,' Larry laughed. 'See if it could save yer.'

Sophie had kept an eye on the cooking and helped me serve up the meal on enamel plates. The men had dragged in a huge log, and with air circulating underneath the flames leapt high and drove back the cold.

'Who was in that hut?' I asked, while we hurriedly ate the meal before it got cold.

'Bloody Noose,' Larry said soberly. 'Didn't want anyone to see him. He'd be lookin for strays. Always pokes around the mountains before the snow comes.'

'He's a bushranger,' Bert added.'

'He's worse than that too,' chuckled Larry. 'Well it depends on yer sense of decency, I suppose,' he said as an afterthought, 'but for me this was the roughest I heard. There was a group come up from Melbourne for a long weekend and word quickly got around they wanted an overnight ride. It must have been one on those very rare occasions when Noose was in town. Anyway he said he'd take em and rounded up some horses. They all left Omeo for a grand adventure. Anyway Noose catches a foal. No one sees him do it and he tells em it was a poor little poddy. He ties it to a tree and they rub its head and take photographs. What a dear little thing, they're saying, but meanwhile it's dawned on Noose he's got to supply some tucker. So he tells em all to go down to the river and see the beautiful water-holes. While they're gone he leads the foal away, cuts its throat, butchers it and puts the rump portions in the camp oven. When the group returns he tells em the foal escaped. A couple of hours later they're blissfully eatin it.'

'Ned Kelly wouldn't have done anything like that,' Bert said grimly. He didn't like the story. It was humourless and macabre. It was probably just a story too.

'Kelly was said to have crossed to this side when the heat was on,' I said, adding a bit of trivia and hoping to change the subject. The famous bushranger Ned Kelly operated mainly on the western side of the alps.

'They only got his body when they hung him,' Larry sniggered. 'His spirit's still with us. Only half a K away down in that hut.'

Light snow began to fall. My rum bottle was more popular than the beer when the flakes settled on our hats. We all had a dash in the after dinner coffee. Not a good beverage in the evening when sound sleep prospects are poor, but tea is somehow tasteless with rum. Drinking coffee and rum by the fire was easy. Facing the cold swags was ominous. Bert, with Sophie's help, had cleverly erected a light tarp and all the swags were thrown underneath. My swag comprised a horserug and a thick sleeping bag. A heavy sheepskin coat made the pillow. I soon discovered it wasn't enough and woke in the early hours of the morning with snow all over me and the sleeping bag half wet. The driving wind had blown it right across the tarp-covered area. The fire was still glowing and I could see the flakes hovering above the faint glow in the dark. Someone was snoring. Sophie was between them.

I slept in fits, mainly for fear the snow might smother the fire. I couldn't come to terms with the prospect of standing in the cloak of swirling cloud in the morning, trying to eat a breakfast of bread and jam swallowed down with freezing water. Every couple of hours I stoked that fire. My boots were soundless in the snow and the wood was so cold I emptied one of the packs looking for my leather gloves. I didn't find them again until it was all over. By dawn the last log of firewood was gone and I didn't need any encouragement to wander away and find some more.

Larry was up at dawn too, fitting the nosebags to the horses. I set off with the four billies for water. The ice in the main stream had melted. Perhaps the wet snow was marginally above freezing. On the ground it seemed to be melting rapidly and the observation bolstered my spirits. Maybe the cloud would clear and we would ride into sunlight.

Sophie had sausages and eggs in the frypan when I got back. I had forgotten about that frypan pushed under the swag on the packhorse. Bert was making the toast and Larry was already saddling up. He said he didn't eat breakfast, nor did he take food on the hunt.

'Sausages and egg for you Mike?' Sophie asked in a soft voice. She was a multiple of contradictions. She looked at you with a cool, appraising eye, yet beneath the tough veneer there was a woman.

'Whatever's on,' I said gratefully. I didn't feel hungry. We were going to go hell for leather after these brumbies and I didn't feel like it. If I tried to stay behind and the other riders got out of sight I wasn't confident I could find them again, or find my way back to base. 'Just follow the cattle pad,' one of them said. There were cattle pads going in all directions.

It was while I was waiting for Sophie to finish cooking I remembered the camera. I had all my gear under a snow gum, a few metres from the fire. Searching for the gloves at about 3.00 a.m. I'd taken the camera bag out of a pack and left it by the tree trunk. It was still covered in snow and I thought nothing of it. The camera had no moisture on it, but in my ungloved hand it did feel very cold. The bag had a clip-down lid, possibly allowing frozen air to enter the bag.

I walked over to where Larry was adjusting the breastplate on his saddle. The old yards with the snow caked along the rails created a pioneer scene not possible to photograph in the NSW southern alps – the Parks authority had removed them all. With Larry and his mount Paleface in the foreground it promised to be a rare shot, but to my horror the shutter refused to work. I changed the batteries – then desperate – the film. I thought the camera was broken. Only later in Albury was I briefed on the sensitivity of modern cameras in subzero temperatures.

I may have cursed Larry to begin with. Now at least I had a hunt to take me to the top to observe the snow brumbies. I put the camera away in disgust and quickly ate breakfast before it was cold and tasteless. Larry came back to the warmth of the fire and Sophie made him eat a sausage. With little to say, we all had a full mug of coffee fresh from boiling water. It was that quiet moment before going into battle.

Bert and I tossed on our saddles. It was time to go. I noticed Sophie made no effort to leave the fire. She seemed lonely and vunerable sitting on a log alone. There were two old strainer posts lying on the ground for seating, which had been cut from the bushyard by previous campers. Bush campers always used the same fire spot to avoid sundry charcoal heaps scarring the camp area.

'She reckons there's a blizzard comin,' Bert said when I enquired. 'There's a front comin, but I don't think we'll get hit. Anyway she's stayin to keep the fire goin,' he paused and glanced into the wind-driven mist. 'If it gets real bad a fire can be the difference between life and death.'

Dooley Pendergast, who told me so much about the alps over a four-month period, said he and Teddy McGufficke would have perished in a blizzard if they hadn't made it to Dead Horse Hut. In heavy snow they collected twelve bullocks missed in the autumn muster. Teddy had a snow lease somewhere in the vicinity of the Cascades. They were heading to

Dead Horse when the blizzard struck. He swears it was no exaggeration when Teddy's horse disappeared from sight in a snowdrift and the first sign of re-emergence was Teddy's bald head. 'A blob of snow sat on his head like ice cream on a cone,' chuckled Dooley when he was telling me the story. By the time they reached the hut the blinding snow gale was nearly sweeping them off their feet. The bullocks found their own shelter and he and Teddy rugged their horses and hoped for the best. Anywhere exposed to the gale had iced over. Sheaths of ice clung to the trunks of trees and the snow drift blown up against the hut had iced over. The hut was the base camp and they had left it only hours before. But there was no fire going. The stockmen never left a fire unattended and before they could get one going frostbite took its toll. Circulation in their feet slowed to a dangerous level. Neither of them could feel their feet and when they thawed them out Dooley said it was agony. Today the scars are visible on Dooley's face, almost as testimony of the peril that awaits those who cannot find shelter in a blizzard.

In the final minutes by the fire I briefly discussed food and a medical kit. They never took either. If they carried a saddle bag a limb would probably tear it off. A backpack would get caught in a tree. They simply took the chance. If someone broke a leg 20 kilometres from base camp, any-time after noon, it meant a night in the open without cover or food. Someone would have to stay and someone ride to arrange a rescue. Mobile phones were unreliable in the mountains and like the saddlebags, nearly impossible to carry in scrub galloping.

With years on the racetrack to focus my thoughts on risk taking and the odds of probability, I did some quick mental calculations. Being plucked from the saddle by a tree because I carried a backpack was 200 to 1. A serious fall from one of three riders in several scrub gallops was as low as 20 to 1. The possibility of a blizzard above 1700 metres was 10 to 1. I immediately began to pack some food into my backpack, along with the medical kit. It was basic stuff – bread, cheese and bars of chocolate.

We set off with Larry in his customary role as leader. I followed last. Larry and Bert wore leather vests and thick leather chaffs which were buckled around the waist and either zipped or buckled through to the boot on each leg. I wore an over-sized sheepskin coat, tucked in and girthed tight with a stirrup leather. Inside the knee-high R. M. Williams boots I wore two thicknesses of socks. Physically I was ready for −10°C. In state of mind it was a different situation.

For an hour and a half we steadily gained altitude. The snow gums shrank in size and stretched gnarly branches to tip off our hats. At first the snow hid in little sheltered hollows, far apart. The light overnight fall had melted quickly after daylight and it was not until we passed what Larry called the 1700-metre contour that the ground ahead of us lay under a brilliance of white. The snow draped the dwarf trees as though someone had gone berserk with white paint, and on the ground it turned drab decay into a wonderland. On the frost hollows it was a white carpet with long brown stains like spilt milk coffee, made by the underlying creeks. There were horse tracks everywhere in the snow and each of us knew there would be a run any moment. We didn't talk. Human voice seem to carry. We may not hear anything, but wild animals hear us. Larry must have nearly been able to smell brumbies. I saw the rope come off his shoulder and his forefinger push the loop a tiny bit away from the coils.

We were almost soundless in the snow with just the horses' hooves making a squishy murmur. The wind had dropped, not a good sign for clearing weather. Overhead, wispy cloud hung only metres above. One minute a frost hollow was clear and you could see for a kilometre, then mist filled it like belches of steam. It happened so quickly it was eerie. We topped a ridge covered in wretched snow gums and Larry reined in. He pointed once, quickly. There was a small mob grazing in a frost hollow where the wetness underneath had turned the snow into slush. There seemed to be plenty of old winter grass.

There were hand signals and whispers. We would split. It was rarely a test of speed. The thoroughbred horses on grain always had the edge, but the brumbies knew where the snow gums grew thickest, and if there was a steep drop somewhere they made for it first. It took anticipation and tactics to catch a brumby. It seemed Larry and I would charge them in the open and Bert would gallop out to the right on rising ground to cut the brumbies off if they opted to dash for the deeper snow.

The signal from Larry was snow flying up from his horse's rear hooves. He was out of the gums and thundering towards the open patch of grassland and the brumbies. I was in full stride too, behind him. Hammerhead galloped confidently and before we burst from the scrub he sailed over a couple of big logs as though relishing the chase.

On a galloping horse time moves in vivid flashes, a bit like the switching on and off of a light. Some images are sharp and others so blurred you never recall them. Galloping in the snow was a new experience and although it didn't feel dangerous I knew every fall of a front leg could be straight into a wombat hole.

The wild horses heard the first stride we made. They flung their heads high and dashed off towards higher ground. The foals floundered in a snowdrift and one fell, causing it to be many lengths behind the mob after it regained its feet. The ridge to the north appeared to rise above the treeline. The brumbies charged out of the last of the trees, reached the skyline and the last to dip from view was a pregnant mare. Larry and I were suddenly out of the chase. In the distance you couldn't see the treacherous bogs, but the brumbies had been grazing on the other side. Larry reined in hard before his mount bellied into sticky black silt. To cross the hollow we had to canter nearly back to where Bert had galloped over it on the high end.

It didn't take long to find Bert. He had roped the foal that had fallen in the snowdrift. It was a bay yearling and a nice type for a brumby. Bert was having a dance with it too. It plunged against the rope, flipped over and upon springing back onto its feet again it bounded away in bold strides, only to flip again on the end of the rope. The antics were not pleasant to observe in those first, panic-sparked minutes of capture.

To hold onto a frantic, plunging young horse the rider must have the rope looped around the knee-pad. The brumby-catching saddles are especially designed for the purpose. At the butt of each of the high knee-pads is a groove for the rope so it won't slip off. The pad in principle is the same as the roping horn mounted on the pommel of American bronco saddles. The horn is a rigid projection and considered too dangerous for brumby roping. In the heat of the moment a brumby runner might rope a fleeing stallion and realise too late his mount can't hold the weight of a big fighting horse, mad with fear. Mounted in the Australian catching saddle the rider can unravel the rope from the pad with a flick of the wrist and let it go if the circumstances are desperate. The horn on the bronco saddle makes a fast release difficult because of the much smaller diameter, increasing the risk of the rider's horse being pulled down. Another danger is the horn itself. If the rider's horse is pulled down there's a possibility of the horn becoming something like a leather dagger.

The lasso ropes are designed to avoid choking. A soft rope, for example, would lock so tightly that a life-threatening hold on the trachea would occur instantly. The hard rope made from nylon, locking on a big leather bound eye, only reduces breathing while the horse strains hard against the knee-pad. Seeking comfort, the foals and yearlings stop fighting the rope after a few minutes and will come up to the catcher's horse. The rider quickly wraps the slack around the pad, locking the little one to the side of his horse. Then the rope halter is put on. Every brumby runner carries four or five rope halters strapped to a saddle dee. The rider must get a halter on to be able to do anything with the young horse and it should be done from the saddle for safety. Brumbies fight with their front legs and can strike as fast as a snake. With their hind legs they can easily kick a man on the catching horse. The older ones are vicious with their mouths. Stallions have a tendency to lock on like a crocodile and the victim has to pull free. Big wild stallions have been known to rip a chunk out of the seat of the saddle.

For a good rope man it takes just a split second to slip a halter on. The lead rope attached to the halter is then wrapped around the other knee-pad before the lasso is removed. Most brumby runners can handle a couple of yearlings on the run home and invariably tie the first caught to a snow gum while they look for another mob of mares and foals. This little fellow had to be taken through snow 30 centimetres deep to a belt of stunted snow gums. He quickly accepted the confines of the rope and stood rather pathetically beside the tree.

We left the little colt and rode along the tree-clad ridge, heading southwest. Larry said we would have caught glimpses of Mount Feathertop if the mist had dispersed. I was feeling cold and could sense the change. A new weather influence was about to encroach into the alps. What worried me more than ever was my sense of direction. There were no physical markers and the sun had only appeared once, briefly. I only knew we were riding southwest because Larry said so. It seemed that riding in these mostly featureless mountains over many years sharpened instincts that otherwise lie dormant.

The next sighting reminded me of a racehorse barrier trial. Larry led over a little rise and there they were, about eight brumbies. There was no hand signal. Our horses sent up a flurry of snow and we bounded out onto the snow plain. The brumbies took off and headed east towards a long thick band of snow gums. At the same instant dark fog rolled in. It always arrived suddenly and silently. Hammerhead was spooked by it and I had to urge him along to keep Larry's Paleface in sight. Near the snow gums I lost sight of the horse. Larry was an experienced man at easing through the trees at full gallop and I instantly tried to ease Hammerhead back to a canter when I realised I had to find my own way. For some reason he fought me. He half turned his head and kept galloping.

It all happened in a split second. The tree rose out of the fog like some horror vision in a nightmare. I don't recall how I reacted. I probably wrenched hard on the reins with all my strength, causing the horse to hit the branches belly first and then flip over backwards. Seeing the horse above me, the saddle just a metre above my head, is another image I'll never forget. I thought he would have to land on top of me, but a branch deflected the fall and he landed in the snow on his side, his back towards me. The snow too saved me from injury. I landed on my backpack and found myself in a ridiculous position. All I needed was for someone to ask me if I'd like a cup of tea.

I was winded, but that would last only a minute or two. Suddenly alone in the fog and the snow was the one thing I had wanted to avoid. The compass in my backpack would probably get me to Falls Creek. Being unable to take a fix on a known feature very much restricted the use of a compass. I wouldn't want to miss Falls Creek or I'd end up in a big wide wilderness of nothing.

Hammerhead didn't leave me. He just stood there shaking. The horse was too distraught to mount, so when my breathing settled down I let out a cooee. It didn't travel. I know how to do them and when they travel there's an echo. For a few minutes it all seemed hopeless. I stamped my feet to keep the circulation moving and rubbed my bare hands down the horse's neck. They'd come back. It was just a matter of waiting.

Suddenly out of the fog emerged a splendid blue-grey horse and a rider in a black leather vest. It was his hat that caught my attention in that first instant, as though I was wrestling to distinguish between reality and fantasy. The crown of the hat made me think of a hacksawed piece of black stovepipe. There was a certain malevolence about it. No one's ever going to believe this happened, I thought. Mounted devils don't appear when you're in need. Had I passed on after all? An old man at a wedding once said to me, peering at me through alcohol soaked eyeballs, 'We've passed on you know. We've passed the test too,' and he raised his wicked grey eyebrows. 'We're in heaven.' There were beautiful girls in long frocks dancing beside the table.

'That horse's a rat,' said the Noose in a tone that sounded like a growl.

'He's shivering bad,' I said.

'Get back on the bastard. Weather's closin in. I was just about to nab the little fella when I heard yer. Only just heard yer. I thought to meself, he's down. That mongrel wouldn't see a gap wide enough for a bus.'

I sure as hell wanted to leave. 'They won't know I've left.'

'Leave that thing on yer back at the tree. They'll think yer went back with the colt.'

'You taking the colt?'

'Well,' he said with a wry smile. 'If they get buried in a white out and find themselves ridin to hell, this little bugger's goin to feed those dingoes I heard howlin this mornin. Reckon we oughta take him. If they overtake us I'll hand him over.'

I think he'd been tailing us ever since we left camp. There are a lot of advantages in having a group of horsemen working ahead. The brumbies tire quickly in the snow and often circle to get back into their territory. The Noose may have been counting on very tired horses suddenly appearing and on a fresh, fit horse he could have taken his pick.

'Weather's closin. We gotta leave,' the Noose said. He watched me get on – Hammerhead was more fractious than ever.

'Where yer from anyway?'

I told him and why I had come down. Dry snow began to fall.

'Nothin's ever changed in these mountains.' He lifted his hand. The one holding the loop of his stockwhip. He had a lasso buckled on the front of his saddle. I followed the line of this arm into a wall of cloud.

'A couple of mile over there is Hotham,' he said. 'Millionaires arrive in planes and they ski down a few places, get hauled up again in chairlifts and go down again. A week later they go home and they think they know the mountains. They don't. It's bastard country and hard people. I'm only here because the mountains have hardened my soul too. I know nothin else.' He paused and looked at me hard. 'Yer ought to get home and buy yourself a horse somewhere.'

'Hardened my soul' – the man was a thinker, brutalised by his environment. I had observed the same lonely people in the Carnarvon Ranges of Queensland some years before. The great Australian loneliness, founded on the rebel genes of British criminals and innocent convicts, sour Irish blood and a reject gentry from the English upper class, made the brumby breeding stock of the alps look like studs.

The Noose collected the little bay without dismounting. It plunged out on the rope a couple of times, but for the veteran it was as easy as walking the milking cows.

'Make yer mind up quick,' he said gruffly. 'The snow's coverin the tracks and if they don't find yer you'll perish.'

'Okay.' I couldn't have been more reluctant – I was abandoning the boys. But he was right: it was a simple matter of survival. I hung the haversack in the tree. They at least would have the food. I always carried a notebook, and with my knife I cut an incision through the centre of it and jammed it onto a spike in the tree. They couldn't miss seeing it. I wrote: 'LEFT WITH NOOSE.' He was well-named! But he didn't have to collect me. He'd tailed us all the way from the camp and must have noticed how raw I was in this white hell of a place. As author Peter Carey said at his Booker Prize presentation, 'Ned Kelly was better than those who sought to cage him'. This eccentric bushman under a diabolic looking stovepipe hat was better than those who had judged him.

We barely exchanged another word after we got going again. The Noose skilfully drove the little bay ahead of him. It gave the brumby a sense of freedom. Sometimes he trotted briskly through the snow. If he got sick of it and stopped, Noose flicked the whip across his rump. When he got piggy and refused to go at all, I rode to the front and he followed my horse. I would have stayed at the front if I was certain of the direction, but the wind-driven snow made it more difficult than ever. The old horse tracks had already been buried and we rode into a shifting whiteness where every tree we skirted struck weird shapes in the poor visibility. The dry snow settled on everything. There was no dampness in it and even when it floated like lumps of cotton wool from the horse's mane it was still frozen. I saw it as the silent, peaceful killer. If you want to die absolutely stress-free, try slow freezing. Once the cold chills your brain you don't even know you're dying. I nearly froze once two kilometres from Mount Kosciuszko: two metres of snow and zero visibility.

It was approximately 20 July 1961. With a trap setter (like a short-handled ice-axe), I cut my steps over Rams Head at dawn. I had left Thredbo at 4.00 a.m. My boots broke through the frosted snow for most of the way, but above the treeline it was hard ice. It broke a beautiful day and I can remember heading for the summit with a rare light-hearted feeling. I was alone and didn't mind that. On lone adventure trips you only consult yourself. You're responsible only for yourself. The downside is you share the experience with no one. On this occasion I was on the final slope to the broad hump of Kossie when very dark cloud billowed over the divide and left me in a room at midnight without a light. At first there was just fog and a gathering wind. Instantly scared, I dropped my compass and was ages trying to find it in the snow. I was only eighteen and death doesn't seem even remotely possible at that age, but I was realist enough to know my life hung in the balance while I sifted through the snow. I had a map in the backpack and tried to hold it down for a reasonable compass fix. All I wanted was a degree setting for Thredbo. When the fog claimed me I was south-east of the summit. I couldn't do it. The gale tore at the paper and the snow blew across it. Every minute wasted was more life-threatening. So in the end I took a setting 180° south. I knew that would take me down to 5000 feet. From memory I expected to reach the road near Dead Horse. It was just as well I was young and very fit. Hunched up against the driving gale, the compass constantly held to my face, it took about four hours to reach the Rams Head escarpment. Once only I sat down and leaned against a boulder, with the blinding snow threatening to bury my legs while I sat there. I was tired and there seemed no urgency any more. I had entered the first phase of the sleeping death. It took a lot of willpower to get going again. Soon afterwards I was on my way down – Thredbo River was more than 2000 feet below. But if I thought my troubles were over, they had only just begun. The 1961 snow season was one of the best ever, with the snowline for two months holding steady at 4000 feet. Thredbo village was in nearly two feet of snow, looking stunningly beautiful every sunny day. I didn't need the compass any more, but I needed the rope. I was a rock climber and never went anywhere without my 130-foot-long rope. Until that moment I thought the Snowy Mountains were feature-less and boring. I can't recall how many times I had to double that rope around a rock projection or, lower down, a snow gum, but at least seven I think. The snow crevices were nothing like those on glaciers. In some ways they were more sinister, because it was a combination of ice and snowdrift. I was scared I'd be buried in it and my gloves would slip on the rope. I walked onto the snow-crusted road half an hour before dark and an hour later got a well-deserved blasting from the authorities, as the Geebung Lodge had already reported me five hours overdue.

'I don't think anyone's ever walked back from the summit in a blizzard before,' the angry officer told me. 'Go back to the Warrumbungles.'

When we got near the camp the Noose skirted wide and headed for the hut. Hammerhead knew where we were and whinnied, and one of the packhorses returned the call.

'I'll have to ride over,' I said. 'Sophie'll think it's Bert back. She might think we rode straight past, half-lost in the weather.'

Twenty minutes later I was back at the camp with Noose's packhorse.

'Where are the others?' Sophie was ashen. She had a big fire going, but the snow was already fifteen centimetres deep. Snow lay plastered over everything. The camp had become frozen and inhabitable.

I told her what had happened.

'You can't stay,' I said imploringly. 'Saddle yer horse.'

'What about them?' Her arms were wrapped tightly across her chest. She was cold and frightened.

'I was young and tough like them once. They'll make it out. We won't if we stay.' I paused to thump my packsaddle against a post to dislodge the snow. 'Hurry up and saddle.'

'It's not my horse,' she said breathlessly. 'Nothing here's mine. I was just a guest – a friend.'

'Right – let's walk out then.' It was getting more and more complicated and I just wanted to get away. I quickly packed Noose's horse, leaving non-essentials. The horserug was old and heavy and I emptied some of the food to make room for Sophie's clothes.

'I feel dreadful,' she murmured as we set off back down the track. I led the packhorse. It was quite loaded with my saddle on top. Hammerhead I left in the yard with the other two packhorses. He'd given me my worst ride in 40 years.

'Forget them. They'll be okay.' I still had to raise my voice to be heard. The snow was still heavy, but the wind was no longer a gale at this lower level. The deep tracks left by the horses were almost snowed out.

'You don't like them do you?'

'I respect their ability.' I felt like saying a lot more, but floundering along in the snow was demanding every ounce of energy. I was worried too. There were two rideable horses, three people and a lot of gear. I decided she better get used to the idea.

'You'll have to piggyback behind Noose,' I said, after we'd walked awhile without speaking. Nearer the hut the track was clearly defined between the trees and I could relax a little.

'More like me up front.' I turned in surprise. If there had been a smile it died like a spark.

The Noose travelled light. He had a neatly rolled swag, small bag of food and his own packsaddle and packs. It wouldn't have worked if Neddy hadn't been a big horse.

'Great stuff,' he growled as we approached. He smiled broadly at Sophie, exposing a side he withheld from men. 'We got their pony. Now we got their woman.'

'Got a bit of clever packing to do,' he said, his mind suddenly focused on the job. 'Jam yer saddle into a pack. We'll let out the girths and strap my packsaddle over the top and the two swags on the top of it.' Then he paused, smiling again.

'You ride on top of the swags. All up it's only 130 kilos. These big buggers used to lumber nearly double that in salt years ago, going up the mountains.'

It took only a few minutes with both of us working on it. The hiccup was my saddle. It wouldn't fit in the pack, so I undid the swag and stuffed the sleeping bag, blanket and groundsheet in. Using the girth we anchored the saddle right on top. Noose legged me aboard and handed me the lead rope. For the next fifteen kilometres I was to ride side-saddle, perched a foot above the horse with a useless lead rope. It was a tragedy the camera froze up.

The Noose mounted his grey charger and extended a hand to Sophie. 'Up here sweetheart.' He'd even kicked his foot out of the stirrup iron for her to mount.

She didn't hesitate. The confident radiance of Noose's smile had overwhelmed her. I had a quiet smile on my lips too when we left. There was an old saying around the bush racetracks, when the races started late morning and the parties ended the following morning: 'Take his horse and he'll skin you alive. Take his woman and he'll break your jaw.' No one ever said what happened if you took both. The Noose was performing right up to his reputation.

Below 1600 metres, conditions improved and by the time we dropped to the old 4000 foot (about 1200 metres) level the blizzard was a bad dream. It wasn't even snowing. There was a bit of wind and it felt cold.

'So often it happens,' Noose said. No one had said anything for ten kilometres. 'Blowin a gale up high and down below nothin.'

The little bay got tired of trotting ahead and stayed by

Grey Ghost's side most of the way. The big grey never tried to bite him. He'd done the exercise countless times before. Neddy simply followed on. A couple of times I was dragged through low branches and copped some scratches, but it was better than trying to stride it out. Below the snowline Noose urged Grey Ghost into a fast walk. Like me, he was anxious to reach the vehicle and clear out.

The Noose had his trailer and battered Toyota hidden on a low level creek bank. By removing the centre rail there was ample room for the three horses. He was a powerful man. I held the little bay's head straight and Noose shouldered him on. The two horses strode up. Sophie got in the front seat and when the Noose pulled away towards the main road that was the last I saw of them.

8 Blue Duck Retreat

No better horseman ever held the reins …

I left another note under the windscreen wiper of Larry's truck along with a payment of $300. The payment was wrapped inside the quarto sheet. In the note I wrote: HORSE FELL. THE NOOSE HEARD ME CALL FOR HELP. GOT VERY COLD, SO WENT OUT WITH HIM. PLEASE FIND PAYMENT, REGARDS, etc. They didn't have to be told what happened to the brumby.

The road over Mount Wills to Mitta Mitta would probably be blocked by snow. It was too remote for authorities to monitor the situation. Uninformed drivers turned around before it was late or got stuck in the snow. I had no option but to head south and stay somewhere.

Although warm for the first time in 36 hours with the car heater on full blast, I felt very flat in spirit. I hadn't really seen anything of how the brumbies lived, and I was beginning to think the brumby culture in the far southeast had a tough, hardcore element. In their world the finer qualities of life either didn't exist or were despised. Was buck running a sport? Was it a cult? Were they genuine in their proclaimed desire to preserve a place for brumbies in the mountains of the southeast wilderness? A researcher financed by a government grant claimed to have figures that suggested Victorian brumbies were heading for extinction in less than 20 years. The foal-catching rate had increased dramatically with more and more young men joining the chase. And what nagged me most was: where did these foals and yearlings go? They all said children's ponies! But at the Corryong Bush Festival there was just one brumby pony offered for sale and it was passed in. The fate of the brumbies remained a mystery. The two foals I saw at McFarlands Flat in February were being taken out to be broken-in for children. I felt confident that at least was genuine. But I kept hearing rumours of foals being caught for the meat industry. The common expression was 'They catch em and dog em' – meaning they end up as tinned dog food. According to the stories, a foal is put into a good paddock for a few months to grow and gain weight (the heavier the animal the better the price) and then it is passed on to a horse trader who supplies the meat buyers.

Fourteen kilometres down the narrow, twisting road, I crossed a stout wooden bridge and drew up outside the Blue Duck Inn. I intended to keeping driving on to Omeo, but when I saw the old weatherboard style with an all enclosing verandah and smoke rising from the chimney I couldn't resist the thought of a pot of beer near the fire. There was also a sign advertising self-contained log cabin accommodation.

It was almost dark and a chilling wind swept down from the mountains to the west. Head down, I strode along the path leading to the bar and hurriedly stepped inside. As is almost routine in most small rural communities, the patrons seated along the bar turned to see who had entered. In a glance I could see there were two groups. Their hats distinguished the mountain people and the colourful array of parkas marked the tourists. The locals sat on high stools along the bar and the tourists were spread about in small groups. Hand gestures and bright smiles from the tourists created a good atmosphere, warmed further by a slow-combustion wood burner. The bar attendant saw me coming and took my order.

I might have only had the one drink and gone on to Omeo if it hadn't been for a startling snippet of conversation which began over canoes. There was room for me to take up a position on a stool at the bar and I got chatting to the bloke immediately to my right. The rubicund complexion aged him a little, I thought, because he still had the strong clear voice of a man under 40. Everything about him was eccentric, from the red goatee to the green military-disposal jumper which looked very warm. I had seen the canoes out on the lawn in front of the hotel and asked if he knew where the canoeists had come from. He told me it was the Mitta Mitta River, but he didn't know where they'd entered. They had booked out the log cabin accommodation, which was in a separate wing from the hotel.

'There's been canoeing in these rivers since the Miocene,' he said seriously. 'There was once evidence to prove it.'

I was so taken aback I caught the eye of the barman and re-ordered. With age slowing me down a bit, my hobby had become Australian archaeology.

'The Miocene's in the Tertiary period,' I said. 'It's even beneath the Pliocene which dates back two million years.'

'The Mining Registrar at the time said the remains of the canoe were extracted from a Miocene deposit,' he said defiantly. 'That's when the gravel was laid down.'

'Where was this?'

'On the Cobrungra River this side of the Victoria Falls.'

'The first hominid to breakaway from the apes was four million years ago.'

'Well I don't reckon the Aborigines dug holes in the wash gravel to bury their canoes. Not even if it belonged to a chief.'

'Obviously no one ever kept the evidence?' I knew the answer before asking. I just had to be sure. Every amateur archaeologist dreams of finding something which will throw more light on the prehistory record in Australia. In 1999 I photographed portrait paintings in one of the most remote rock art galleries in the west Kimberley. I claimed they were more Arabic in appearance than Aboriginal and may have been painted 10 000 years ago or even much earlier. I had no supporting evidence and therefore didn't deserve any recognition from the scientific faculty of archaeology in Australia. I believe hard evidence will emerge one day and my conjecture on the arrival of dhows from the Middle East will be confirmed.

'It was the goldrush, mate,' the next bloke along the bar said. He and Red Goatee were drinking together. 'Most of those miners in the 1880s were poorly educated.'

'Maybe the first man walked on the great southern continent,' posed Red Goatee.

'There were no apes here for a start,' I said. 'But I'd like to know where that wash is. There might be stone tools buried associated with the deposit.'

'Never find it again,' said the other bloke. He had an angular face, firm set jaw and bushy eyebrows. 'It's like the gold leads. Yer stumble onto em and when yer go back you can't find it again.'

Red Goatee laughed. 'Max has been looking for the Brandy Creek lead for years. Charlie McNamara from

Cobrungra Station rode over it in the 1890s. So he said, anyway. It's been like Lasseter's Reef: no one can find it. But it's out there.'

We talked for ages about the mines. From the 1850s to about 1910, gold was found all over the district. Men working alone washed for it in the streams and mining companies either mined it or sluiced thousands of cubic yards for it. It's widely contended that after the banks collapsed in 1893 only Victorian gold saved Australia from complete economic collapse.

There was a tap on my shoulder and I turned to see Larry and Bert.

'You got yourself out nice and safe,' Larry said and sealed his lips with a smirk.

I moved away from the bar so we could talk privately.

'I had a nasty fall and the Noose heard me cooee. I wasn't very confident of you blokes returning after last night.'

That was laying it on a bit thick They would have searched for me of course, but I have no nerve in freezing conditions and didn't like to admit it.

'We'd have found yer,' Larry said, looking a bit disappointed. 'Anyway yer safe.'

'Sophie must have known him?' I queried. 'She left with him as though he were her father.'

'Dashing bloody Noose,' Bert said bitterly. 'He wins every event that's ever put on. Recites poetry. Bloody girls love him.'

Larry handed me my backpack.

'The tucker was good anyway,' he said. 'It blew up awful. We stuffed our pockets with cheese and bread and ate goin along.'

'Did you catch any more?'

'Caught a foal,' Larry said. 'But when the mother come

runnin back for it. Oh shit – how can yer do it when yer see that? Let the little bugger go.'

Bert thrust up his jaw. 'Yer getting soft.'

'No it's not. Just being human that's all.'

I offered to shout and they eagerly accepted. We moved to a table of six or eight chairs. A couple were already seated and they nodded when I asked if we could sit down. Since I had arrived men and women had congregated to be three deep at the bar.

'Popular place,' I remarked to the bloke already seated.

'Best pub outside Melbourne,' he said. He was balding, with a strong, open face. 'Some really interesting people turn up in here.'

The hotel itself had goldrush beginnings and was named the 'Blue Duck' out of frustration and disappointment. In 1910 Bill O'Connell and Paddy Moore acquired the land and built the hotel. Bill sold his share in the Yellow Girl goldmine, probably thinking a hotel on the way to the goldfields from Omeo was a safer investment. There were no rumours of war at this time and the towns of Glen Wills and Sunnyside looked like becoming boom mining towns. The hotel promised to be a goldmine in liquor sales. But along came the First World War, the mines closed, and O'Connell lamented the hotel was nothing but a 'Blue Duck'.

We drank a round of beers and the boys left. Their tired horses were waiting on the truck and trailer. They didn't wait long. Dehydrated from altitude and hard riding, the boys drained their glasses like Queensland stockmen in January. There was no question of me driving anywhere. I was under the limit, but unfamiliar hairpin bends at night mixed with alcohol mean certain disaster. The accommodation was booked out. I wondered where else in the world whitewater adventurers, hardy mountain trout fishermen, deer hunters and wild horse rope men all mingled together in the same bar. If I was in charge of promoting tourism in Australia I would put the Victorian Alps ahead of the Red Centre and Kakudu.

'Tell Mike about the bolting packhorse with all the gold,' prodded the woman with the friendly balding chap. We had all got talking together about brumbies and gold. She was about 40, long blonde hair and a weathered face. There were happy, smiling creases coming away from her full lips. We had introduced ourselves at some stage and it is remiss of me not to remember their names, but I was meeting too many people to take in names unless I wrote them down. For story purposes I will call them Peter and Judy, after good friends of mine on the land.

'It was in the early 1890s,' Peter said, 'there were a lot of private gold mines at Glen Wills and Sunnyside. The company mines used a coach and full police escort to shift gold to the bank at Omeo, but the small consignments went by packhorse with a mine manager and one mounted constable. The gold thieving was terrible on those fields up there. There were no armed robberies, but some said the Maude mine failed because of thieving. In desperation the manager stored the ore underground and moved it up to go straight into the crusher. He discovered too late the employees were sneaking into the shafts at night and taking the ore containing the highest concentrations of gold. A lot of the men had separate licences for a mullock heap – low grade ore no one wanted – and they'd work the stolen gold through a small crusher. They were desperate men, a lot of them, in a harsh world up there on the side of that mountain.'

'Sounds like not much has changed,' I interrupted. 'Stock stealing. Desperadoes chasing brumbies for little more than small change.'

'I think a lot of stock goes missing,' Peter said soberly. 'Anyway, in this instance the packhorse carrying the gold went missing. The story goes that the constable got very bored during the long ride to Omeo and discharged his revolver at some birds. The packhorse had never been exposed to gunfire and bolted. They couldn't catch it and it outgalloped them through the scrub.' Peter smiled, his eyes gleaming with the thought of the chase.

'Fair bit of dead weight in those packs,' I speculated.

You have to wonder whether the constable had an arrangement. Someone waiting out there! Either the plan came unstuck or it was an awfully strong horse.

'It wasn't found for two days,' Peter laughed. 'Imagine the word that flew around the goldfields. The escape of Banjo's colt down by Kosciuszko was one thing in folklore, but the escape of the Omeo packhorse loaded with 200 ounces of pure gold was real. They reckon there wasn't a horse left in a stable or a yard at Omeo.'

Luckily for the miners who made up the consignment, an honest man found the horse.

The proprietor of the inn, Graham Brown, stood by our table as Peter related the final part of the story. Graham wore a chef's cap and a white apron.

'It was a bit of an anti-climax,' he said cheerfully. 'If someone had run off with the gold it would have been a big story.' He pulled out one of the chairs and sat down. 'I can tell you a yarn from the goldfields of Glen Wills that's not bad. The bailiff arrived on the coach one afternoon to serve a summons. He had a glass eye. The businessman to be summonsed to appear in court was very popular among miners and they threatened to lynch the bailiff.

'The scared bailiff decided to try and serve the summons just before the departure of the coach next morning, back to Omeo. He went to bed early in the local hotel and pretended to be asleep when a drunk wandered into the room by mistake. The drunk noticed the open glass eye and announced to the late drinkers in the bar that the bailiff was dead and no one had to worry any more. They all flocked into the bedroom and discovered he wasn't after all. The bailiff, thinking the mob had come to lynch him, jumped out the window and the coach picked him up about here, at Anglers Rest. The summons was never served.'

There were too many customers for Graham to sit any longer. He took my order for one of the homemade pastas.

Graham was one of the friendliest, most enthusiastic hotel proprietors I had ever met. With his personality he made the bar and fireplace area hum like a cocktail party. He took the trouble to introduce patrons, and there was something especially stimulating about his love for the Omeo region and its vibrant history. He had rescued the Blue Duck from languishing and perhaps even closing. He had even had it put on the official maps.

'The only hotel in Victoria on the maps,' he laughed, then added seriously, 'It's been placed on the map for the safety of travellers, because this is the loneliest, most remote road in Victoria.'

'What are you writing about this time?' Judy asked me. Before the packhorse story we had been chatting briefly about a previous book of mine. A lot of copies had been sold out of the local bookshop in Omeo.

'Sometimes I wonder myself,' I replied with rare frankness about the task. 'Your story about the packhorse reveals the culture of the time. It's one of those anecdotes people enjoy hearing, but in my travels they're few and far between. What I do know is that the story of the Australian brumbies has degenerated into a horrible, miserable saga.

Like many Australians I've always had a naïve image about the brumbies and the culture all my life. It began with images conjured up from 'The Man From Snowy River' – and what child hasn't read or heard about Elyne Mitchell's *Silver Brumby* books? When I set out to research the wild brumbies I had these unrealistic images of horsemen galloping across the high plains cracking stockwhips. I imagined big timber stockyards and real men from the bush working among the horses. In my mind I saw the drafting of the aged brumbies to be removed to farms and the roping of the self-weaned colts to become saddle horses. The rest released to run wild again. I expected to see a practical, common-sense approach to wild horses, which is all I've ever known in the bush.' I shrugged. 'I couldn't have been more out of touch.'

'You'll come out with the truth,' Judy said softly. 'That's the main thing.'

'Might be indeed harder than you think,' Peter said grimly. 'Getting the truth, I mean. The brumby running scene's a murky one. We live at Bright. I work up on the ski slopes in season and Judy helps in a village shop. We're friends with some of the rangers. They talk about a cult which is growing rapidly.'

'I'm not clear what you're getting at,' I said.

'They talk about a rider of freakish ability. A man who's a legend within his own lifetime. He rides the mountains from here to Thredbo and has roped hundreds of brumbies. No one knows what he does with them and no one's ever cared. Now young men bred in the mountains want to emulate this man. There's half-axe rope men all over the place and a lot of foals are being caught. The riders smash themselves up and very often their horses as well. There's a cult emerged, a sort of gladiator sport. But no one knows what happens to the foals. They seem to disappear.'

'I've been told they're broken for kid's ponies,' I said.

He looked at me, almost sympathetically. 'Suggest you keep on with your research!'

'But you stop them and there'll be helicopter shooting,' I argued. 'There's no yards to run horses into. Catching them with ropes must surely be better than machine gunning from a helicopter.'

'Problem is, there's no way of ever policing animal handling.' Peter said, unconvinced. 'They either do it properly or they don't. There's no one there to observe. I've heard of foals been tied to trees for 36 hours, no water and no hay. Another day of being driven down and out of the mountains. Then the long haul on the road.'

'What about the painkillers,' Judy added. 'The professionals carry syringes with them and when one of the chase horses goes lame it's dosed directly into the stomach with a painkiller and thrown back into the bush galloping. It's just awful.'

When Graham brought my pasta the couple left. They were staying overnight.

I was deeply troubled by Peter's comments. I thought back to the odious stories I'd heard during my travels in the Snowy Mountains region in the late autumn. I was beginning to think they might not be exaggerated after all. One young woman from Jindabyne confided she knew instances of mares with unweaned foals being roped. She said her husband had pleaded for their release. Had even offered to swap his mature brumbies for their release, but some of the mountain men were brutal and callous. The mares were sent away to be killed for pet food and the young foals sold for $20 to be butchered in some backyard for dogs meat.

After the meal I went out and slept in the car. I had two

pillows and two big sleeping bags. It was cramped, but I was exhausted.

The snow on the road over Mount Wills was cleared by noon next day. Including coffee breaks, it was a ten-hour drive to my home at Myall Plains. The failure of the ride made the trip a marathon. I didn't have a single photo and my obser-vation of the snow brumbies amounted to a couple of fleeting glimpses. Meanwhile Sal had taken a call from Greg Everingham up in New England, while I was away. He told Sal that Ernie Maskey was on the road with cattle and if I wanted to meet him there would never be a better opportu-nity. Ernie Maskey first reported the sound of gunfire on the day of the Guy Fawkes masssacre. There was nothing Greg didn't know about brumby mustering and catching, but he thought I would enjoy talking to Ernie about the brumbies. Ernie and Billy were perhaps the only men in southeastern Australia still living who actually rode in amongst the brumby mobs and communicated with them. They were 'brumby whisperers'.

I found Ernie Maskey about 20 kilometres east of Glen Innes on the Grafton road. He was droving about 400 mixed-breed cattle to a holding property not far out of town. The cattle came from Why Worry, the property Ernie had recently sold to the National Parks and Wildlife Service. He was battling serious illness, his boys had moved to other industries and I felt that maybe the shooting of his beloved brumbies was the last straw for Ernie.

To look at Ernie you wouldn't think he was having a strug-gle against cancer. Old bushmen with direct links to the original tribes always have a twinkle in the eye. 'We got a spare horse for you,' he said, grinning as I approached the little gathering on the side of the road. They all laughed.

There were brothers, cousins, nieces and nephews and Rose, Ernie's jovial wife. They were having smoko. I looked at the unsaddled pony.

'Brumby?'

Ernie nodded and we shook hands. I introduced myself to all of the family.

'When they told you about what happened to the brumbies,' I began, 'you apparently said just three words: "they was beautiful".'

His face clouded into sadness and I felt he was embarrassed. Those words told so much about him. He was little, lean and weathered. With his light shade of skin and deeply etched character lines he could have ridden straight from the arid mountains of Afghanistan. Yet there was a distinct proudness about his stature. Even the way he wore his hat made me think of an old general who had seen it all. After all, he had managed Broadmeadows for 20 years, the biggest cattle station on the eastern fall.

'It was a bad business,' he said at last. The memories were clearly painful so I shifted the focus onto the cattle. 'This the final walk out of the canyon country?'

Ernie brightened up. 'Oh no, we got until March on Why Worry. We just goin to hold these for awhile and let a bit of feed get goin down there.'

'Still got cattle in the park?'

'They been good to us, they have. We got a month to move em. They doin good job too those cattle. Oh that red grass yer know, it get a strike in it and it go up as though all the country doused with benzene. One day all this country go up – big big fire, like white man never seen,' he paused and smiled to himself. 'You know, they worry about a cattle pad here and there and along somewhere they say rainforest come back,' he shook his head once and looked away at the distant blue line of the hills above Guy Fawkes. 'When the big one comes the dirt will burn and the seeds will cook.'

I felt it was okay now to come back to the horses. 'There's rumours the brumbies were in excellent condition. That what the media was told about brumbies starving after the fire was bullshit.'

'I saw them one week before on both sides of the river. They was in good condition and there was pockets that never had the fire,' he paused and looked at me warily. I could have been a journalist desperate for another story. 'I don't know who the people are, mind you. But there were people who wanted that fire. They hated our horses. They wanted them all gone.'

'They were your horses, Ernie?' I queried gently.

'Oh yes, they were our horses. Over the years we culled the bad stallions. If a stallion didn't have that creamy colour, or buckskin, goin back to the Saladin and Radium blood, we shot it. But what happened was our fault. We should have cut the numbers right back.' Ernie didn't want trouble and he may have been fearful I would stir it all up again. I decided to keep away from who was to blame.

'You think 50-odd survivors is enough foundation stock for a recovery?'

He looked at the ground and adjusted his hat. 'The old days and the old people have gone. In ten years we all gone. New breed of people everywhere now. Some can't even strain a fence up.'

He clearly thought it was all over. I hate questioning people and decided to tell him a little about the Snowy Mountain brumbies and the men and women who roped them. He was both interested and puzzled.

'No one up here has ever done that,' he volunteered with

an incredulous expression. 'Injuries to themselves and the lovely horses all ruined. On our last muster we took out 50 horses. You ride amongst them, nice and quiet. Maybe few days before they ready. Then you drive em, nice and steady. Two riders either side at the lead and the rear men bluffin em. One looks like breakin you crack the whip. You gotta be alert. When out of their territory they walk along good. We always yarded em, just like the cattle. But you gotta know stock. Greg, he knows how to handle em, but he don't have the time. Blokes managin or runnin their own places are flat out. Yer see we used to live down there. No one down there any more and I reckon it's some of the best valleys in the falls country goin to waste.'

'What are the brumbies' chances of heritage listing, Ernie?'

'I dunno. They was beautiful horses all right,' Ernie lamented.

The cattle were scattering. The lead had followed the road over the brow of a low hill. They had all finished smoko and it would have been rude to hold Ernie up any longer. He mounted his bay stockhorse and trotted away, leading the brumby.

In a few words Ernie Maskey had confirmed what I suspected. Brumby running Snowy Mountains style was a new gladiator sport. It definitely wasn't the way to handle wild horses for culling purposes.

When I returned home Sal had a message for me from Ken Connley from Benambra.

'He's going on a brumby run in the alps,' she said. 'He said the big snow will come any day and he wants to catch a couple of yearlings before it does. He thought you might like to go with him.' She paused, looking at me a bit like my mother used to when I told her I was going climbing in the Warrumbungles. 'I think you should drop it. I hate to say it, but you're too old. You've already had one tumble.'

It was a moment that reminded of an evening in Derby two years before, in WA. My Aboriginal friend and guide, Peter Brooking, had looked at me carefully and said, 'You really want to go that far?' We were planning a packhorse expedition into a remote area of the King Leopold Ranges. When do you draw back? When is the risk foolhardy? I am resigned to never knowing. I hated the cold and I hated snow with a passion. But those brumbies in the Guy Fawkes canyons were so beautiful. If I could get Ken to catch me a filly brumby from one of the snow mobs I could mate her to Greg's colt, Survivor. If all else failed to save the brumbies in the wild, perhaps a few of us on properties could breed horses from genuine brumby stock, and when the political dogma changed in regard to wilderness, we could reintroduce some lovely horses back into the wild.

I tried to call Ken and got the usual frustrating message on his answering machine: 'Hi there. Well, it looks like I'm not about . . .' I tried again and again. He had already left. Desperate to be amongst the action I made a call to Dean Backman, the guide I met when I went out on Chris Stoney's ride in March, through the Suggan Buggan and border mountain country. Dean was a farrier by trade from Bairnsdale and only caught brumbies on weekends. I would need to be lucky, and I was – or at least at the time I thought I was lucky. He said he was going to chase in the alps with Chris Stoney and Rachel Parsons on the weekend. The problem was a horse for me. He said he had a lot of shoeing to do for Helen Packer, who ran a horse trekking operation locally, and would speak to her about spare horses. Helen's farm was on the Bundara River a few kilometres west of the

Blue Duck Inn. Dean made it the meeting place. I told him I wanted a filly from the snow brumby line and I couldn't catch her myself. 'I might get her for you,' he said. 'You never know.' I had a feeling Dean was chasing Ken Connley's tally of 1400. We had a deal. If all went well Sal and I would be collecting two brumbies from Bairnsdale.

Omeo (the gold town) and surrounding districts

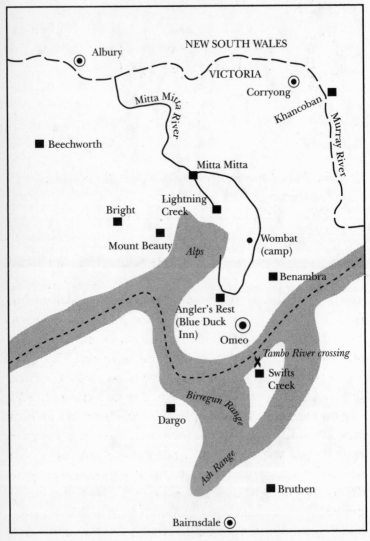

NEW SOUTH WALES

VICTORIA

Albury

Corryong

Khancoban

Murray River

Mitta Mitta River

Beechworth

Mitta Mitta

Bright

Lightning Creek

Mount Beauty

Alps

Wombat (camp)

Benambra

Angler's Rest (Blue Duck Inn)

Omeo

Tambo River crossing

Swifts Creek

Birregun Range

Dargo

Ash Range

Bruthen

Bairnsdale

Great Divide - - - - -

CHAPTER 9

The Gold Town

For the bushmen love hard riding where the wild bush horses are,
And the stock-horse snuffs the battle with delight.

It was the sound of the Bundara River that made me stand still for a moment. From the car it had looked like a painting – the scattered horses, the old slab cottage, the caved-in front of a sulky shed, a woolshed and, across the narrow river flats, the willows and eucalyptus along the banks. But on leaving the cocoon of the car, it all came alive. The river was flowing noisily through the valley from snow melt and the echo of the turbulence had a hypnotic effect. A willy wagtail bleeped from an apple tree and down on the flat a grey horse snorted. I heard the tap of a shoeing hammer and the murmur of voices. A plover called its mate from near the river trees, and from the heavily forested range the lonely call of the currawong rose above the sound of the water. Behind me the range rose higher still, with the morning sun putting a little fire into the drab granite boulders. This horse haven of Helen Packer's lay in a vast wilderness and the charm of it all was enough to make me want to leave the packsaddle in the car and just stay here to drink it in.

Helen's farm, Bundarrah, was once the headquarters of a sheep station. The woolshed still stood in solid order, but where sheep had one time been held waiting for the shearer's blade, a little mob of horses now watched Dean Backman at work over the fence. Dean had two horses tethered to a hitching rail.

Dean had arranged a horse for me to ride but I was the last to arrive. The farm was about five kilometres west of Anglers Rest, on a dirt road which terminated where the valley narrowed into a deep ravine. A low range separated the Cobungra River valley and this smaller valley. It was the Cobungra where the fly fishermen flocked and if you didn't wish to go riding on one of Helen's sturdy mountain horses she could arrange a river excursion. But her love was the horses. From a base on Dinner Plain, near the Hotham airport, Helen operated her horse trekking business. She and her partner Russell Tonkin could take you into the sub-alpine for up to five days, almost any time of the year. Of Aboriginal descent, Russell followed the old moth hunter trails – the Aborigines used to come here to feast on the Bogong moths in the summer months when the moths clustered in their thousands in the rocky clefts of alpine crags. Sometimes Russell and Helen boiled the billy at the site of an abandoned goldmine. The trekking area was rich in history and folklore. When I walked over to meet Helen, Dean was shoeing the packhorse hired out to me. The old gelding knew the mountains like the brumbies. Helen had disarming, liquid eyes. Her brown hair fell to her shoulders and there were none of the penalty facial lines so many outdoor women over 40 tend to carry. She had an open, friendly nature and wanted to help us as much as possible.

I probably took advantage of her good nature as ten minutes after shaking her hand I had her down by the slab cottage relating to me all the history of the place.

The pioneers didn't have electricity, television or the telephone, but they had what many of us have lost in the modern rural scene, and that's tightknit communities. We were all tribal not so many centuries ago, and isolation from one another is an abnormal condition. In my lifetime the communities have faded. There has been an exodus from the land and a once vibrant culture is now fragmented.

Bill O'Connell owned Bundarrah at one time. In his day the sheep station ran from the head of the valley to Anglers Rest, where he had the Blue Duck Inn. Bill lived in the cottage until the Blue Duck was opened for business. Judging by some of the stories he would have been at the hotel seven days a week once the road to the high-country goldfields was through. Many of the miners were shifty characters. Gold rushes invariably attracted those bent on the waistcoat and gold watch from the first swing of the pick, and when the adrenaline-charged confidence tumbled, they wallowed in bars and ran up big chits. Bill knew the type well and when the down and outs bolted they paid up half an hour later across the barrel of a shotgun. The road to Omeo ran due east from the Blue Duck for half a kilometre, then swung in a tight loop around a steep forested spur and ran due west. So crazy was the original road builder the road ran back to within 300 metres of the hotel. When the bolters took off for Omeo, Bill would be seen jogging and limping along the short cut over the hill to shotgun loop, where many of the chits were honoured. It was said he had a gammy leg and maybe his limp fooled the bolters.

The man was some character and so was this little cottage.

Russell had just completed the renovations and with
Helen's feminine touch it was ready for the first holiday-
makers. Russell had made the dining room table from snow
gum. The slow combustion heater was set in local pipeclay,
lanterns hung overhead and restored antique furniture
stored every item needed for cooking and dining. Through
the back door and along the verandah there was perhaps
the only three-walled stone shower room in Australia. You
could take a hot shower while looking out onto the mountains. When I asked Helen what the water race was for,
coming off a little waterfall and flowing along a tiny stone
canal, she said it used to drive the chaffcutter to make
wheaten chaff for the O'Connell horses.

We went into a barn which had also been converted into
guest accommodation, and by the time she had given me
coffee I didn't much feel like the ride to the alps. In O'Connell's Cottage I could have dug in with a few books, a fire and
a couple of bottles of wine for a long time. From the front
verandah I could watch Helen's mares. She kept the little
family in a separate paddock. The foals were either piebald
or skewbald and constantly played together when they
weren't fast asleep. I loved the way the mothers stood watch
while they slept. The father of the foals was a wild brumby
stallion.

About 10 a.m. we mounted up for the ride to Dinner Plain,
to the east of the Mount Hotham ski resort. Helen made
it easy for us. All the gear and packsaddles were placed
into her 4WD and she took them as far as a locked gate, on
the park boundary. All we had to do was lead the two packhorses, and with no load on their backs we climbed quickly
into the mountains. Rachel rode her old favourite,
Mahogany, Chris was on a very stylish silver grey called

Snow Gum and Dean rode a battle-scarred campaigner he called Ronald. I was on a bay gelding. Quiet enough, but he jogged rather than walked. He was a big improvement on Hammerhead.

Somewhere up in the mountains was Ken Connley. He and I seemed to narrowly miss each other all the time. The very day I headed back to Victoria he called. He told Sal he had returned from the alps, forced out by bad weather. It seemed that in July the alps traded one good day for two horrible ones. When Sal told him I'd left he said he'd go back up. I think he was anxious for the fee and I didn't blame him. The problem was I had hired horses from Helen and offered Dean $300 for the filly if he could catch her.

Two and a half days later I returned to this peaceful farm in a very shaken state. Dean had an agonising shoulder injury. Chris came back with a leg straight like a stump and I had taken a heavy blow to the head. Five brumbies were caught.

Before my accident I had one gallop, following Ken Connley. We met up on the evening before. The four of us were having coffee by the campfire, beginning to think it was time to head for the swags, when we heard an extra-ordinary growl from the darkness of the snow gums. Rachel jerked her hand impulsively to her mouth, to choke down what could easily have become a scream. Chris and I were instantly on our feet. Only Dean was unmoved. I think he may have experienced the prank before. It was a dreadful animal sound. I've heard lions make the same guttural growl on documentaries – we all had and I think that's why we all jumped the way we did. Anyway, Ken is the lion of the mountains, so when his figure appeared in the firelight no one was surprised. It meant we didn't head for the swags for another two hours.

Ken was one of the most natural bush riders I'd ever seen. He rode a big bold mover with a lot of white markings. Ken said he was training him and didn't want to push the gelding too hard. We cleared logs and swerved through the snow gums. I was tested to the limit again, but when I looked at the figure steadily widening the gap between us, it all looked so easy.

There was plenty of roping and excitement. A cold wind got up, but it wasn't too bad a day for 1800 metres in July. It was sometime in the afternoon when I got knocked out. On an exposed mountain ridge called Youngs Spur, Dean had caught two young brumbies. It takes great skill to get two frightened wild horses to run along with a domestic horse. It's not difficult to imagine the fear they would have of the strange creature on top. Dean had exemplary patience and never once got irritated with them. It was a different story with a pregnant black mare. Reared in the snow country and able to run free since birth, she had no intention of leaving her home territory without a fight. Rachel had roped her, been pulled out of the saddle and without help from the boys I think she might have got herself injured. Dean was first on the scene, followed by Ken. They finally got her tied to a tree and had a meeting about getting the captured brumbies down to the camp. Ken suggested he set off in front with the young colt and the mare should follow. Both Dean and Chris took a filly each. Chris had a lot of difficulty getting his filly to move along and when the black mare baled up tempers began to boil over. I got more orders thrown at me than in a month of Sundays at the Singleton army base. When the blow came I don't know what happened and I don't think anyone else saw it either. I think the black mare may have bitten my horse on the mouth causing him to throw his head back, connecting with my head. I recall very heavy bleeding – blood on my clothes and in the snow. The noise in my head was the worst. It sounded like a wind whining through an old stable in disrepair. And the cold – I will never forget the cold. Then a numbness flooded everything and recollections from that point on began to fade.

Rachel put me on her horse, Mahogany, and the battle with the black mare continued. Mahogany was a quiet, easy horse to ride, and dazed as I was, I managed to ride ahead of the mare, enticing her to follow another horse. Eventually the mare ran along well and we reached camp about dark. My greatest regret from the accident was missing the brumby running stories Ken Connley told that night. I was seated by the fire like everyone else, but sadly recall nothing. A couple of days later Dean told me there was a particular story Ken told at the campfire that I really had to hear. Once again I would have to search for the elusive Ken Connley.

Dean and I stayed the night with Helen when we returned from the mountains. Next morning I was okay again. Russell and I chatted about the fire threat in eastern Victoria and after a lengthy breakfast I went down to see Dean. He was shoeing Helen's trail horses and I noticed three brumbies in a wire mesh trailer. The black mare was one of them.

'They didn't take her?' I said.

'They couldn't fit her on.' Dean had a rear hoof on a leather apron in his lap. 'They're going to pick her up from my place.'

'She might have a nice foal,' I speculated.

The subject lapsed and I turned my attention to the charcoal filly. I think the other foal was a filly too; rather scrubby looking from memory. 'That the filly for me?'

'That's yours,' Dean said cheerfully. 'You earned her, even if you didn't catch her.'

'I'll write the cheque now.'

'There's no hurry. Pay me when you collect them both from my place.' I still had O'Rourke, the brumby colt Dean was keeping for me, to pick up.

He was a tough young man, Dean. His shoulder was bad, yet there he was shoeing. Lieutenant General Sir Henry Chauvel, commander of the Australian Light Horse in Palestine, would have liked to have had Dean around in 1917.

I had nausea and a headache. It was only 40 kilometres into Omeo and I would decide there about seeing a doctor. I was worried he might diagnose concussion and put me in hospital. On the way in I had a bit of difficulty with the driving and knew it would be irresponsible to travel beyond Omeo. I also knew then that a doctor was a certain passage to the Omeo hospital, so I wandered into the chemist and asked for something for nausea. The woman asked me where I had been and the whole room went dark. I had a job to stop her calling the local doctor.

Steady on my feet again, I only had to drive a block to the Colonial Bank building, converted into shops at the front and a motel at the rear. I took a room for the night and slumped onto the bed.

The Colonial Bank in Omeo opened for business in 1889. It is an imposing building for a country town the size of Omeo. Just up the street the Post Office building was equally impressive. Had mines like the Yellow Girl at Glen Wills kept yielding and men with capital, like Edmund Crooke, a local landowner, been inclined to stay, Omeo may have grown into a very big town. The charm of Omeo was its village atmosphere, with all its crooked streets and quaint buildings. Nestled on the side of a hill above Livingstone Creek, it is one of the prettiest towns in Australia. But its beginnings were turbulent and sometimes ugly. The diggings and the mines failed to yield the wealth accrued at the Ballarat goldfields, and the absence of effective law for many years attracted thieves and outlaws.

A prospector by the name of Ed Schieffelin was told in 1877 that the only thing he would find in Arizona's arid Dragon Hills was his grave. When he discovered ore impregnated with silver he called his claim Tombstone. But in the rush that followed not many found more than their graves, and in the Omeo goldrush only a handful fulfilled their dreams.

The two early mining towns of Tombstone, Arizona, and Omeo, Victoria, had extraordinary similarities in their frontier cultures. It was all to do with isolation. In terms of distance from a civilised community Tombstone was more remote, but Omeo was cut off by mountains and ranges on every side. Both towns sprang from a single shanty into wild, lawless settlements. In 1860 Magistrate Brown declared Omeo to be the roughest and toughest goldfield in Australia. It at least survived. When the silver ran out at Tombstone a law enforcer said the town was 'too tough to die'. But die it did – until Hollywood re-enacted the famous OK Corral Gunfight, when Wyatt Earp and his deputies had a showdown with the Clanton and McLaury brothers, who were ranchers and well-known cattle duffers.

Omeo didn't have a famous gunfight, but given the choice of Omeo and Tombstone in that frontier period I would have taken the Arizona town. In Australia in the latter half of the 19th century there was a stifling conflict between moral hypocrisy and the raw reality of early settlement days. The first magistrate to Omeo had all the friendly parlour girls rounded up, brought before him and taken by coach to the Beechworth Lunatic Asylum. Even the local sergeant pleaded for their release. Not many miners had wives and all had the same needs, but it was the Victorian period in a British colony. In 1857 a clergyman from Gippsland was morally distressed by rumours from the Omeo goldfields. He decided to end the bawdy culture at once and braved the arduous horse ride from Bairnsdale to bring the word of the Protestant God and civilisation. He arrived exhausted, and hoping to buck his spirits he accepted a noggin of homemade whisky from the miners. There had never been a clergyman to Omeo before and his coming had spread across the diggings. The miners said it called for a celebration that they should be so blessed, and the whisky flowed. It flowed down His Reverence's neck too and when members of the Worrajabaree tribe arrived for what they thought was a white corroboree, the clergyman was mesmerised by the beautiful, naked young women. Like my old friend at the wedding and the dancing girls, he may have thought he had died and gone to heaven. By the 1850s, naked Aboriginal women were no longer a common sight in the Gippsland coastal settlements.

Next morning His Reverence woke with an Aboriginal woman entwined around him. The Omeo culture of the day approved of such cognition. The miners rejoiced with more homemade whisky and the clergyman saddled his horse and fled back across the Ash Mountains to Bairnsdale. I'll bet on his last breath he remembered Omeo with a smile, such was the hypocrisy of the era.

Omeo may have been deprived of men who preached the Gospel for a long time and free-loving women for short periods, but for 40 years it was never short of Wild West atmosphere. Had the suppression of self-expression not been so dominant in the British Victorian era, I believe Australian history would have been recorded more honestly and subsequently have been far more interesting. Some academics contend it is better to be remembered for something, than nothing at all. There are obvious limits on that philosophy too, but Omeo is a town from the roaring days of the gold-rush that has been overlooked. Dramatic events stamped the culture of the time and are immortalised in folklore.

If Wyatt Earp had never gone to Tombstone the town would probably not exist today. Now, 120 years after the gunfight, the regular re-enactment is a major tourist attraction. Yet Omeo is a wilder and far more interesting historical cauldron of human greed and brute survival than Tombstone.

One of the early Omeo magistrates had such an assortment of felonious characters to regularly deal with that he retired to write about Australia's wild colonial days. He wrote under the pen name of Rolf Boldrewood and his best-known book, *Robbery Under Arms*, has been immortalised in two films. His characters portray the resentment of the colonial class division in the squatter era.

I doubt whether Omeo's notorious gold hold-up gave Boldrewood much material for the book. It must have been the most bungled and grisly bushranger hold-up in Australian history.

It happened in 1859 about fifteen kilometres south of Omeo. A gold agent had a packhorse team headed for the coastal town of Sale. In those days, gold consignments were carried over the mountain passes by packhorses. On this occasion the gold agent had only one trooper with him to guard the consignment. In 1859 that would have been all Omeo could spare. When the bandits sprang, the trooper went to snatch his rifle from the scabbard and recoiled from a bullet through each arm. The agent was dropped with a bullet through the chest and when all the horses bolted, including the packhorses, one of the bandits scalped the agent with a tomahawk. The agent's girlfriend was astride one of the bolting horses and despite his wounds the trooper somehow clung to his saddle. The girl, the trooper and all the packhorses arrived at the mining camp of Swifts Creek about 20 minutes later. The bandits got nothing but the hangman's rope at a later date.

The first trooper rode into Omeo from Bairnsdale in 1858. Up until that time it appears all murders and robberies went unrecorded, and if not dealt with by a local posse, most criminals were never caught and punished. One notorious criminal by the name of Tom Toke was an escaped convict and known to be linked with several murders. A popular method of enemy disposal on the mines was to lure the victim to the edge of an open mine pit and push him in.

For the original Omeo settlers, cattlemen, the goldrush created intolerable problems and the first man to stock the land where Omeo now sits was ultimately defeated by lawlessness. Edmund Crooke, born in England, left the family tea plantations in China to take up land in Australia. When he set off from Sydney the Omeo countryside was marked on the only official map as 'wasteland'. The Pendergasts and a handful of other stoic squatters from the bleak Monaro tablelands had already arrived, but Crooke secured Hinnomunjie Station in 1840. Soon afterwards he bought Benambra Station and in 1855 bought Targio and Bindi Stations. He owned the core of the Omeo district. The rolling upland hills provided some of the best cattle-breeding country in the lower end of southeastern Australia. If it hadn't been for the mountains, which totally enclose the upper Mitta Mitta valleys, he might have been too late by

1840. In all other districts south from the Gwydir River in northern NSW, squatters had seized all the prime grazing land by 1837 and few were interested in selling, as they would have to pack up and move further out into territory still held by the tribes.

When gold was discovered on the Livingstone Creek end of Hinnomunjie Station, Crooke and his squatter neighbours must have had doubts about what lay ahead, but no conception the whole area would degenerate into lawlessness. By the late 1850s the miners along Livingstone Creek had squatted on every waterhole used by the cattle and they killed the animals for meat as though they owned them. Law enforcement had still not been dispatched from Melbourne. Frustrated with the intrusion of people all over his land, Crooke had his men impound the roaming horses and cattle belonging to the miners. The action failed and the following year Crooke sold all his Omeo-based stations. He was an enterprising man and a loss to the fledgling district. In another part of Gippsland he soon became a major breeder of horses for the lucrative Indian market.

For the next 20 years there was no improvement in the Omeo area. Horses everywhere were stolen. Cattle duffing became rife. Other regions had notorious bushrangers to contend with – Ned Kelly across the alps in the Ovens River country and the Ben Hall gang in the central goldfields of NSW – but in Omeo it was a Wild West. Some of the miners at Omeo were ex-Californians and several were known to have migrated from the notorious Klondike goldfields in the Yukon territory.

To the Victorian Police the worst gang was known as the 'Omeo Mob', of which Tom Toke was the most dangerous. John Ahern raided the squatters' cattle along the entire length of the Mitta Mitta and John Paynter ('Bogong Jack') used the deep ravines of the alps as a base to raid over a wide area. If cattle prices were low, domestic horses became the principal quarry. They targeted well-bred horses, hid them, and if a reward was posted they 'found' the horse and collected the reward. If no reward was posted, brands were fiddled with and the horses sold in Melbourne. The only means of inland transport apart from barges and ferries on the Murray River, horses were a highly valued commodity. The animals were in such short supply the Victorian Police administrators were unable to mount their troopers adequately. The bushrangers stole the best horses, which were thoroughbreds, and when a pursuit was necessary the troopers found themselves left far behind.

By the 1860s there were at least fifteen mining communities scattered across the mountains east from Mansfield and the population was predominantly Irish. The first generation of Irish were now young men and women. Their parents had been convicts, had no money and in most cases provided little or no education for the children. For the Australian-born Irish the goldfields presented the chance of a lifetime. Reared in a harsh environment, the first native generation was trained to survive. They knew the mountains almost as well as the Aboriginal tribes before them. British colonial authority was as deeply detested as the occupying forces in mother Ireland and inflaming insurrection in the remote goldfields was the purpose of the clandestine activities of the Irish Fenian Movement. There were Irish in Victoria at the time who dreamt of a breakaway state. Those who fought colonial authority were heroes among the Irish. My great grandfather, Richard Keenan of 'The Bridge' near Cudal, provided lodgement for Ben Hall on one occasion. They were both about the same age at the time.

My father had to be prompted almost with a stick to speak of this incident. His mother was of English descent and, as with so many of the early colonial Irish families, there was a conflict of allegiance. Sometimes Dad drank too much and if the police interfered with his 'drive home' after a session in the pub they were likely to be told the flag of the Republic of Ireland was about to be raised on the flagpole at the local Court House. Next morning the Irish rebel would have vanished and it was all Rule Britannia in speech and spirit. On his mother's side his great grandfather (Hinley Gall) was aide-de-camp to Queen Victoria. In my family the confusion aroused bursts of mirth on many occasions, but there is something mystical, I believe, about old Irish sentiments.

In 1970 I rode at the St Patrick's day race meeting at Wellington in NSW. In the final race I won on the favourite in heavy rain and I had barely sat down afterwards in the Jockeys' Room when in rushed a priest with a strong Irish accent: 'Son of Ireland!' he exclaimed, blessing me at the same instant. I was wet and cold and the whisky was liquid from heaven. I didn't think much about it at the time, but 31 years later I can remember that priest charging into the room as though it was ten minutes ago. If I forget every other victory, I will never forget that one.

In 1863 Captain Standish was well aware of the situation and no doubt played a hand in the recommissioning of two of his best officers. Senior Constable John Reid took over the Omeo Police Station and James Pepper took up residence at the Snowy Creek Station (now the town of Mitta Mitta, although the police station was probably at Granite Flat). The two police stations were no more than a good day's ride apart and the constables worked in collaboration to quickly put all of the Omeo Mob behind bars except

Paynter who slipped the net. Egan, Ahern and Toke were arrested between 1863 and 1865. Toke was not Irish; an escaped English convict and a hardened criminal.

In the final showdown with the Arizonian cattle duffers Wyatt Earp lost his brother, but he put an end to the duffing. Like the Gippsland cattle duffers, the Clantons and McLaurys thought they could operate with impunity. In adjoining New Mexico the Irish did in fact create enclaves after the Civil War, such as Lincoln County. In a lesser way, the Victorian highlands were something of an Irish enclave for two or three decades too, for the arrest and imprisonment of the Omeo Mob did little to quell cattle and horse theft.

In 1868 the most notorious of all the highland cattle duffers emerged on the scene, Jimmy Lee. He was not of Irish decent, but in the new goldmine town of Wombat he was the butcher and was readily accepted into the Irish community. The little towns of Wombat and Thunder and Lightning, just east of Mount Wills, sprang up overnight and perished almost as fast when the gold ran out.

Lee had probably been stealing cattle for years, but in 1868 he pulled off a coup, taking 25 bullocks from Bringenbrong Station near Corryong. To put the seriousness of the crime in perspective: a bullock was worth six pounds in 1868. These days, six pounds is equivalent to $2000 or more.

Jimmy Lee was never brought to justice. The locals were always willing to help fugitives, provided they weren't killers – no one in Gippsland would have been sorry to see Toke locked up. On one occasion Lee was arrested following a stakeout, but in thick scrub he slipped off his horse, escaped and within hours his handcuffs had been filed off. Two or three years later another mob of cattle was stolen from Bringenbrong Station.

Living with cattle duffers creates a great deal of stress. One successful raid on your stock can break you, and 130 years after those lawless goldrush days the situation is worse in some respects. Big thefts are rare, but small theft is more common than ever. With the precarious profit margins of a rural business a loss of several head of cattle can lead to financial embarrassment. The modern police are not bushmen and their powers are very restricted. Many graziers feel it is a waste of time reporting missing stock. The tactics used by cattle duffers today are no different from those used in the 19th century. In fact they are probably better mounted. They use cutting horses and work in the moonlight. A good cutting man can make a cow and calf go anywhere he wants them to. The rewards are huge, detection rates the lowest for any criminal activity and the punishment – and it's more likely that a meteorite will hit the earth than a conviction actually occur – is usually no more that eighteen months' imprisonment.

It was nine in the morning when I put my head out the motel room door. The sun shone blindingly, but underneath the shrubs and trees the frost was slow to melt. The woman who managed the premises said a gnarly old peach tree at the side was as old as the bank. She asked me about breakfast and brought it over in a basket. I felt a bit better and hungry for the first time since my retreat from the alps.

When I am in a strange town the first place I head for is the bookshop. I have always been interested in local history, no matter where I find myself. At the Octagon Bookshop I met owner Trish Leon. We got talking about everything from brumbies to Black Friday in 1939. She knew of a local historian by the name of Fred G. Ward, who had retired to

Bairnsdale. Trish thought he might know something of the early history surrounding brumbies. I gave him a call. He told me that a family by the name of Brumby had leases and ran cattle in wild country to the east. I think he meant the mountain country north of Buchan. In the very early days · the other squatters would say, 'Oh them's some of Brumby's horses,' when wild horses were sighted. Fred's father Arthur began as a horse breaker and often talked about brumby running in the high country. If I thought at the beginning of this book I would nail the origin of the brumbies I was unaware of how little has been recorded of the past in some of Australia's remote and forgotten pockets.

Our discussion about the brumbies was interesting, but Black Friday at Omeo sounded like one of the American military's Daisy bombs igniting the countryside.

Fred was in Omeo on Black Friday and I quote from an article he wrote soon afterwards:

At the Hilltop Hotel I stopped again, because I had seen a tiny wink of fire on the summit of Mount Mesley to the north. As I watched, an explosion of fire erupted. It came off the mountain behind the town like a fiery tongue and it licked the town into one great blaze. It could only be described as an explosion of fire – a terrifying sight (luckily that area of Omeo had already been evacuated).

The memory of the fire burns in Fred Ward's memory as though it happened yesterday. He had me riveted when he explained eucalyptus gas under certain conditions could accumulate in the atmosphere and explode like liquid fuel. He said the Victorian national parks and Kosciuszko were ripe for the repeat of such an event and it distressed him how very few people were aware of the impending danger.

He blamed the de-stocking. The fire threat is another example of the real issues surrounding 'wilderness' in southeastern Australia being ignored while radicals rule the day.

The last cattle driver over the alps

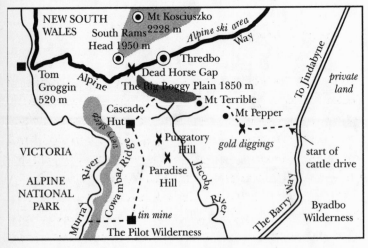

Droving route - - - - -

CHAPTER

10 The Permit

So all the cracks had gathered to the fray ...

It was to be a few days' holiday and it almost had a dreadful beginning. Travelling south in the old station truck to collect the brumbies, Sal and I stayed at Cootamundra the first night, planning to cross the alps at Mount Wills and stay at the Blue Duck Inn on the second night. The next day I had arranged to meet up with Ken Connley again.

There appeared to be cattlemen and brumby runners in the high country who would never buckle to bureaucrats. They saw government resumption of land, originally acquired by their forebears, in the same light as the Aboriginal people did before them. In NSW it was already over. In Victoria a similar demise loomed as inevitable. Some of the mountain leases had already been relegated to mere annual leases, which made it difficult for cattlemen to plan ahead on essential investment strategies such as herd size. When the axe fell most respected the law and moved their herds off. They had no choice anyway, but there were recriminations and rumblings of bitterness that would persist for another generation, and rangers would have to deal with boundary incursions for many years to come. Maybe future governments would acknowledge the impossibility of a handful of office-bound staff looking after vast tracts of mountainous country. History often follows paths beyond the anticipation of anyone. Who were those last fighters for the alpine meadows? I had raised the matter with Ken and he said he had a story for me, set in 1983. It was the story Dean Backman had told me about. Ken said that it was the last time the battlers had cocked a snoot at the park authority. He didn't think such a thing would ever happen again.

On the second day we arrived at the village of Mitta Mitta about one o'clock. It was 8 August. From the village the road climbed gradually for 40 kilometres to a pass only 100 metres below the summit of Mount Wills (1750 metres). There was a cold westerly blowing and to the south a darkened sky. At the village's only store I enquired about snowfalls.

'Reckon road be right by the time you get there,' the storekeeper said cheerfully. 'You'll be right.'

I had to make a decision before I went back to the truck. Sal's greatest fear was to be stuck in a wild, lonely place. I knew her fear sprang essentially from her knowledge of me: I would risk it – go beyond the pale. On one occasion I was within minutes of losing my life.

It happened at Lord Howe Island. I had been warned by the locals of the channel rips when the tide turned, but I wanted to free dive the outer reef, two kilometres from the shoreline. I set out alone in a sturdy rubber boat, dropped the anchor and forgot about the time. When I realised the tide was on the run the anchor was dragging. I was very fit and pulled feverishly on the oars. On the edge of the turbulent centre stream I busted an oar and literally froze in fear at the speed the little boat gathered in just a few seconds. I flung the anchor out and it gripped in four metres of water, but in the gathering pull of the tidal outflow I didn't expect the anchor to hold. I had to get out of the reef area before the big tide run started. I pulled on my diving gear – wetsuit, goggles, snorkel and flippers – and dived down to the anchor. To move it five metres away from the centre of the channel before I had to drop it and rise for air was a desperate underwater swim. If I hadn't had the boat to grab and take half-minute rests between each dive I could never have kept it up. It was pretty frightening. As the sea level dropped I could hear the waves crashing on the emerging reefs. The battle seemed to go on forever, but it was probably about 45 minutes. Suddenly I was out of the tidal stream and paddling towards the still distant island with the remaining oar. Next day Sal and I joined a fishing excursion and shooting the waves on the outer breakwater I had a glimpse of what lay in store if I had lost that battle. Sal was white faced and taciturn that day.

'There's a grader up there pushing a track through the snow,' I said to Sal. 'The bloke in there says the road's open.'

'Looks like horrible weather. How does he know? We haven't passed a single car from Omeo.'

That had me stumped. 'If there's a big dump tonight we'll have to go back to Albury, down to Melbourne and pick up the highway through to Gippsland. About nine hundred kilometres. I think we better give it a go.'

The first ominous sign was a bloke in the cabin of a low-loader, lights on and looking as though he was about to leave.

'The grader driver hasn't been able to finish,' he said when I stopped and walked over. 'I think it's only six inches deep. You should push through.'

The low-loader driver was going home and the grader operator was staying overnight in a VicRoads hut. Obviously there had to be a lot more snow graded off the road. As my father used to say, 'It's not marvelous, you know.'

I continued on with a small white face hovering beside me. For the first few kilometres it was nothing. The snow was thin on the ground and the grader had done a good job. The dual-rear wheels were gripping well and there was no sign of icing. The only nagging doubt was the altitude. How much higher did we have to go to top the pass and start coming down on the Omeo side?

The vision of a white hell came quite suddenly. The truck crawled up over a steep rise and we gasped at the scene. A snow storm had covered the track cleared by the grader and we stared into the forest through a gloom of foliage shadow and a deep carpet of snow. There was no stopping now, or any chance of turning around. I had to force my way through or spend a bitter, almost dangerous night. The old truck had no heater. If the rear wheels slipped into the ditch I would have to run the engine all night to keep the cabin temperature above freezing. Sal was so scared she couldn't speak and guilt made my stomach feel the size of a golf ball.

Gradually we climbed with the diesel engine running perfectly. The noise of it had become our security. There was no radio – and even if there had been, I doubt whether we would have picked up any frequencies in such a remote area. I had to turn the windscreen wipers on to deflect falling snow, and to stop cabin condensation and fogging of the windscreen I wound down my window. The snow blew through the window and onto my lap. I couldn't look at Sal then – the intensity of the anger in her eyes would have given me a heart attack.

At half a metre snow depth I expected the rear wheels to spin at any moment. I needed more power and I knew that was because the spare tyre underneath was dragging through the snow. On the switchbacks I must have been clearing the deep roadside ditches by mere centimetres.

The timber on either side began to thin. I knew that the treeline was 1800 metres and the pass fell short of that height. We leveled out and Sal spoke for the first time in a hour.

'This must be it – the top,' she almost whispered. 'The going down will be worse.'

Sal had a truck licence as well. She knew the gravity pull on the rear wheels was likely to cause a slide. We could expect icing, too, at any moment. It was four o'clock, one hour from dark in the cloud. Sal had been a skier for years at Falls Creek, just 20 kilometres away in a straight line, and she said icing in a southerly change began about an hour before dark. One strip of ice and the truck would half broadside into a ditch.

At least we were talking again. Sal's fear had turned into excitement. I think she had full confidence in me and we were talking about a bottle of Shiraz at the Blue Duck and relaxing beside the big slow combustion wood fire. I had set her expectations about the Blue Duck very high and I knew she wasn't going to be disappointed. But we had to get there first. On the south side the snow was deeper still and that was where we ran into the grader driver. He was churning up a snowbank a metre high, coming towards us. I gave him a wave and he didn't wave back. I don't blame him. I don't wave at idiots either. If I went into a ditch he was the one that would have to pull me out to clear the road, but that wouldn't be until the next morning as it was nearly knock-off time.

With the grader having come through I had the track again. The problem was the switchbacks. The truck had to grind over the snowbanks and on one drift I thought the Shiraz at the Blue Duck had been snatched from our grasp. We almost stopped. If we did stop the rear wheels would spin hopelessly.

'Keep going. Keep going,' gasped Sal.

I found myself slapping the steering wheel and growling words as though I was locked in a bob-of-the-head dual coming to the line in my racing days. But it was the last obstacle. The snowbanks got smaller and smaller and 40 minutes later we were safely by that cosy fire, but my nerves were so frayed I began the evening with a rum. Next morning the snow that had compacted on top of the spare tyre was still there, dripping slowly onto the road.

Russell Tonkin, Helen Packer's partner, was by the fire when we went in. He had an open, friendly manner about him and we soon got chatting about bush stories. Little did I know then Russell's father, Daryl Tonkin, was widely known for his extraordinary bush skills and compassion for Aboriginal people. Russell's story began with Black Friday. Everyone in the Omeo district knew about Black Friday, even though the catastrophe happened more than sixty years ago.

Russell's father and his uncle were logging on a newly acquired property near Drouin in South Gippsland. It had been known as Eliza Peter's block but when they bought it and built a timber mill, the mill was named Jackson's Track, after a nearby access track through the forest. The brothers were used to bushfires and not too concerned about the advance smoke that day back in 1939, but when booming blasts began to echo from the north, like a frontline under artillery siege, they knew this was no normal scrub cleaner.

It was too late to run. With no time to gather anything but their horses and axes, they fled to the centre of a ploughed paddock and waited.

The fire roared straight at them. Mighty forest trees blew up with the ferocity of 50-kilogram bombs, propelling fireballs over their heads, and they watched spot fires ignite on the other side of the ploughed ground. Within seconds the flames completely encircled them. Daryl told Russell the heat was unbearable and they struggled to stop the horses fleeing in panic. Afterwards there was nothing left. The mill lay in ashes and the big driving engine was buckled and twisted beyond recognition. They were left with five axes and several horses to start all over again.

Russell was the fourth child of Daryl and Euphie. The story of his family is one of the most remarkable in 20th century Australian history. I read his biography, *Jackson's Track*, and discovered Daryl could have run from the advance of the fire together with the men employed at the mill. Instead, he and his brother Harry chose to stay with their horses, knowing that if the centre tongue of the fire hit them there would be no oxygen left in the atmosphere. Quiet running fires will progress on an even front for days. Wild fires driven by wind and fed with heavy fuel on the ground generate a heat vortex. The cyclonic-force wind creates a giant furnace and spears ahead in a narrow strip. On a miniature scale the same principle applies to stubble burning.

Russell had dinner with us at the Blue Duck and I asked him if he had made any more snow gum dinner tables. I took a risk asking him in front of Sal. If she ever saw the one in Bill O'Connell's old cottage she would want one made for her and cash reserves were low. Russell may not have had the time either, but Sal was fascinated by how he had acquired his wood-crafting skills. Making quality tables from gnarly snow gum trunks required great skill. It turned out to be no self-taught accident.

His father's whole life had revolved around wood. When he had the mill running he felled trees for the sawn timber market. In difficult times he cut fence posts and firewood. The fine moulding of wood was another story and one that made Russell a wood craftsmen.

Daryl Tonkin fell in love with a Kurmai woman, Euphie, from a large tribe which incorporated several clans from Port Albert to Orbost. His family were so opposed to the match that they kidnapped Euphie and dumped her at a sleeper-cutter's camp in the care of an aunt, hundreds of kilometres away. Euphie wrote to Daryl, disclosing where she was out in the bush. What followed was one of the most romantic stories to come out of the Australian bush. Ostracised from white society and distraught about conditions on the mission stations, Daryl encouraged many Aboriginal families to come and live at Jackson's Track. Some helped with the mill, others felled and snigged trees and those bent on resuming traditional lifestyles hunted. Everyone collected bush tucker which was plentiful in the surrounding forests. One man, Gene Mobourne, was a craftsman. He made boomerangs. For the observer the most exciting ones were those which skimmed away at ground level, rose high on a turning arc and returned to the thrower's feet. Daryl was so intrigued, Gene taught him the craftsmanship. They would go out into the bush together and collect blackwood roots. That was the easy part. The shaping and fine turning took many hours. The heat toning had to be within a fraction of a millimetre. It became an evening hobby for the two of them. Gene's wife Effie made baskets from swamp grass. Their intricate crafts were popular with tourists all along the Mornington Peninsula. It's ironic that 50 years on Gene Mobourne would have been so overwhelmed with contracts that Jackson's Track would have become a boomerang and basket-making factory. In half a century white attitudes to Aborigines had changed from open hostility to proud recognition of their culture. Alas, though, perhaps all too late.

In the midst of all this activity Russell was taught to mould wood in the manner his people had applied to the craft for thousands of years. Bundarrah, Russell and Helen's farm, is not only a horse haven; it contains examples of raw wood craftsmanship rare today.

That night we stayed in one of the Blue Duck's cabins. I had never slept in a slab-walled cabin with an open fireplace before. With rum starters, followed by Shiraz, I was in no fit state to chop wood, but I was determined we would have a blazing fire in the bedroom. The room was warm enough without it; I simply had to have the atmosphere. The fire danced shadows on the wall all night and I envied Sal when I rose early. She could stay put in bed and boil the billy and make toast on the flame at her leisure. I had a meeting with Ken Connley, way out in the mountains beyond Benambra.

My decision to cross the high pass had been the right one. Snow lay on the tops of the high timbered hills and a light wind travelled over the unseen snowfields and down onto the Mitta Mitta and Cobungra valleys.

Edmund Crooke must have been exasperated with the lawlessness emanating from the Omeo mining camps to sell the land he acquired in 1840. The road from Omeo to Benambra runs through the heart of old Hinnomunjie country and it was some of the best agricultural country in Australia. The flat to undulating downs never had to be cleared by white man. The Aborigines no doubt adopted the same hunting practices on the Omeo plains as they did in other areas where rich land was surrounded by hard hilly country. They regularly burnt the useless autumn grass and the green shoots which followed the first rain attracted kangaroos out of the hills in hordes. The Aborigines erected barricades cut from scrub and drove the mobs into the arc-shaped traps, spearing the quantities needed for a week or more. In the cooler months, meat hung from a branch will last up to ten days. The new grass on the burnt country remained fresh well into winter, when the energy from protein was most needed by the animals. The fire-hunting practice of the Aborigines was the sole reason catastrophic fires were unknown before white man arrived. A diversity of marsupial life and numerous ground bird species certainly reduced the undergrowth material, but without Aboriginal interference with fire the big droughts would have still laid the foundation for occasional devastation.

The historical fire sequence is now rated at approximately every ten years for most of the vulnerable areas in Victoria. It should be noted by the advocates hell-bent on de-stocking millions of hectares that in Victoria, summer humidity levels are sometimes near zero. This gives a fire potential of a magnitude that would never be possible in much hotter Queensland, where humidity levels remain high over most of the state.

Taking a dirt road running northeast from Benambra, I was soon back into the narrow valley country flanked by steep granite mountains. From here on was Connley country. Ken, his brothers, and the generations before them had been riding the valleys and ranges from Benambra to Tom Groggin near Thredbo since 1850. Ken knew the country better than anyone alive. He had three properties. The main block on the Omeo plains was near the Old Hinnomunjie racecourse. He and his family lived there. Where I was headed was one of his breeding blocks near McFarlanes Lookout.

Polish explorer Hohann Lhotsky discovered the Omeo plains in 1834. Rumours of his expedition circulated in Sydney and James McFarlane, James McKillop and Thomas Easton mounted an expedition to assess the grazing potential. They first viewed the plains from a high peak near the farmhouse where I met up with Ken. Geographically speaking, the Omeo plains are a wide river basin spreading east from the Mitta Mitta to form low lying areas and even a lake. McFarlane was so impressed he moved cattle from his Monaro property within months, fearing someone might arrive before him. Not one acre on the Monaro came within a bull's roar of the rich Omeo plains.

I arrived early for a winter's morning. I knew Ken was an early starter from that first morning on Dinner Plain. We were still having breakfast when up rode Ken at about 7.30. When I saw the smoke rising from the chimney and horses in the yard I knew I hadn't missed him. We had arranged a meeting, but on cattle properties plans can be altered overnight beyond the control of the owner.

'In here, Mick,' came the friendly voice.

I walked inside and he was standing with his back to the fireplace. With thick curly sun-bleached hair, Connley was one of the most rugged looking men I have ever encountered. He still had a spark of youth in his eye and he moved with the spontaneity of a young man. He had a billy on the fire. There was a heap of food on a long table, including bread. Ken nodded at a mug. 'Help yourself to some coffee.'

I didn't need any encouragement. I needed some coffee

to get myself fired up. I glanced out through the window to the yards. The horses looked okay, but the handler caught more of my attention. She and Ken were going mustering. That is, after Ken told me the last colourful story to come out of the Snowy Mountains. There won't be another one.

I knew Ken had a tale to tell, but getting bushmen to tell a story can be harder than winding up a grandfather clock with your fingernails. I've tried everything. Alcohol's the worst, because I have to drink too and I am the first drunk. I've tried insults, telling stories myself and prompting gossip. I tried the latter with Ken and he looked at me as though I was insinuating he had come down in the last shower. Suddenly I woke to the prod that might work.

'Bet that girl in the Parks office was a good-looker,' I said.

He looked away and out through the window to the stockyard. I prayed the handler'd stay out there so that Ken would talk freely. 'She was all right,' he began, eyes twinkling. And so the story of the permit unfolded.

It was autumn. Most of the higher areas of the Kosciuszko National Park had been resumed from leaseholders more than 25 years earlier. The old stockmen from the mountains had probably forgotten when the last mob of cattle was walked from Jindabyne across country to the Victorian border. No one ever dreamed there might be a final drive over the alps. No one but Ken Connley, that is.

Southeastern Australia was in the grip of drought that year, from the Monaro to the Queensland border. The Monaro was a dustbowl and with winter around the corner there was worse to come. The graziers had to unload their cattle. Hay and feed grain prices were already exorbitant. The cost of feed through the long winter would exceed the value of the stock on a per head basis. Desperate, the graziers looked to the saleyard, knowing there were few, if any, buyers. The late autumn sale in Cooma was to be the last before winter.

Conditions in the Omeo district were only marginally better. Ken, his brother Rusty and his uncle Sneaky had pooled their cattle and bushed them in the Davies Plain area.

The risks for the Connleys were considerable. Higher in rainfall and marginally lower in altitude, the mountains southwest of the Murray are heavily forested. If a major bushfire started it would be suicide to even look for cattle, let alone try to get them out. If there was a heavy dump of snow in July or August they would stand to lose the lot. But the Connleys felt so secure they plotted by the campfire one night how they could make money out of the drought in NSW. Their cattle had settled down well and when a few did cross the Murray into NSW, the steep ramparts of the Snowy Mountains forced them back.

Sneaky had noticed that the mountain springs had begun to flow. For the old bushmen it was a sign of rain.

'We better make a hit day afta tomorra,' he said to Ken. They had just finished the evening meal by the campfire. 'About 500 head listed for the Cooma sale. It's in that *Land* I bought when I last got the tucker in Khancoban.'

'We'll walk em straight over the Great Divide,' Sneaky snorted.

'No one's got permission since the 50s.' Ken reflected. 'The rangers would think it was a prank.'

'We could drive em day and night. Be across before them bastards knew.'

'Better still if we could get a permit.' Rusty loved a challenge. He began to focus on the logistics. 'It's going to be as difficult to walk ten as 500. Might as well buy the lot. We'll need five riders.'

'We'll put it to our mountain mates,' Ken said. 'Richard

McGufficke and Noel Pendergast. Pity old Teddy's not still alive. Wouldn't he have loved it.'

'Be the last big drive over the alps,' Rusty said. The romance of the concept had more appeal than the profit.

Sneaky drained his pannikin of tea and stood up from the log seat. 'I'm headed for the swag. We gotta get out early and ring old Noel. Give him a day to think about it.'

Noel and Richard agreed to give them a hand if they went ahead with the purchase. Noel had spent much of his life in the high country before the national park took over and Richard was only a young boy when his father, Teddy, had his lease resumed.

Ken said they didn't buy every single yard put up, but at the conclusion of the sale, 400 head of steers and heifers were in their hands for an average price per head that was as low as the sales recorded in the great cattle crash of 1974, when many producers were sent to the wall. They even bought the steers used at the local rodeo.

The Monaro tableland was so bare the cattle could not be walked along the road between Cooma and Jindabyne. Ken had to organise cattle trucks and lift them over that stretch of 60 kilometres. He had them unloaded on the Barry Way road near Jindabyne. In those days the somewhat hair-raising dirt track to Omeo was not open to doubledecker semi-trailers. Even today the road clings to sheer drops with no safety fences as it winds up Black Mountain from the Suggan Buggan River. The road over Dead Horse Pass was also unsuitable and heavy transport through Thredbo was banned. The only route Ken could have selected to transport the cattle all the way to Benambra would have been via Bairnsdale on the Victorian south coast, a distance of almost 500 kilometres. The cost of the transport on a per head basis would have spoilt the bargain price he paid in the Cooma saleyards. The Connleys' problem was to find enough feed and water for the cattle while they decided whether to risk the huge fine or try and get a permit from the National Parks and Wildlife Service office. They could only hold them on the road for a couple of days.

'They reckon mainly women up there in the Parks office,' Sneaky growled to his fellow stockmen. It was a formidable team, comprising the staunchest family names ever to ride over the alps. In the 1988 Bicentenary celebrations the Pendergasts and the McGuffickes rode to the summit of Kosciuszko in the ultimate mood of defiance to raise the national flag in remembrance of the mountain people.

'They're our only hope,' Noel said. He was the most pragmatic of the group. 'I vote Ken goes for the permit. If he can't sweet talk it out of em, no one can.'

'Just don't get smitten,' Sneaky spat. When he wanted to make a point he always spat first. 'We gotta move. Ain't much feed along this road.'

The cattle were being held on the road south from the Moonbah Church. Moonbah was the original Pendergast settlement before the family split in the late 1830s and three brothers out of five left for Omeo. Under Rural Lands regulations travelling stock had to walk ten kilometres a day. In drought times stock inspectors waived the rules in certain circumstances. The drovers were given a few days to either walk north and skirt around the national park on back roads with little or no feed, or truck out to a destination further away.

The odds were stacked against Ken and he knew it. At the village he went into a café. He had to find out who was in the Parks office. If he simply blundered in and met a senior park ranger it would be over before it began.

Ken ordered tea and toast and waited until the waitress brought it to the table.

'I'm a stranger in these parts,' he said. 'I need a little help.'

The girl stood back and looked warily at this rugged man from the mountains. His black slouch hat with a narrow strip of Hereford hide for a band was as impressive as the insignia on a general's jacket. She was young, but in village communities the young girls are worldly before their time. She waited for Ken to come out with it.

'Do you know anyone in the Parks office? There was a woman ranger I met once. Just can't recall her name.'

'I don't have much to do with the National Park people,' the girl said. 'I'll ask Elaine.' She turned swiftly and went through the rear door to the kitchen.

A woman in her late 30s came out. She had long red hair tied back in a pony tail. In 1983 Ken's hair was also a light shade of red. 'I know the people in there,' she said. There was a faint smile. 'You in some sort of trouble?'

'I've had to unload cattle near the park boundary,' Ken replied, looking past her. 'You know, drought cattle. Goin down in the trucks they were. They need a feed bad and there's nothing along the road.' He paused and looked at her the way he might have looked at his mother when he didn't want to go on the school bus.

'Oh it sounds a desperate situation,' the redhead said, her eyes heavy with concern. 'Ask for Mary-Lou. She and I are good friends.'

'You couldn't call her then? It would help so much. Put the phone call on the bill.' Ken spoke so quickly it caught her off-guard. She looked suddenly rattled and smiled fleetingly at a couple who had just entered the café. They moved to a table.

'Well now that's not really fair.' She dropped her hands

onto her apron with a slight slap. 'I don't know you.'

Ken looked at the redhead gravely. 'I know it's a bit rough to spring it on you. I live in the mountains and rarely ever go to a town. I am shy with women. I am okay with you because you remind me of my late mother.'

The redhead was intrigued with his gall. She knew men. This one was full of bullshit, she felt sure, yet he was likable – as rogues often are. In a different place with country music in the background, evening and the suaveness of a Chardonnay he would have asked her to dance and she would have blushed. Conscious of her own vulnerability, she suddenly wanted to help him.

She smiled mischievously. Ken caught the look in her eye and half smiled. 'I don't believe a word of it,' she said briskly. 'But I'll ring Mary-Lou anyway.'

The couple looked on as though pre-meal entertainment had been provided. The waitress took their order and went into the kitchen. The woman at the other table kept sneaking glances at Ken but when he smiled at her she didn't look again.

The redhead was away for a few minutes. Ken ate all the toast and drank the tea pot dry. So much depended on the next half hour. When she came back from the kitchen she seemed pleased with herself and announced, 'Mary-Lou said any time. There's a girl at the desk. Just ask for her.'

'I'm much obliged I can tell you,' Ken said rising. He took his wallet from his pocket and pulled out a five-dollar note. 'Keep the change please.'

'Oh no I'll give you . . .' she was slightly breathless and Ken touched her forearm with his hand. 'It's okay. Best pot of tea in years.' He dipped his hat and left. She watched him leave and turned away, embarrassed, when she noticed the couple were looking at her.

In the Parks office Ken felt about as comfortable as a rat in an open-top drum. A tall middle-aged ranger strode out of one office and disappeared into another. Ken held his breath. To ask him for a permit would be on par with asking the local cop if he'd look the other way when the bank was held up. The waiting was the worst moment of the whole exercise. When Mary-Lou did emerge from her office to meet him she gave Ken a pleasant smile and his hopes soared.

They went into her office and she sat down behind the desk. Ken sat in one of the two chairs. He would soon know the fate of the cattle and the anticipated profits.

'You have cattle on the road somewhere,' Mary-Lou said, getting straight to the point. 'I'm wondering how I come into the picture. If you're in trouble with these cattle you really should be going to see someone in the Pastures Protection Board.'

'I had to unload,' Ken began. 'They're young cattle, none more than fifteen months old. Four hundred head. Trucked into a saleyard, held there and trucked out after the sale. For drought cattle it was too long. They got to have feed immediately. Hay's eight bucks and I don't have that sort of money. If I could walk quickly through the park to the Murray they'd get the tucker they need and be nearly home at the same time.'

Mary-Lou's eyes narrowed. 'Where are you from?'

'Benambra – it's dry there too, but we got feed up in the leases.'

'So you bought these cattle on spec that it might rain?'

Her informal response took him aback. Ken's past experience with rangers suggested they knew little about anything outside ecology and environmental matters. More perplexing, she looked to be only about thirty.

'Not quite like that,' Ken said, thinking furiously. 'We got

burnt out. Not a big general fire. Just my farm from a lightning strike. Saved the cattle, but had to sell em – no feed,'
he paused and focused his mind on a sad event back in his
childhood. It always made him look sad. 'To stay in business
I had to buy in again.'

'I know how it is,' Mary-Lou said gently. 'My father was a
Monaro grazier. He's had to sell up the cattle several times.'
She stood up and moved to a large map hanging on the
wall. 'The original stockroute across the alps was through
Wollondibby, up where Thredbo now stands and over Dead
Horse Gap to Tom Groggin.' She giggled at a sudden image
in her mind. 'You'd be thrown into jail if you walked your
cattle through Thredbo. Four hundred head of them.' She
paused and for a moment looked at Ken askance.

'You're obviously a good horseman,' Mary-Lou stated.
'How many other riders?'

'Four good men – the best.'

'If I can get a permit through would you promise to walk
straight across – no loitering?'

Ken straightened his shoulders and tilted his hat. 'I'll kiss
my brumbies and swear before the Virgin Mary.'

Mary-Lou shot her hand over her mouth. 'Oh God,' she
laughed. 'Would you really?' she asked, then sobered
quickly. 'Leave it with me, Ken. It's a drought issue and I'll
see if anything can be done.'

Ken went back to the droving camp. The cattle were scattered along the road for three kilometres. They were restless
and hungry. At the camp Sneaky had made himself cook for
the day. The other men had their horses saddled, tied up to
the boundary fence of a farm. They had just come in for
lunch. At both ends of the spreading mob the cattle had to
be continually hunted back or they would walk and walk in
search of grass.

There was a tense sense of expectancy as Ken got out of his ute. 'I gotta go back.' He glanced around at the cattle. 'Look at em, they're starved, the poor bastards. We'd better get movin.'

Sneaky shook his head. 'If it gets signed I spose you'll have to give her one for thanks.'

Richard McGufficke burst out laughing. 'He's not Robert Redford!'

'I dunno about that,' Noel Pendergast chuckled.

'If we get the go ahead we'll move at first light.' Noel got up from his squat on the ground. There were no trees. It was bleak, undulating country. 'We can get to the Big Boggy by dark.'

Sneaky broke a dead stick across his knee. 'We'll go right away,' he growled.

'We'll hit the dark in a bad spot,' Noel said removing his hat and scratching the back of his head.

'They're that bloody starved they'll stop and eat the minute we stop drivin em,' Ken said. 'I vote we move. The moon will roll out about ten o'clock.'

The men had the cattle bunched up into a mob when he got back the second time. Sneaky had got his way without any argument. Permit or no permit, he was headed for what he called the front line. His mates were eager to go too. Even Noel conceded it was better to be in the mountains under the moonlight than holding cattle against their will on a miserable strip of ground either side of the road.

The drover supply vehicle and Ken's horses were at a nearby farm. The plan was for Ken to leave his vehicle there too, load what he wanted to take onto his packhorse and catch them up. By the time he'd got to them they were nearly at the gold diggings.

It was hard, aggravating work. The moment the cattle walked through the park gate they wanted to stop and graze. They hadn't seen feed like it since they were calves on their mothers. The men cracked their stockwhips until their arms ached, and at the same time had to lead a packhorse each. A couple of the packhorses didn't like the sound of the stockwhips and sometimes pulled away. At the foot of Mount Pepper the lead in the mob entered a scrubby ravine, and with no grass to eat they lengthened their stride. It was a lucky break and ensured the mob reached the Mowamba River before it became completely dark. The cattle stopped at the river as though blocked by a gate, and slowly spread out in snow grass knee high. Before the moon rose they may not have been able to see it, but they could certainly smell it.

The men dismounted on the riverbank and halter-tied the horses to trees after taking them for a drink. A fire was lit and they slumbered around it, drinking tea with biscuits. They couldn't afford to get too comfortable. The cattle had never been in an open wilderness before and once their stomachs were full they would become fearful of the forest and all the strange sounds. A couple of dingoes on the prowl or just a mob of kangaroos passing through would be enough to trigger a stampede. Even the four working dogs brought along to help had to be tied up to trees in case they wandered and spooked the cattle.

Luckily, the night passed without drama. At first light a big damper was prised from the coals with a stick and each man had a mug of tea in his hand before the mopokes had called it a night and headed for their homes in dead tree trunks. There was a bit of argument about how quickly they should move off the Mowamba River.

'Reckon we saddle up and push on up to the Big Boggy

while it's cold,' Rusty said. 'They're tired already. Once it warms up we'll fight the devil getting up this next 1500 feet.'

'Stay here for a day,' Sneaky suggested. 'Get a bit of guts into em on the river here. Nothin's goin to stop us now.'

'What about those campers we passed at the diggins?' Richard McGufficke threw in. 'They looked like Greenies to me. It's only a phone call to the Parks office and the shit'll hit the fan.'

'Yeah, let's keep goin,' Noel Pendergast mumbled. 'If they drop onto us at the Cascades we're nearly there anyway. In fact they'll order us to keep goin to Victoria.'

Ken didn't say anything. He'd promised Mary-Lou they'd cross as quickly as possible and he and Sneaky rarely agreed on anything. They rode together for necessity.

Without another word the decision had been made. They drove the reluctant cattle through another tight, steep ravine. With Mount Terrible towering nearly 600 metres above them it must have been a daunting cattle drive in the frost. By late March the alpine valleys slip into the morning frost cycle. The Boggy Plain is one of the highest big frost hollows in the alps. In the lease days the Nankervis bullocks fattened on the Boggy, but there was an unwritten rule: be mustered and gone by 15 March. Locked in between the Chimneys Ridge and the Brindle Bull Range above Thredbo, the Boggy Plain was exposed to heavy dumps of early autumn snow. Noel was anxious. He knew of whole mobs wiped out in late March and the drought conditions make snow all the more likely. Records show that some of the biggest falls of dry snow occur in drought conditions. But there was no other route. The steep, dangerous terrain which plunges to the Jacobs River lay to the west and blocked any chance of walking in a direct line.

In the lease days Richard's father, Teddy, had a hut and a set of yards at the eastern end of the plain. His lease joined that of the Nankervis family. It upset all the men to see the hut in a state of ruin. With his advancing age, Noel knew this would be the last time he'd see it. He reined in and watched the cattle pick their way around the ruins and spread out onto the plain. Shaded by mountains on all sides and 1700 metres above sea level, the Boggy Plain never properly dried out, even in the height of summer. In a normal season the vast swamps would have been treacherous for unsuspecting cattle, but the drought had dried them back to scattered soaks. The Thredbo River began here, flowing west to Dead Horse Gap where it looped eastwards and gurgled its way through the Thredbo village.

The drovers didn't bother checking the lead. In the warm sunshine the exhausted cattle camped across the plain and the horses fell asleep by their tether tree. The saddles had been removed and each man used his saddle for a pillow. They were all back in the high country they loved so much. It was quiet and peaceful. The dogs lay full length on the grass, in deep sleep. Not a bird sang or chirped, for they too were asleep in the drowsy noon.

At first the sound was a distant hum. No one stirred. It could have been a joy flight over the alps to the north. Then there was the unmistakable chop in the air from rotor blades. Richard was the first to sit up.

'That's a helicopter,' he announced.

One by one they all sat up to listen. 'It's down towards the diggins,' Noel said gravely.

'Comin this way too,' Rusty said. 'Those bloody Greenies must have gone to town.'

The echo of the helicopter began to carry into the mountains. The horses were suddenly alert and restless. The drovers rose and searched the sky to the southeast. When it appeared over Mount Terrible there was a flash of sun from the cockpit glass.

'They won't be comin down nice and steady, the bastards,' growled Sneaky. 'I've been wantin to give em the plastic for a long time.'

Rusty wheeled. 'No plastic. You'll have us all jailed.'

'You're Victorian anyway,' Noel gasped. He watched in horror as Sneaky pulled a big sheet of plastic from his saddlebag.

'We're next on the hit list,' Sneaky shouted. 'They're goin ta grab our leases too!'

Minutes ago they were all asleep. They stood frozen in disbelief. The helicopter was only seconds away from being overhead. If Sneaky released the plastic into the violent updraught it would be sucked up at the speed of a rocket to the engine air intake. The helicopter would stall almost immediately. Ken was the first to react. He pulled his axe from a cowhide scabbard attached to the front of the saddle. The sun fired off the bright blade like a mirror.

'Leave it, Sneaky!' he bellowed.

Adrenaline surging, Sneaky dropped the plastic and rolled his saddle over. He flung back an oilskin tied tightly to his saddle front and snatched out his axe. Both axes were short handled. The blade of Sneaky's was black with dried blood.

'No, it's not comin to this,' Richard said sharply and ran between them. He was the same age as Ken. They had been good mates since boyhood. He knew the Connleys had had axe fights before with serious consequences.

Some of the Connleys were noted for their axe skills. Ken and Sneaky carried them on the saddle for cutting firewood and, if threatened, weapons. With 1400 brumbies caught in the bush no one would have expected Ken to admit someone from the fair sex could teach him a trick or two, but only a couple of years before this epic cattle drive Ken took a female Canadian cowhand into the mountains to help him round up the cows and calves for branding. Before her arrival in Australia the young woman had won the women's axe-throwing championship event in Canada, and before that the Jack and Jill crosscut saw championship in the USA. The axe used in sporting events was double-bladed, like those used by the native Americans. There is considerable skill in the throwing of the short-handled axe. By the time the woman (who had a splash of native Assiniboine) returned to the Rockies Ken could throw a short-handled axe with the same deadly accuracy as the 19th century Sioux could throw tomahawks.

As the helicopter passed overhead, Noel saw the plastic start to gather up and threw a lump of wood onto it to hold it down. The helicopter passed over and started to descend towards an open space nearby. Ken's big baldy-faced gelding had managed to pull away and had bolted. The cattle rose and ran across the plain.

Sneaky glared at them all, beaten. When he turned to face Ken he knew he was too late. Ken's axe was poised in his throwing hand. Sneaky knew it would be hurtling towards his chest before he could even release his own axe. He spat on the ground.

'You're traitors, all uva yer! They snatched this land and never a shot was fired. You've made it easy for the bastards to do the same to us. In Kildare our ancestors made the rivers run in blood and they got it back. You buggers done nothin.'

'We had our turn,' Noel said breathlessly. 'We had the mountains for 130 years. The bush is all growin back and when the big fires scorch it from the Murray to the sea our people will be back again. Land don't change. People just blow over it like the dust.'

The pilot lowered his machine into the snow grass. The big rotors whined down and the cattle on the plain stopped trotting away and turned to watch in bewilderment. The horses still skittered about, tied to the trees. Ken's baldy-faced horse had stopped where the snow gums formed a foliage wall and the men quickly gathered their wits. Noel screwed up the plastic and pushed it under a log. Sneaky dropped his axe by the saddle and Ken swung his down hard onto a dead branch the thickness of a man's forearm. The blade went through to the dirt and Ken snatched up one of the pieces. He pretended to be setting wood for a fire, but all the while held the axe.

Three men stepped down from the helicopter. Ken was relieved when he saw Mary-Lou hadn't come – if there was to be a showdown he did not want her involved.

A tall man in ranger uniform walked briskly towards them. In his wake was a short plump man, whose eyes darted around like a frightened bird. The swarthy pilot remained by the helicopter. The ranger had a military air. He eyed them all fearlessly and for a perceptible second his gaze dwelt on the axe in Ken's hand. Ken went on nonchalantly gathering wood and occasionally the sun danced on the blade as he swung it down on a thick stick.

'Who's responsible for all these cattle and horses?' the ranger demanded.

Ken straightened and let the axe hang in his arm. 'I am,' he said quietly.

'Are you aware under the Act, in the state of NSW, the severity of the fines for such an intrusion into Park lands?'

Ken swung the axehead gently up into his armpit, locked

it in by tightening his bicep and removed something from his shirt pocket. Silently he walked forward and handed it to the ranger.

The permit had been folded into a piece as thick as cardboard. The ranger unfolded it and very soon his lips parted, wide enough for a fly to pop in. 'I'll be damned.' He raised his eyebrows sharply at Ken. 'What did you tell them when you applied for this?'

'Just what we're doin here,' Ken said with a shrug, careful not to ease the bicep pressure on the axe. The handle stuck out half a metre, nearly poking the ranger in the ribs. 'Walkin through to Victoria.'

The ranger held the permit away as though it were used toilet paper. 'Something's wrong – it should never have been issued. No cattle have walked over the alps for 20 years,' he paused and slapped the heavily creased piece of paper. 'You got 48 hours to run on this.'

'We can't move again today,' Ken said firmly. 'These young cattle are exhausted. We'll get to the Cascades tomorrow and the tin mine day after that. The next day we'll drop onto the Murray and cross the border.'

For the first time the ranger looked uncomfortable. To hold the drovers to the dates on the permit would punish the cattle. It was a love of animals than inspired many to seek careers in the National Parks and Wildlife Service.

'You must realise you're on thin ice,' the ranger said at last. 'I'll waive the expiry date by a day, but don't push it. This helicopter runs at $500 an hour. If I've got to chase you out you could be held to the cost of the flying time.'

'We'll be out,' Ken said. 'Now if you'll just excuse me I'll go and catch my horse. When the rotors kick up again he might clear out altogether.'

'You don't give a fuck about anybody do yer,' Sneaky spat

at the ranger. 'Yer just drop in here and scare the shit out of everything.'

'If we did nothing you rogues would have 10 000 head of cattle in here,' the ranger replied, ignoring Sneaky's aggressiveness. 'I'm paid to do a job and that's to protect the Park.'

'You reckon we're rogues,' Noel said, indignant at being called one. 'What about all the huts that were destroyed. Everyone knows who torched them. That was a beautiful solid hut at Dead Horse and someone burnt it.'

'I don't know anything about the huts. I wouldn't be accusing the Park administration if I were you.'

'No, yer untouchables ain't yer,' Sneaky hissed. 'Law unto yer fuckin selves. Well it won't last!' he began to shout. 'The whole roof's goin to come down on you rotten bastards. I wish I could live long enough to see it all happen.'

'Drop it now Sneaky,' Rusty said. 'It's over. Over for the time being anyway. Come on, we better go settle these cattle down.' He walked over to the ranger and shook his hand. 'Thanks mate for givin us a break.' The ranger appreciated it.

The short, plump ranger never uttered a word. He kept staring in disbelief at the axe handle protruding out from Ken's armpit. As he left, he focused on Sneaky and the blood-stained axe leaning on the saddle. But for the older ranger he probably would have run back to the helicopter when Sneaky spoke out.

Two and a half days later the cattle were grazing on the headwaters of the Ingegoodbee River and the drovers camped at the abandoned tin mine. Nothing had changed since Charles Carter lived there as a hermit. It remained the most isolated old settlement in the Snowys.

'Never seen cattle pick up so much in three days,' Richard McGufficke said, standing by the breakfast campfire.

'Shame to push em back into drought country.'

'Don't reckon I can,' Ken said. 'I'll split em up a bit. Run the heifers down to Cowombat Flat and bush em. They won't leave the good feed and should be the first to fatten.'

'We'll put some of the steers on the lower Ingegoodbee,' Sneaky piped up. He'd got over the brush with Ken. Men in the bush had to shrug off rows and even fights, or they could never get along.

'Well, we all seem to be agreed,' Ken said. 'Let's rope the mickeys, pull em up and mark em. Then we'll draft.'

They were all standing around the fire drinking tea. The horses had been saddled before breakfast and their dogs waited close by. They knew the routine. While breakfast was being eaten they got titbits, like the fatty end of a bacon piece or a toast crust. When the plates were washed and the pannikins topped up for the last time the dogs seemed to know action was near at hand and they either sat or lay down, waiting for the order. Without the dogs the men would have been hard-pressed to hold the big mob together. The owner only had to say, 'go back', and the highly-trained dogs went to the lead like rockets and turned back the restless leaders. Their vital role was when the men mustered the cattle into a mob for a particular job. While the men galloped in to rope or cut one out, the dogs held the mob together. Out in the bush two men had to rope a mickey bull to hold him while a third dashed in on foot to grab its tail and throw it. The fourth and fifth men did the castrating, de-horning, ear-marking and branding. Meanwhile the dogs held the mob.

By noon on the third day the ten or so mickey bulls had been castrated, the heifers drafted off, plus a run of 50 steers. The stockmen split up. The heifers left first and when they were out of sight Ken followed with the steers. These were only to be walked a few kilometres down the river and then let go. The heifers had about ten kilometres before they reached Cowombat Flat.

'Think you'll ever see them again?' Richard asked Ken as they rode away from the steers.

'I'll be up here runnin brumbies every bloody week,' Ken said, smiling broadly. 'Life in the mountains. Yer know Richard, I never get sick of it.'

When Ken returned to camp with Richard they spotted two riders coming in from the north. He livened the fire up, put a billy on and waited. It was George Day and his son Gordon. George was into his 70s in 1983.

'Never thought I'd see it again,' George said to Ken when he reined in and dismounted. 'Cattle up to their bellies in feed in the Pilot country. It was always one of the best pockets in the Snowys. How the hell did you get in here and avoid serious trouble?'

'It's a long story, Mr Day,' Ken replied, wondering how to explain the permit to the old King of the Mountains. George Day was a legend in his own lifetime.

'Great spirit, young fella.' George nodded his approval when he shook hands. 'Keep up the fight. Maybe one day common sense will prevail and the stockmen will reclaim the mountains. I don't mean the alps. We'll never get those lovely meadows back. But down here – boy . . .' He gazed out onto the rolling grasslands of ridges and valley. 'Down here is good cattle country going to waste.'

Ken made the tea and they sat down on the camp logs. 'We're camped up at the Cascades,' Gordon added, changing the subject. 'Must have got in a few hours after you left. We saw all the cattle tracks and, fascinated, decided to ride down. We unloaded at Dead Horse and rode down to fish and reminisce a bit. They say it won't be long before horse-riding's banned from here.'

For a while the four men were quiet, all with the same thoughts. 'Guess I saw the best of it,' George finally said. 'Been a sad end.'

The following morning the cattle were herded up, driven west over Cowombat Ridge and assembled on the yawning tumble of forested spurs to Australia's mightiest river, the Murray.

'Four hundred metre drop in half a mile,' Ken said, grinning like a light horseman reflecting back on a desert charge on the Gaza Strip. The young woman helping him with stock work had come in from the yard and sat down, without interrupting. She was just as riveted by the story as I was. We paused to replenish our coffee mugs from the billy left on the edge of the fire.

'We had to take the mob away from the rim a bit, then up em with the stockwhips. They were running when the spur dropped away. Over they went and down through the timber. It got steeper as they went down. Some skidded down on their arses and others rolled, got up and ran and fell over again. Two of the packhorses must have rolled half the way down. All our saddle horses knew how to do the rear hoof slide.'

'Did you lose any?' I asked.

'Not even an injury.' He paused – the cheeky grin again. 'We left most of em on the river until the next autumn.'

'So the cattle were there for twelve months?'

'We kept takin little drafts out and sellin em at Omeo. Those heifers we put on Cowombat Flat were first to go. They fattened there and the 60 head paid for the whole purchase. Rusty and I covered a bit of ground lookin for some of the steers. One little group wandered as far north as Tom Groggin. We think the only ones missing from the big mob might have got caught in blizzards. About seven of em.'

'Sneaky make a dollar out of it too?' I asked.

'Oh he got crook, but we looked after him.'

'You've roped more than 1400 brumbies, Ken,' I said, still prodding him. 'You think you'll hang the rope up soon?'

He squinted at me under his shaggy eyebrows. He didn't like the inference. 'Got a few ribs busted about a year ago. They've healed up good and I'm still gettin em quick as I ever did.'

His general countenance was that of a man who has survived many battles. It was Alexander the Great who once remarked his best warriors were in their 50s and 60s. Men who never soften evade the grave longest, so Ken could be galloping on the alpine frontline for many years to come.

It takes much more than mere physical stamina. The mountain men have a rare quality: mental resilience in moments of extreme adversity. The broken ribs accident should have resulted in Ken Connley's death. His horse fell at full gallop and landed feet in the air, cast on top of him. For four hours Connley lay there, struggling to breathe and doggedly planning his survival. Slowly and painfully he removed his belt and tried to reach out with one arm and put a twitch on the horse's nose. He thought if he could force its head up and urge his dogs to bite, the horse might swing over and gain its feet after a desperate struggle. Eventually one of the twitches locked on and he yelled the order to his dogs. It worked, but the horse trampled all over him and broke five ribs. He still managed to mount and ride back to his trailer.

I think Ken rides just about every day. When I left he had his black slouch hat and spurs on. He looked a bit like an old lion and I think the cub was in awe of him. One thing was certain – if she helped him with the cattle for even just a week she would leave more confident with horses.

At the Blue Duck I collected Sal and we crept over the Ash Range to Bairnsdale. The bitumen had replaced the bullock dray bogs, but the switchback road probably took more lives in modern times than were ever lost on the lawless gold-fields. There were many crosses by the road, some decorated with fresh flowers. The sight of them made me use the gears and not the brakes to hold the truck more surely on the hairpin bends.

Dean Backman's farm was a few kilometres out of Bairns-dale. The soft hills rippled all the way to the sea. To the north a range rose. When Dean got restless for the chase I'm sure he gazed out upon that range. The captured brumbies probably did too. There were 20 or more in the paddock where the yards were. I noticed the black mare among them, leading the charge as they galloped away towards a fence. Sal took a photograph of them. Their destination was Wangaratta and there they would be drafted and consigned on. The romance of the brumby world was well and truly finished.

We stayed at Dean's place and loaded O'Rourke and Feathertop next morning. O'Rourke was a curious little fellow, on the plain side. Feathertop, on the other hand, was a pretty filly. The black mare would not live to have the foal she was carrying, but maybe Feathertop would have many foals.

Back in my home territory, the wild is slowly creeping back to reclaim much of the land in the shadow of the Warrum-bungle Mountains. The altered landscape has little to do with money. It's about lifestyle and modern man's expecta-tions from life. The bush no longer has the same appeal.

The few of us left are slowly but surely being forced to focus on the consequences – the environment. Kangaroos hopping through wheat crops was unthinkable when I was a boy. Now it's just another risk, like the weather. I get cranky when I see the little ears rise above the crop, about a month before harvesting. But in the final analysis it is probably three or four tonnes lost, from a tally running into hundreds.

I think the National Parks and Wildlife Service in NSW will have to adopt a philosophy of tolerance as well. If they don't, the hatred of the state administration in rural electorates will ultimately manifest into a major political issue. Governments who fail to acknowledge the simple expectations of genuine country people will find themselves in opposition. O'Rourke and Feathertop are destined for a life on a farm, but equally there should be a place for some of their cousins in the wild.

Epilogue

But his pluck was still undaunted and his courage
 fiery hot,
For never yet was mountain horse a cur.

Twelve months after hearing Dooley Pendergast speak on the ABC's 'Country Hour' I was still looking for a couple of saddle horses – the kind that become quiet old plugs for children after a few years of chasing cows. For the cost of my brumby escapades I probably could have bought them at the appropriate sales and lost little more than travelling time. In fact it was time to come clean and admit the brumby chasing was just another new adventure.

I think the quest for adventure or the urge to delve into mysteries is a mental precondition that surges like electricity through the genes. Only decades later, when I had children of my own, did I appreciate what my parents went through with me. Once in my early teens, in April 1959, I saddled a horse at 2.00 a.m., rode for seven hours to the foot of the Tonduron Spire in the Warrumbungles, climbed it via the south face, and arrived home at the same time I left, the next day. What they must have gone through, with just a little note left by the bed!

But compared with my great great grandfather, James Keenan, my exploits are pretty tame. James arrived in Sydney in 1825 from Kildare, Ireland, aged 25. If you were a second son in Ireland, as he was, it was the priesthood or a boat. In a country under enemy occupation there were few careers available, if any. Most left for America or Australia.

When James arrived in Australia fate treated him well. The sheep scab epidemic had swept through the colony's flocks and no one had any experience with eradication. Despite the troubles in Ireland, James was well educated and had experience with sheep parasites on the family property. He made a significant contribution to the young colony by organising the eradication programs. This was noted by the principal landowner at that time, William Wentworth, who led the explorers' expedition across the Great Dividing Range in 1813. Wentworth must have also observed James' enthusiasm for venturing into the unknown, because he sent him into the lower Macquarie and Bogan rivers regions to form stations. He would be gone for months, in uncharted country.

There are no horizons left to cross now, so people like me have to be content with experiences in Australia's inhospitable corners. On reflection, however, a picnic basket, a bottle of chilled Chardonnay and the hand of my beloved wife in Sydney's Centennial Park would have been a lot more fun than all my brumby running adventures. But I had a go, and if I went in with dreamy delusions I emerged with the true history of the Snowy Mountains brumby culture and its present-day disintegration.

And what of my two brumbies? Well, Feathertop and O'Rourke had three months in a paddock with my old troupers Malameen and Billy. O'Rourke was always a friendly little fellow and you could catch him in the paddock, but

Feathertop was so shy and fearful she would try to hide behind the other horses whenever I went near them. She was truly a wild animal and my gut feeling was that no amount of human contact would ever vanquish her wild spirit.

Sal and I do all the work on our property. By the time we have laboriously prepared the wheat paddocks for sowing, kept abreast of the cattle work, undertaken water and fence maintenance and dealt with the GST and other financial records, there is no time left for a task like the handling of young horses, which demands both time and skill. In the end I took O'Rourke up to Greg Everingham at Ebor and Feathertop went to Christine Stuart near Tooraweenah, at the foot of the Warrumbungles.

O'Rourke was a disappointment right from the start. When Greg saw him he said he wasn't worth the cost of the diesel to bring him from Coonabarabran, explaining that the brumby's general conformation was so weak he'd probably fall over if anyone heavier than a child rode him. Ponies for children are usually ridden first by an adult for at least a couple of years, so O'Rourke's prospects were bleak. 'If he's an average Snowy Mountains brumby,' Greg said soberly, 'they might as well clean them all out.'

Feathertop, on the other hand, had the conformation of a thoroughbred – fine legs, powerful rump and a graceful neck. You could picture her being very smart around cattle, but would she ever consent to being caught without being cornered in a tiny yard?

Christine let me know that the little brumby hated being touched anywhere near her head and had a tendency to strike out with her front hoof.

'What was the nature of the catching in the alps?' Christine asked.

When I explained how the freshly caught foals went

berserk – rearing, plunging and throwing themselves down – Christine didn't hesitate: the poor little thing had been traumatised, she declared.

Feathertop was accepting a rug, which is always more difficult to put on a touchy young horse than a bridle, so there was hope. But I decided to cut my losses immediately. Christine consulted with her son John and they offered to take the filly. They felt they could work with her successfully over time.

'Oh she'll be fine!' Christine exclaimed. 'We'll win the Tooraweenah Endurance Ride with her. Bred in the alps, the steep trails over the Warrumbungles shouldn't trouble her.'

The village of Tooraweenah hosts one of the main annual endurance rides in NSW.

For the Stuarts, farmers, horses were a mere extension of the family.

'She doesn't mind the little kiddies,' Christine added brightly. 'Little Sophie is feeding Feathertop out of a tin.' (Sophie was only five years old.) 'Don't worry – we love her and she's going to be a great success.'

Christine Stuart would have been too reserved to say so, but her son Johnny is one of the best horse handlers around. Each season he joins the yearling handling crew for the famous Widden Stud, prior to Sydney Easter yearling sales. So Feathertop had been left in the very best of care.

She had her own mates on the Stuarts' farm as well. There was Oscar, a three-year-old colt. He had come from a western station where the horses had been abandoned for some years. Oscar had only been ridden three times. He had that brumby stallion 'snort', which apparently had the desired effect. There was also Roy from the same station, a wild chestnut really giving Johnny the works. But a filly called Blondie was the success story. After the wild beginnings on the western station Johnny Stuart broke her in at the Scone TAFE college and even took her with him to the prestigious Widden Stud – horse royalty, if only she knew! If Feathertop behaves herself she might get a trip to Widden too.

The future for brumbies in Australia's southeastern national parks and wildlife reserves continues to be plagued with ambivalence. There is no evidence to suggest any softening of the approach to brumbies in NSW but in Victoria, Park authorities have formed an unofficial coalition with the mountain horsemen to contain numbers.

The horsemen have formed brumby running clubs and operate on a self-regulatory basis. Permits are issued by the Regional Manager of East Region, Parks Victoria. The clubs must comply with the rules issued by the Park. For example, they are required to give notice of intent to conduct a run and submit a report afterwards. One such entity is the Buchan Brumby Running Club, established in 1986. The better type of brumbies are kept and tried as saddle horses, but the majority of the brumbies caught are sold to knackeries for pet food.

The general consensus of opinion on brumby numbers in the Victorian Alps is that they are being contained. Some brumby runners are concerned that numbers are dropping and one field researcher went much further when I discussed the matter with her, stating that the current rate of capture would lead to extinction if fresh mobs were unable to wander south from the Kosciuszko National Park. It is currently Parks policy in both Victoria and NSW to eradicate wild horses.

Kosciuszko is facing a more serious problem with

unwanted brumbies. They are often sighted in the alpine zone on the western side, and anyone driving from Khancoban on the Victorian border to Thredbo has to be careful, particularly if driving at night. They're difficult to see, darting out of the snow gums and onto the road like shadows. And they're so quick, you wonder sometimes whether it was a hallucination related to driver fatigue.

On the question of actual brumby numbers, to my knowledge no assessments have been made public. NSW brumby runners, who operate illegally and run the risk of a heavy fine, claim that the southern end of Kosciuszko provides the best running for their purposes. The Jacobs Ladder and Pilot Wilderness probably have the greatest concentration of wild horses in the Australian alps. My estimates of course cannot be confirmed.

What methods should be adopted to control brumby numbers continues to a be a vexed issue in NSW national parks. Wild Horse Management Steering Committees have been formed to give the various factions a voice. The brumby runners are eager to do the job and would definitely reduce numbers at a faster rate than trap yards with salt used as the bait, which appears to be the option most favoured by Park authorities. Mustering is not an option, mainly because there are no facilities in any of the parks where brumbies run.

The capture of brumbies in national parks for the horsemeat trade is also a cause for concern. There is no doubt that our alpine national parks have become an unintended source of supply for the meat industry.

There is nothing wrong with the Australian horsemeat industry itself. If it didn't exist, thousands of domestic horses would be put down every year and left to rot in paddocks. To obtain the services of a bulldozer and have a hole pushed costs about $500 at the time of writing, and in some cases the burial of large carcasses can contaminate groundwater. In many countries carcasses are burnt, but in fire-prone Australia fire bans can be enforced for months.

Furthermore, horsemeat is a valuable export commodity and Australian companies supply Japan and Europe. There is a huge trade in horsemeat in Europe, where Belgium is the principal distributor. On the local scene, smaller knackeries specialise in the pet food industry.

Brumbies caught in the alps and surrounding subalpine districts are killed in Victoria. One knackery in central Victoria receives consignments of brumbies running into the hundreds. Brumby catching is not an insignificant industry. Prices vary according to weight and condition, but overall, young brumbies sell for $70 to $80 a head.

The problem is not the industry, but rather some of the professional brumby catchers who supply it. The mountains are saturated with misinformation, nourished by some professionals. They don't want the public to know the truth, because the practice of roping yearlings and foals and driving them out of the mountains for ultimate dispatch to the meat industry is repugnant to the thousands of people who love horses. On a successful raid a crack chaser can earn up to a thousand dollars. Not much money in the modern world of high salaries perhaps, but a fortune to battlers.

In Victoria, the senate inquiry into brumby culling recommended commercial harvesting as the most cost-effective method of control. The operators are licensed and bear all the running costs.

The National Park and Wildlife Service administration covers a wide range of management, from the welfare of tourists to bushfire control measures. But some state governments never seem to be able to provide adequate funds and this leads to inadequate staffing. Wild horses are time consuming, and if Parks administration can pass on the problem of wild horse management it is an enormous bonus.

The commercial harvesting by professionals is by far the most satisfactory option. I discussed the matter with a horse-trader from Queensland, who wished to remain anonymous.

We costed out a large ironbark post and rail stockyard, 1600 metres square (or 40 metres on one side). In addition, the plan had a small holding yard, a loading race and truck loading ramp. Depending on the source for the ironbark and cartage, the yard could be erected for about $16 000.

This is not a huge capital outlay when you consider that a correctly managed feeding program can draw in horses across 20 000 hectares – possibly many more. As one mob is removed from a given territorial habitat, another mob moves in. In other words, the operator doesn't need to extend his feeding range – the horses move in from the outer perimeters. At Guy Fawkes River National Park, for example, a good-sized yard near the junction of the Guy Fawkes and Sara rivers, would have drawn most of the 600 horses shot in the helicopter culling. In comparison, according to a 27/06/01 report in the *Sydney Morning Herald*, the helicoptor culling program cost $30 000, plus $40 000 was spent on an RSPCA investigation and a further $62 500 for a working party to establish whether the surviving horses had any sort of heritage value. However, it must be acknowledged that Guy Fawkes has a vehicle access problem, so achieving a removal result comparable with the helicopter shoot would have required a combination of mustering and feeding. There were experienced riders available who, if offered wages, would have been able to move the horses into a suitable feeding location for eventual yarding. This would still be less expensive than helicopter culling, and further outlay would be avoided.

Our proposed procedure for trapping brumbies is simple. It begins with laying little hay trails. Once the brumbies start to feed on these, the hay is put out at the same time each day. Animals love routine and have a wonderful sense of time. Not much hay is required. It is important that the brumbies eat it all and then return to their normal grazing haunts. This ensures that all the horses in the location swing into the routine, and when the number targeted is coming onto the hay the operator starts laying the feed trails into the big yard. This is when a coax horse plays a vital role. If the coax horse isn't locked in the small yard, many of the brumbies would remain wary of the yards, but the coax fella gives them confidence. The feeding should continue for a few days in the yard, so that when the entrance gate is 'sprung' there will not be the usual panic. The horses are then removed to the small yard and loaded onto a truck.

It is essential to use timber yards, and ironbark rails melt into the natural bush background. Some wild horses will never walk into a steel yard, and if they panic and hit the rails the injuries are horrible. Also, steel yards in the bush attract thieves.

In the western states of the USA, conflict between opposing interests is also bitterly entrenched over mustangs. Considering the cultures of both the USA and Australia are founded on old British values, it is sobering that the ingredients of the US conflict are so different from ours. In the Rocky Mountains steppelands and western fall there are more than 45 000 wild horses and burros. The aim of the Bureau of Land Management is to reduce numbers to

24 000. The cattle ranchers are driving for reduction and the World Wide Fund for Nature (WWF) is frustrating their efforts with lawsuits. However there is not a murmur from any party about complete removal, unlike Australia.

It is both interesting and poignantly sad that Australia is the only country to declare wild horses as ferals. In Argentina wild horses are called Criollo horses. The Tehuelche Indians prize them over all other breeds. They claim the horses are tough and have adapted to the harsh Patagonian climate. In the northern savannah lands of the Northern Territory a near-perfect horse environment created an explosion of numbers in the 1980s, and mass culling was undertaken to save natural waterholes as well as prevent woodlands from being ringbarked and destroyed. But even when numbers rise beyond the capacity of the land to carry, horse societies maintain ordered and tightly controlled groups. Each stallion marks his territory and his mares are never allowed out of it.

No brumby refuges have been declared anywhere in southeastern Australia and environmentalists staunchly oppose the concept. But the creation of at least a handful of refuges would be a reasonable compromise, given the expressions of support in regional centres where brumbies arouse considerable interest. But there are highly organised militant groups who believe public lands are put aside for their interests and aspirations, and theirs only. They have nothing but contempt for any group or person who opposes their views.

In the northern tablelands of NSW the Guy Fawkes River National Park is the perfect refuge for brumbies. The two principal rivers flow year round and the beds are either rock hard or heavy broken shale – scree-like. The tough granite terrain is almost impervious to erosion. In four days' riding the only erosion I saw was a gaping gash in the riverbank left by a bulldozer. The river flat ecology has been altered forever by early pioneers and horses are needed to consume the worthless red grass, which is probably the most explosive 'fire' grass in Australia. If hardline environmentalists continue to screw their heads into the sand and manage to dictate intransigent policies for land management, the ultimate fire will destroy the whole region for everyone. Recently I had a wheat stubble fire jump the break and get into a copse of white box trees. In the high plains grass the flames belched with the intensity of volcano vents and I was devastated at how easily a wild fire can bring down full grown trees. That was just over two hectares. Imagine what could happen in 4000 square kilometres! And where will the Greenie advocates be when it's on? In an air-conditioned office in Sydney or Canberra.

Guy Fawkes is also a genuine refuge, free from meat trade poachers. Brumby catchers like Greg Everingham only take selected yearlings to be broken in and used for station work. In the tracks of the Maskey men before them, Greg and his colleagues are unpaid caretakers of the horses. They provide the opportunity for Australia to have a wild brumby herd with a sound and interesting genetic base. Genetic scientists have warned the United Nations that the world needs wild refuges for our most domesticated herbivores and Guy Fawkes presents an excellent opportunity for Australia to make a contribution. The National Parks and Wildlife Service is considering the heritage status of the surviving brumbies in the park. The plan is to remove them all to a new location, which basically amounts to an adoption plan. It would be the end of them. But if the locals have their way, these brumbies could become the first ever to have sanctuary status. Guy Fawkes is a test case.

So what of the future for any of our brumbies? Somehow I feel there's something symbolic about the fate of those in the southeast mountain ranges. If we lose them all, this nation has lost another part of its cultural heritage. Only a small part, but it all accumulates.

APPENDIX I
The Fighting Ringer and 'the Scalding'

There was a sombre mood at the yards that day,
for every man knew that the fighting ringer might be thrown,
and if he were to taste the dust, then God help anyone
who got near, when the rum fired the breath of that ringer.

It was at Maneroo Station, out on the gibber plains of the
Darr, that the ringers assembled on the high rail.
Below in the round yard, Roy James took hold of reins
on a black young un, named by the breaker as 'the Scalding'.
Behind and below the silent men, a string of saddled horses
   fretted and pawed, their wide eyes straining and rolling,
for the breaker had thrown the rope, saddled once, and
moved on.

It was up to us now, the ringers, to mount and ride
these creatures, no more familiar than brumbies.
But before we spurred out to look for the sheep in the
gidgee, we had to mount up in the yard,
yell for the gate to be flung and canter out onto the gibber.

Back in the cookhouse the station cook spat as he grumbled,
'Same every season. When the breaker leaves the bastards
   don't eat.' And he was right that old villain of burnt chops
   and cakes with no egg or sugar, for some of us would limp
   back to the station.

Out on the Winton road, the breaker rocked along in his
sulky, humming a ballad he composed, for there was a
score to be settled and he would have happily
laid the sulky and all on the Scalding.

It was the smuggled in rum that caused the trouble,
and no manager west of the Thomson dared interfere,
when the breaker and Roy James had a penchant to
    drink from the bottle.
Tempers would flare and arguments were settled with fists.
but it was always Roy, the fighting ringer,
    who had the last word.

Down in the round yard, the gun ringer felt the heat
from the sun and the heat of the breaker's gift – the Scalding.
The black horse showed damp along neck and flank
and his nostrils were flared like a stallion.
The ringer knew the odds were stacked and he
quietly cursed the breaker's parting gift,
for no one so tough could dishonour the challenge.

With reins crossed and a handful of mane, Roy James
pressed the sole of his boot to iron.
He felt near his eye the twitch of a nerve, for the time had
    come,
and he knew his only hope was a swing to the saddle,
at the speed of a fighter's left jab.

The Scalding reared high, as though struck with a bullet,
then a squeal of unbridled fury rent the rising dust.
With knees pinned like a vice and a hand aloft for balance,
Roy James braced against a buck filled with rage.
Blinking through dust of decay, we ringers yelled
for our hero and when we heard the saddle flaps clap we
knew the next buck might be it.

The wild horse squealed and sucked the hot air.
The shoulder drop sent a gasp from all of us,

and we watched, quiet all at once, when Roy lost an iron.
A dizzy spin – the ground near, the dust in his eyes
 and in his nose, the black outlaw above in the greyness,
and beyond a fiery sun after dawn.

Caked in dust and not a small trace of blood,
that fighting ringer re-mounted, time after time,
until finally the saddle itself was pelted to the gibber.
We rose as one to take our own mounts and
we prayed for no encore, for even the shoes on that
outlaw had sent sparks from the gibber.

For the man with a splash and terrible beginnings,
he knew a score had been settled, and as his
horses jogged and the sulky squeaked somewhere
out on the old Winton road, he hummed
a tune he named 'The Scalding'.

When Wild Horses Roamed East Gippsland
J. M. Mackenzie

*Some things are gone forever in the bush. It often puzzles me
why it is so. We still have strong stockhorses, similar to the famous
walers, and the young men can ride just as well as their grand-
fathers. I think Ernie Maskey summed it up that day on the
stockroute near Glen Innes when he said, 'The old days and the old
people have gone. In ten years we all gone. New breed of people
everywhere now.'*

*J. M. Mackenzie's vivid recollection of a brumby muster is a
chance to put the reader in the saddle. He's not telling you how it
was; he's showing you. You sense the fear, recognise the discipline
and feel the great excitement of the final gallop through the timber.
It is a splendid piece of impromptu writing from the heart.*

I went up to North Gippsland over 35 years ago to join
my brother who owned, in partnership with the O'Rourke
Bros., a big track of country stretching from the head of the
Murray (which then went under the name of the Limestone)
to the Snowy River at a place called Willis, on the NSW
border.

The O'Rourkes, three brothers (John, David and Michael),
owned, with my brother (Hector Mackenzie, married to
Mary O'Rourke) this country, which was called the Black
Mountain Run. The Black Mountain was, I think, taken up
by the father and uncle of these brothers (Christopher and
James).

At the time I write of, there were only two fences between
Bruthen and the Snowy River, one at the Buchan boundary
– Buchan was then owned by Ricketson – and the other
at the top of Turnback Mountain, the boundary between

Black Mountain and Suggan Buggan. The latter place was owned by Ned O'Rourke, a cousin of the Black Mountain O'Rourkes. Good old Ned of Suggan Buggan was a real white man, and a character in his way.

He has passed in his checks a good many times, but I can see him now riding after cattle and handling a mob of touchy ones, born to the game, as cunning as a fox, and as keen as mustard.

Soon, this wild and rugged country and the surrounding districts became the home of a community of wonderful bushmen and wonderful horsemen and horses. Every man's living depended on his ability to ride and track and steer a pathway by the sun and stars.

At that time North Gippsland was full of wild horses right up to Kosciuszko and all through the Black Mountain country. As boys the O'Rourkes used to run them, but they had not been molested for years. The O'Rourkes and my brother decided to see if they could make anything of them. They were all comparatively young men at the time – probably not over 35 years.

David O'Rourke was a fine stamp of a bushman, over six feet and wiry, a good steady rider, not dashing, but generally in the right place after a mob of brumbies or cattle. John O'Rourke was one of the best horsemen I have ever seen and a regular fire-eater after stock. I can see him now after a hard run, his eyes flashing, and his horse pretty well all out. He could let some language fly about if his mob was not kept in by the tailers when he had brought them in sight. He was always right on the tail of a mob, sending them through the thickest scrub as hard as his horse could pelt, giving a mob of brumbies no time to swerve or turn. Michael O'Rourke rode well over eighteen stone. Good old Michael! He had the best judgment in the bush after stock of any man I have ever seen. He was never bustled or at a loss, and was always in the right place, and generally about at the finish. It took a good beast to get away from Michael if he was riding old Darkie, a cranky devil of a black horse, which was as powerful as a bull, and would follow a beast like a dog.

What a company gathered for those old 'Brumby' runs (they were 'wild horses' in those days. 'Brumby' was a much later word).

Hector, mounted on old Phil; his brother Farquhar, a wild and reckless horseman with all the dash but lacking the cool judgment of his elder brother; George Johnstone of Tubbut station, a hard riding Englishman; Fred and Ned Smith; Billy Cobyam, one of the full-blooded Aborigines, with judgment and horsemanship combined.

Perhaps Bob Moon from Buchan might be one of the party. The wonder man who seldom seemed to do more than trot or canter and still was always just where he was wanted and riding a fresh horse when the others had bellows to bend, Bob was probably the best white tracker that Australia ever knew. His keen eyes never spoiled by reading small print or any other kind of print for that matter.

Bob Moon has long since been gathered to his fathers and surely, if horses are over the divide, Bob is mounted on a prancing steed stamp with RTC (the brand was that of Ricketson, who held a large area of the land in the Buchan district in the early days).

Through the haze of the years, I can see Dave and Billy Kiss in charge of a wild-eyed mob of Monaro cattle; Barry passing through with a mob of steers for the Gippsland market. Barry haggard from long night watches and wild rides with mobs that rushed till they would jump when a leaf falls.

A long procession of boys who took places, rides past. I can see young Farquhar Mackenzie of Ora, Sam Gilbert on a Buchan grey that would have delighted the heart of a Desert Arab; young Charlie Gilbert on bluey; George Harrison from the Murray; Charlie Woodhouse from the Monaro; Joker Johnstone on Sea Spray; Harry Biggs from Glenmore, the furthest outpost of the Buchan, on a raw-boned bay that was miles better than he looked; Charlie Biggs on old Stumpy, a horse without a single hair in his tail; Andrew Davidson, Jimmy Dixon, young Bob Moon, Tom Connors in the days when his beard was black; Ted and Tom Cox; one Jim O'Keefe; Frank Welby with a team of fiery RTCs and Tom Hamilton from Ensay with his four greys.

H. Mackenzie came from the Billabong with the reputation of a crack horseman, which I think he gained partly by sweating Willie and Ned Kennedy's horses, they having a good many more in those days than they could handle. He kept his reputation up well in the mountains, and was a hard man to beat in any country. For dash at a critical time and for judgment he had few equals. He could ride any sort of horse and knock good quarters out of him. Hector was perhaps the dandiest horseman of them all. Six feet two inches of wire and as strong as steel, he had an easy graceful seat that drew old horsemen's eyes when he rode into Moree from his NSW property forty years later.

I have ridden behind all these men, and it is not easy to say which was the hardest to follow. I think for real dash and smashing through John O'Rourke took the cake. For myself, I didn't feel altogether out of the running as I was able to follow them.

Well, after a good deal of hard work putting up trap yards with long, light wings, we prepared for the first run. Horses were got in and shod, every man doing his own shoeing in those days. The horses were of the good old sort – like cats on their feet and game as pebbles. I shall never forget the first run we had, and wish I could describe the country as I can see it now. There was a patch of fairly level ground called Wongulamerang Forest, which sloped off in almost perpendicular spurs to the lower country on the Little River and Farm Creek. I had some adventures on that same Farm Creek in later years, which, however, do not belong to this yarn.

Down these spurs the brumbies went for water. If they were disturbed they always kept to the sidelines, never going straight down if they could avoid it.

We built our yard on one side, and ran wings just under the brow on each side nearly to the top.

On this particular run D. O'Rourke went out to start the job. He knew almost to a mile where every mob ran, and which way they would make. Michael was on Darkie and H. Mackenzie on a fine bay horse called Phil, a very hot headed horse with the reputation of being a bolter if he was in a bad humour. These two were to take the mob from Davie and bring them along towards the wings where John O'Rourke and I were waiting, one on each wing, about half a mile from each point, and well hidden in scrub. Our job was to take the mob from the other two and send them down the spur towards the yards as hard as we could pelt.

I must say while I was waiting for my turn to come I had great doubts as to how I was going to do my part. The spur was as steep as the side of a house, and timber and undergrowth as thick as it could stick. I remember I was riding a horse called The Toad – a sweater, by-the-by – named from a habit he had a swelling himself out when first mounted, and giving three or four flying bounds before settling down. I had many a good ride on him afterwards.

My instructions were 'as soon as the mob passes you, after them like blazes and don't give them a chance to turn on the wing'.

I looked at the spur, which seemed steeper and steeper, and at the timber which seemed much thicker than the day before and had many doubts.

John O'Rourke was riding a little bay horse called The Arrow, and he took some riding through scrub and down-hill. The least bit of humbugging with him and up would go his head, and he would race through the scrub straight on end – no doubt thus getting his name. After waiting what seemed a very long time, well hidden in the scrub, we heard the thud of galloping horses – there is no other sound like it, and once heard it is never forgotten. On they came nearer and nearer. The Toad, beginning to jump about with excitement, and my feet jingling in the stirrups with fright. Now scrub is smashing and stones rattling as the mob gets nearer, galloping so close that you could cover them with a tablecloth. The king of the mob is now in the lead – early in the run he was at the tail of his Harem, and keeps good watch on his mares to see that none single off. But now that the matter is serious he is taking the lead for he sees a man on each side of his mob riding hard and quietly. There is no shouting or cracking of whips at this game; one shout, and the whole mob would probably wheel short round on its tracks, and the run would be spoilt. The old king is not very much alarmed yet; he has often before been sent for a spin, and he looks for safety round the side of the spur as usual. The mob is beginning to waver a bit just as they come abreast of my stand, but they flashed past at top speed and I take up the running. I just see my mate on the other flank, and I know I will have to ride as I have never ridden before to keep my end up, but old Toad was full of go, and I had lost my fright, and found no difficulty in keeping well on the mob's tail.

They were now mad with fright, and fairly threw themselves down the wings smashing many a sapling on the way. I glanced across and could see my mate well abreast of me and riding hard. The arrow head up and going for his life. The mob made a wheel towards my side, and I thought it was all up, but I put on an extra spurt and straightened them up again. I could now see the wings closing in, and down went the mob straight into the big yard and through into the smaller yard beyond. We had a temporary gate up before they turned again, and there they were, securely yarded – a big chestnut stallion, eight mares and a couple of foals. More foals started with the mob, but the pace was too hot and they dropped out.

The mob was in the pink of condition – fat, with coats like satin. Some of the old mares had manes to their knees. We were all together again now, and rode the run over again. Someone asked me 'How did you get on through the timber?' I said, 'I never saw a darned tree' which was absolutely true. I had no recollection of pulling my horse off a single tree – he did it all himself. Later on I found that the secret of success in riding in rough country is summed up in the words 'let your horse alone'. I asked H. Mackenzie if Phil had bolted. He said: 'The beggar hadn't time.'

The horses were in the yard but they had to be branded and taken, all of which is another story.

Acknowledgments

New South Wales

Ted Taylor and his wife Helen made Sal and me very welcome at Currango. Ted felt so strongly about the demise of the high plains culture since the Second World War that he released his own book, *Reflections of Ted Taylor, Man of the High Country*, edited by Judy Hearn, in 2001. It's loaded with wonderful stories from Ted's childhood period.

Jim Nankervis from Corryong always found time over a cup of tea to yarn about the old pastoral culture of the Australian Alps. His family owned Tom Groggin Station for some decades and when he spoke of 'Groggin', as he affectionately called it, there seemed to be an absence, as though there was an empty chair. It was of course the master of verse himself, Banjo, for it was from Tom Groggin he set off more than a century ago and heard Jack Riley's tale, the Man from Snowy River.

Dooley Pendergast from Jindabyne had that rare knack of conjuring up a sense of presence in all his stories. He just didn't tell you that the river water from melted snow was cold, but 'The man was storm-blue when he came back to the surface and his arteries all pressed against his skin like a dead shorn sheep, all bloated up'.

Greg Everingham from Ebor took me on a horse trek into the Guy Fawkes canyons. Without his assistance and passion for the horses I would not have been able to come up with a sound claim for a heritage refuge for the brumbies.

There is a sense of genuine pathos surrounding the Guy Fawkes brumbies.

Ernie Maskey and his extended family had direct links with the brumbies going back more than a hundred years. In a legal sense the brumbies belonged to the National Park, but in a spiritual sense they belonged to Ernie and his people like their great grandfather belonged to the land.

Well known Dorrigo cattleman Alan Cavanagh provided a lot of information on the problems confronting land owners joining national parks.

From Thredbo village, Helga Frolich, Julie Bourke and Jill Foster all made contributions as characters in the book, as well as assisting with research and kindly lending photos, and there was always a bed when I arrived, sometimes with little or no notice.

Gordon Day related numerous stories about the golden days of the Alps when his father George ran the Chalet and had 50 horses saddled before breakfast. His most memorable story was the rescue of Jim Nankervis.

A special thanks to Leisa Caldwell, who was brave enough to relive a dreadful experience she and her husband Gary had near the Snowy River. She inspired in me the mettle to fight for the modest dreams of the mountain horsemen who find themselves isolated and vulnerable in the most urbanised nation on earth.

Tom Barry, who owns the newsagency at Jindabyne, must

have most of the Monaro and Snowy Mountains history stored in his memory. Tom's family was one of the very first to drove sheep and cattle into the Alps for the brief summer.

Liz Wren from the Jindabyne office of the Kosciuszko National Park helped me on matters of Park policy.

Robin MacDougal from Newton Boyd, just north of Guy Fawkes, headed a Heritage Working Party to try and save the surviving brumbies in the canyons. Robin provided an insight into the depth of community feeling.

Victoria

Graeme Brown alerted me to much of the colourful history surrounding Omeo and thanks to his prompting, the chapter called The Gold Town was written. Graeme owns and manages the Blue Duck Inn, which became a retreat for after two escapes from the wrath of the Alps.

Local historian Fred G. Ward from Bairnsdale recounted chilling images of Black Friday in Omeo. He also sourced more speculation on the origin of the term 'brumby'. Thanks, Fred, for forwarding so much documentation.

Ken Connley from Benambra provided numerous stories from the Alps. I thought The Permit was the most entertaining.

Buff Rogers is one of the last of the old cattlemen from the Victorian Alps. His management and understanding of the environment is living proof some of the old ways should shape the future and not be discarded as they have been in NSW.

Chris Stoney and Rachel Parsons made it possible for me to go on a brumby chase and see the wild country of the Suggan Buggan. Chris is one of the most courageous men I've ever seen ride.

Max Dyer and John Murphy are the authors of *The Tale of*

Jimmy Lee, and generously allowed me to use material from their book. In Australian colonial folklore we're led to believe every bushranger ultimately faced Crown justice. Not so! The escapades of Jimmy Lee make entertaining reading and more aptly describes that period in history than the bland, history-effacing texts I had to read as a school boy in the 1950s.

Helen Packer and her partner Russell Tonkin had me to stay on their farm near Anglers Rest. Helen's love of horses and Russell's extraordinary craft skills always provided inspiration.

Also available from Bantam

WILD HORSES DON'T SWIM
Michael Keenan

The Horses Too Are Gone, the true story of Michael Keenan's fight to save his cattle and his farm from drought, won the hearts and minds of readers all over Australia. In *Wild Horses Don't Swim*, Mike embarks on another quest: to rescue the magnificent wilderness of the west Kimberley from being destroyed forever.

The Fitzroy River, one of the last great rivers flowing freely to the sea, is the lifeblood of the west Kimberley. When Mike heard of plans to dam it to allow cotton-growing, he was horrified. A dam on the Fitzroy could cause an environmental disaster greater than any Australia has ever known.

With the help of the local Bunuba people, fierce opponents of the dam which threatened their homeland and sacred sites, Mike organised a horseback trek to explore the area and discover what was at stake. What he found was a paradise of unique plants, pristine rivers and dramatic gorges.

In *Wild Horses Don't Swim* we join Mike, his intrepid wife Sal and their Banuba friends in action-packed adventure as they dodge wild bulls, ford raging torrents, brave bushfires and climb sheer cliffs – searching for the legendary rock art that might be lost forever.

Bantam Paperback
ISBN 1 86325 183 9

THE HORSES TOO ARE GONE
Michael Keenan

The drought had reached crisis point. Cattle farmer Mike Keenan decided there was only one solution: he would have to get his starving cattle – and his beloved horses – to greener pastures north of the border. But when he finally got there he found his troubles had only just begun. South-west Queensland seemed like a modern-day Wild West, and as Keenan moved his cattle along the traditional droving routes in search of long-term pasture, he had to match wits with a host of characters – as well as Nature herself.

The Horses Too Are Gone is the true story of Keenan's struggle to survive against mounting odds, and it's an action-packed adventure that rivals any fiction. A fresh voice from the Bush, Mike Keenan writes with a deep passion and knowledge of Australian life on the land, tinged with a sadness and nostalgia for a way of life that is under threat. *The Horses Too Are Gone* will strike a chord with all Australians.

Bantam Paperback
ISBN 0 73380 167 6

IN THE MIDDLE OF NOWHERE
Terry Underwood

'His smile was big enough to light the universe. He lay in an extended plaster bed which engulfed his body but obviously not his spirit.

"I'm big bad John," he chuckled.'

A city girl with dreams of the country, eighteen-year-old Terry Augustus was a trainee nurse working at St Vincent's hospital when she met John Underwood, a young, born-and-bred cattleman. Flat on his back in Ward 3, nursing a serious spinal injury sustained while mustering cattle, John was itching to get home. And home he finally went, to his family's cattle station, Inverway, up in the Northern Territory. He promised Terry he'd write. A postcard arrived a week later.

After five long years of writing letters, John and Terry married and moved to their new home – a tent and a newly drilled bore in the middle of nowhere. Modern-day pioneers, John and Terry built their station from scratch and raised and educated a new generation of Underwoods there. Times were tough and there was heartbreak, danger and struggle, but the power of love and the strength of family ties helped them overcome every obstacle.

In the Middle of Nowhere is their story. It's a story of beating the odds, told with warmth and a genuine knowledge of the Outback and its people, and the issues they face today. It's a *real* story of the Territory, and is as vast, dramatic and inspiring as the land that lies at the heart of this unforgettable book.

Bantam Paperback
ISBN 0 73380 191 9

KINGS IN GRASS CASTLES
Mary Durack

When Patrick Durack left Western Ireland for Australia in
1853, he was to found a pioneering dynasty and build a
cattle empire across the great stretches of Australia.

With a profound sense of family history, his granddaughter,
Mary Durack, has reconstructed the Durack saga – a story of
intrepid men and ground-breaking adventure.

*. . . far better than any novel; an imcomparable record of a great
family and a series of great actions.*
BULLETIN

*The best saga of pastoral Australia ever published . . . hard to
describe without superlatives . . . in a hundred years the book will
still be a classic.*
MEANJIN

Bantam Paperback
ISBN 0 73380 156 0